INNOVATION AND COMPETITIVENESS OF SMALL AND MEDIUM ENTERPRISES

INNOVATION AND COMPETITIVENESS OF SMALL AND MEDIUM ENTERPRISES

Editor
Rathakrishnan, L

KALPAZ

Innovation and Competitiveness of Small and Medium Enterprises

Rs. 790

ISBN: 978-81-7835-834-5

Published in 2010 in India by
Kalpaz Publications
C-30, Satyawati Nagar,
Delhi-110052
e-mail: kalpaz@hotmail.com
Phone : 9212729499

Laser Type Setting by: Rudra Computer Graphics, Delhi
Printed at : Chawla Offset Printers, Delhi

Dedicated To
My
Mother

Contents

Foreword

Ever since second five-year plan, the Indian sub continent has started showing rapid strides in industrialisation. In fact, the Government of India aimed at achieving faster economic growth rate from eight to nine per cent per year. The globalisation process further strengthened the growth pattern of the Indian Small Scale Industries, changing the Government policy from *"Production led Growth to Competitive led Growth"*.

Even change obviously demands better performance, growth, efficiency, productivity, quality and greater market share. This requires Chaos, Creativity, Communication, and Channelisation. India has the first three but needs to strengthen the fourth one.

Duly realising this, the author has brought out the present book entitled "*Innovation and Competitiveness of Small and Medium Enterprises,* which provides the relationship amongst innovation, competitive advantage and SMEs capabilities. The volume is a compilation of papers contributed to the National seminar. The book provides platform for further discussion on policies and strategies for accelerated growth and enhancement of SMEs competitiveness in the globalised era. It provides insight on innovation, total quality management, patent rights, WTO,

ICT, technology revolution, strategies to enhance competitiveness, value added services etc. All these issues are addressed in 20 chapters.

The efforts of Dr. L. Rathakrishnan need special appreciation. I hope this publication will bring new insight on SMEs development in India and meet the needs and expectations of our country.

Dr. S.M. RAMASAMY
Vice-Chancellor,
Gandhigram Rural Institute
(Deemed University)
Gandhigram – 624 302.

Preface

The process of industrialisation of the country was launched in the second five year plan (1956-61). The industrial polices of 1980, 1991, and 2006 have given enormous boost to private investment in the industrial sector. The government of India has been very keen to develop the small scale industries (SSIs) or Small and Medium Enterprises (SMEs) through various incentives and promotive measures. In fact, the SSIs constitute 95 per cent of the industrial units, produce 7500 products and contribute about 40 per cent of the industrial output. These industries employ 32 million persons and export 36 per cent of the total export from 32 million registered units. The SMEs alone contribute to seven per cent of India's GDP. They provide ample opportunities to the nation through harnessing local competitive advantages for achieving global dominance.

In order to enhance the global competition, the definition of SSIs has been broadened to include medium enterprises. As per the definition of Ministry of Small and Medium Enterprises, the industries which invest in plant and machineries from Rs.25 lakhs to Rs.10 corer are treated as SMEs (2006).

The globalisation process has affected the growth of the SMEs to a great extend. It has led to shift in the policy, namely "production–led growth to competition led growth". The small industries are facing great challenges on innovation, standardisation, value added products, total quality management and subsidies. At the same time the SMEs have lot of opportunities on innovation, developing new entrepreneurial activities and adaptation of competitive spirit. The future of the Indian economy lies in the growth and diversified competitive activities of SMEs. The optimists argue that increased competitive pressure will trigger the upgradation of SMEs through the introduction and absorption of new technologies. The SMEs are now witnessing a dramatic change in their attitude owing to growing knowledge-intensity of production and emergence of innovation based competition. These changes influence SMEs to experiment with a continuous process of innovation. Besides, the SMEs interaction with supportive organisations and institutions further help in bringing out new products, new processes, and new ideas into economic use.

In any case innovation does not limit to R and D activities alone. But it includes continuous improvement in product design and quality, changes in organisation and management routines, creativity in marketing and modification of production process that brings cost down, increases efficiency and ensures environmental sustainability. Thus, "innovation is the process by which firms master and implement the design and production of goods and services that are new to them, irrespective of whether or not they are new to their competitors, domestic or foreign".

Studies have proved that effective or efficient use of social networks and clusters have been recognised as a key drive in the promotion and implementation of innovation. According to Marshal (1920) it is "concentration of specialised industries in particular localities". In denotes "the geographical and sectoral concentration of firms and its potential benefits for the smallest companies".

Intensive competition in the market place is another compelling force for the firms to go for innovation. Sustained competitive advantage can be generated through continuous innovation. It is also proved that the rates of innovation by SMEs are higher than that of very large corporation. Studies conducted by the U.S Department of Commerce revealed that 50 per cent of all innovations and 95 per cent of all radical innovations since World War II have come from new or smaller firms.

Being small in their size and having greater flexibility the SMEs in India have been most optimistic of economic recovery and growth during this year - 2009 among other countries in the region (UPS – Asian Business Monitor 2009). Despite the slowdown in their business, the SMEs are the key contributors to the economy, optimistic even amidst challenging business environment. The survey further reveals that SMEs in India have a more positive outlook towards their development and business prospects than their regional counterparts. This book is prepared in order to analyse the SMEs competitive spirit and innovation.

The book is divided into three parts. The first part deals with the innovation and patent rights, in which innovation practices adopted by SMEs and total quality management are analysed. Few case studies have also been discussed in this part. The technology interventions for enhancing competitiveness are discussed in part two. ICT intervention, technology revolution, internet trading, e-commerce are analysed in the second part. The third part discusses strategies to enhance competitiveness of SMEs. Strategies such as clustering, value added services are discussed and analysed with case evidences. Altogether, twenty chapters present some of the issues pertaining to innovation and competitiveness of small end medium enterprises in the world in general and India in particular.

The expected outcome of the book is that it may provide substantial information on innovation and competitiveness of the SMEs for the academicians, researchers, NGO's, industrialists and other ministerial staff on some of the research issues and policy options for starting innovative enterprises by understanding the ground reality.

Acknowledgements

I wish to express my deep sense of gratitude to all contributors of this edited volume. The papers presented in the National seminar on "Small and Medium Enterprise under Globalisation: Challenges and Opportunities" form this book. All the papers were thoroughly revised to suit the book format. I am thankful to the chapter contributors of this book.

The seminar was sponsored by the UGC, New Delhi and co-sponsored by the Federation of South India Producer Associations (SIFA), Chennai and Kins Foundation, Gandhigram. My special thanks to them all for their financial support.

I am under obligation to acknowledge gratefully the kind co-operation received from the Vice-Chancellor, Registrar and Administrative staff of GRI, Gandhigram for having given me the opportunity to conduct the seminar and support extended to get the book published in time. I also thank my colleagues in the Department of Rural Industries and Management, GRI, Gandhigram for their continuous support and encouragement.

I would like to extend my special acknowledgement to my teachers, Dr. M. Ramadoss, Dr. B. S. Nagarajan, Dr. S. Ramachandran, Dr. S Ramasamy, Dr. S. Ramamoorthy and

Dr. P.N. Ramani for their care and unflinching support throughout my career and development. I am deeply indebted to them all.

My heartfelt gratitude to Prof. S. Lakshmi, Faculty of English and Foreign Languages of Gandhigram Rural Institute, Gandhigram for her kind co-operation in proof reading the entire material.

I gratefully appreciate the silent contributions given by my family members for all my sincere efforts.

A special thanks to Kalpaz Publications, Delhi for their timely publication. I whole heartedly acknowledge the kind co-operation extended by the publisher.

(L. Rathakrishnan)

List of Contributors

Balasubramaniyan R, Reader, Department of Economics, D.G. Vaishnav College, Arumbakkam, Chennai-600 106.

Dayanandan, R Associate Professor, Department of Natural Resource Economics and Management, P.B. 3011 Mekelle University, Ethiopia.

Ezhilarasan M, Reader, ANJA College, Sivakasi -625 005.

Geetha R, Lecturer (S.G) in Commerce, V.V.Vanniaperumal College for Women, Virudhunagar.

Nisha J, Lecturer, Department of Management Studies, Shrimati Indira Gandhi College, Tiruchirappalli.

Parivallal R, Lecturer, Department of Management Studies, Thiagarajar College, Madurai-9.

Raja alias Pranmalai K, Reader in Rural Industries and Management, GRI, Gandhigram – 624302.

Rajasekar N, Reader, Department of Business Administration, Thiagarajar College, Madurai-9.

Rajasekaran N, Lecturer, Department of Business Administration (S/F), NMSSVN, College, Nagamalai, Madurai.

Rathakrishnan L, Reader in Rural Industries and Management, Gandhigram Rural Institute, Gandhigram-624 302, Tamil Nadu.

Renganayaki R, Full Time Research Scholar, Department of Rural Industries and Management, Gandhigram Rural Institute, Gandhigram-624302.

Sangeetha D, Lecturer in Business Administration, NMSSVN College, Madurai.

Sarata A.V, Research Scholar, Department of Management Studies, National Institute of Technology, Tiruchirappalli.

Saravanan Naidu A, Sr. Research Associate, ICFAI Research Centre, Bangalore, Karnataka.

Selvalakshmi M, Lecturer, Thiagarajar School of Management, Madurai.

Sriram K, Research Scholar, Gandhigram Rural Institute, Gandhigram-624302.

Sriraman, V.P, Assistant Professor, Bharathidasan Institute of Management, Tiruchirapalli, Tamil Nadu.

Srinivasan R, Reader in Econometrics, University of Madras, Chennai.

SoundaraPandian M, Professor and Head, Dept. of R.I.M, GRI, Gandhigram-624302.

Sumithra Devi N, Faculty Member-Finance, ICFAI College, Thadikombu Road, Dindugul.

Thillai Raja, Lecturer, Department of Business Administration, Thiagarajar College, Madurai.

Thirumal Azhagan C, Senior Faculty Member, Department of Management Studies, Adhiparasakthi Engineering College, Melmaruvathur – 603 319.

Uma P, Head, Dept.of MBA, Fatima College, Madurai.

Varadaraj A, Senior Faculty Member, Department of Management Studies, Adhiparasakthi Engineering College, Melmaruvathur – 603 319.

Abbreviations

Small and Medium Enterprises (SMEs)
Organisation for Economic Cooperation and Development (OECD)
Madurai District Small Industries Association (MADISSIA)
Japanese Union Scientists and Engineers (JUSE)
Total Quality Management (TOM)
Quality Management Systems (QMS)
Hazard Analysis Critical Control Point (HACCP)
Good Manufacturing Practices (GMP)
Good Laboratory Practices (GLP)
Plan-Do-Check-Act style (PDCA)
World Trade Organisation (WTO)
Intellectual Property Rights (IPR)
African Regional Intellectual Property Organisation (ARIPO)
Canadian Intellectual Property Office (CIPO)
Eurasian Patent Organisation (EAPO)
German Patent Office (DPMA)
Indian Patent Office (IPO)
Japan Patent Office (JPO)
United States Patent and Trade Mark Office (USPTO)
World Intellectual Property Organisation (WIPO)
Women Entrepreneurs Enterprise (WEE)

Small Scale Service and Business Enterprise (SSSBE)
General Agreement on Tariffs and Trade (GATT)
Information Technology (IT)
Intermediate Technology Development Group (ITDG)
Small Scale Industries (SSIs)
Information and Communication Technology (ICT)
Trade Alternative Reform Action (TARA)
Sustainable Access in Rural India (SARI)
M.S. Swaminathan Research Foundation (MSSRF)
Clear Targets for New Internet Traders (CTNIT)
Indian Space Research Organisation (ISRO)
Internet Access Provider (IAP)
Personal Digital Assistants (PDAs)
Electronic Data Interchange (EDI)
World Wide Web (WWW)
Internet Service Provider (ISP)
Videsh Sanchar Nigam Limited (VSNL)
Mahanagar Telephone Nigam Limited (MTNL)
Gross Domestic Product (GDP)
Organisation for Economic Co-operation and Development (OECD)
Customer Relationship Management (CRM)
Small and Medium Enterprises and Regional Innovation, Japan (SMRJ)
Scheme of Fund for Regeneration of Traditional Industries (SFURTI)
Technology Bureau of Small Enterprises (TBSE)
Credit Guarantee Fund Trust for Small Industries (CGTSI)
Self Help Groups (SHGs)
National Institute of Fashion Technology (NIFT)
Micro, Small and Medium Enterprises (MSMEs)
Indigenous Technological Capacity (ITC)
National Research and Development Corporation (NRDC)
National Information System for Science and Technology (NISSAT)
Industrial Development Bank of India (IDBI)

Industrial Credit and Investment Corporation of India (ICICI)
Industrial Finance Corporation of India (IFCI)
Department of Scientific and Industrial Research (DSIR)
Programme Aimed at Technological Self-Reliance (PATSER)
Scheme to Enhance the Efficacy of Transfer of Technology (SEETOT)
Small Industries Development Bank of India (SIDBI)
Khadi and Village Industries Commissions (KVIC)
World Health Organisation (WHO)

Part – I
Innovation and Patent Rights

1

Innovation in Small and Medium Enterprises

Rathakrishnan, L Uma, P

Abstract

The major objective of this paper is to analyse the relationship between experience of entrepreneurs in a particular business and innovation in that field and also the factors influencing innovation with respect to Small and Medium Enterprises. Data was collected from 50 SMEs in Madurai district of Tamil Nadu. The hypothesis formulated for this study was experience and innovations are independent. Chi-square and factor analysis were used to test the formulated hypothesis. The result of the Chi-square test shows that experience and innovation are independent. Irrespective of experience, entrepreneurs practice innovation out of their own interests and confidence. Some of the factors influencing innovation are cost, return on investment, efficiency, compatibility, complexity, perceived relative advantage, susceptibility inter- personal relations and risk and uncertainly.

Introduction

Small and medium enterprises play a critical role in the economy of India. The post liberalization era (1991) has thrown up new challenges to the Indian Small and Medium Enterprises (SMEs). Innovation is the basis for all competitive advantage. Innovation can cause change. Organisations need innovation to stay in business. Quality programmes are vital for providing conducive climate for making change, and for continuous improvement. Innovation leads to better performance, growth, greater improvement in efficiency, productivity, quality, competitive positioning and greater market share. This paper attempts to bring out the factors influencing innovation in small and medium enterprises. Organisations need innovation to survive, delight customers, establish competitive advantage, deliver quality products, quality services, be more productive, and also to meet business goals.

Objectives

(i) to analyse the relationship between experience and innovation in SMEs and

(ii) to identify the factors influencing innovation among SMEs.

Hypothesis

(i) Experience and innovation are independent.

Methodology

Data was collected from 50 small and medium enterprises in Madurai district. The lists of industries were collected from Madurai District Small Industries Association (MADISSIA). In choosing the sample for the study, two considerations were borne in mind, namely :

(a) the firm must have a total investment of not more than rupees three crores and

(b) the sample must be restricted to the organised sector only.

Random sampling technique was used for selecting samples. Simple interview scheduled comprising of 19 factors was administered in the field for data collection. The respondents were asked to select an answer among five scores namely, Very Low, Low, Average, High, and Very High. Factor analysis was used to identify the crucial variables, which influence innovation. Chi-square analysis was used to test the formulated hypothesis.

Analysis and Interpretation

Experience and Innovation Practices in SMEs

Innovation is the process by which an employee learns to execute a work in a different way. This may lead to a change in the product or process. The experience of an employee may equip him with knowledge required for change. But application of the same depends on the attitude of the entrepreneurs. The relationship between experience and innovation can be established through a hypothesis by Chi-square method.

Table 1 shows the experience and innovation practices adopted by the Small and Medium Enterprise (SME) respondents at Madurai. The respondents were selected randomly from the list maintained by MADISSIA. Out of 50 respondents 32 were

Table 1: Experience and Innovation of SMEs Respondents

Experience in Years	*Respondents who Practice Innovation*	*Respondents Do Not Practice Innovation*	*Total Respondents*
Greater than 16	5	3	8
5-15	19	11	30
Less than 4	8	4	12
Total	**32**	**18**	**50**

Source: Computed from primary data.

practicing innovation in their enterprises and 18 were not practicing innovation. Those who practice innovation were either practicing product innovation or process innovation. Product innovation involves incremental break through in modifying existing features. Process innovation features mean the change in the method or a way of functioning of the system. Lack of awareness and lack of investment were the main reasons for not practicing innovation by the non- practicing SMEs.

Table 2: Testing of Hypothesis: Chi-square test

Observed Frequency	*Expected Frequency*	*(O-E)*	*(O.E)²/E*
3	5	4	0.8
22	19	9	0.5
7	8	1	0.125
5	3	4	1.33
8	9	11	0.82
5	4	1	0.25
		Total	3.825

Note: Table value: 5.991(d.f=2 & level of significance = 5).

It is found from Table 2 that the calculated value is less than the table value. Hence, the null hypothesis is accepted. Therefore experience and innovation are independent. From the chi- square test, it is evident that innovation and experience are independent. Irrespective of experience, entrepreneurs practice innovation out of their own interest and confidence.

Change makes experience outdated. Managing change depends on how it is perceived. Perpetual opaqueness, which is also known as the dominant logic of a firm is the major barrier for managing change. This is mainly due to the internalisation of past experiences and formulated set of assumptions and belief. The only way to overcome this perpetual opaqueness is through unlearning and relearning process. The change may cause fear of work load or obsolescence to cope with the new change. Top management can clearly communicate the outcome of change process to avoid mis-perceptions and to reduce fear.

Factors Influencing Innovation

The existing competitive environment of business changes the rules of the game. Environment change informs and forces an enterprise on the need to keep pace with changes both internal and external. The following factors influence innovation. These factors were identified after discussing with the sample respondents in this field.

- **Cost:** Cost factors involve two elements, namely economic cost and social cost. Economic cost includes the initial cost of adopting an innovation or new programme and the continuing costs of keeping it in operation. Social costs involve changed status arrangements within the organisations as individuals and group gain or lose power because of the new developments.

- **Return on Investments**: It is obvious that innovations will be selected on the basis of high returns on investment. It is much more difficult when it is the non-business sector.

- **Efficiency:** The more efficient innovation will be selected over the less efficient innovation.

- **Risk and Uncertainty:** The less the risk and uncertainty, the greater the likelihood of adopting an innovation.

- **Communication:** The clarity of the results is associated with the likelihood of innovation.

- **Compatibility:** The more compatible the innovation is with the existing system, the more likely it is to be adopted. This implies organisations are conservative in their innovations since what is compatible is unlikely to be radical.

- **Complexity:** More complex innovations are less likely to be adopted.

- **Scientific Status:** If an invitation is perceived to have sound scientific status, it is more likely to be adopted.
- **Perceived Relative Advantage:** The greater the advantage, more likely the innovation will be adopted.
- **Point of Origin:** Innovations are more likely to be adopted if they originate within the organisation.
- **Terminality:** This involves the timing of the innovation. In some cases, innovation is worthwhile only if it is adopted at a particular time or in a particular sequence in the organisation's operations.
- **Status quo-ante:** This refers to whether or not the decision to innovate is reversible. Can there be a return to the previous state of the organisation or is the decision irreversible.
- **Commitment:** This involves behaviors and attitudes towards the innovation. Participation in the decision to innovate tends to raise the commitment of organisational members towards the innovation. A higher level of commitment is associated with more successful innovation.
- **Interpersonal Relations:** If an innovation or a technological policy is likely to be disruptive to interpersonal relationships, it is less likely to be adopted.
- **Public vs. Private:** If an innovation is likely to affect a large part of the public, it will typically involve a large decision making body than an innovation is limited to a private party.
- **Gate keepers:** This refers to the number of steps of approval an innovation must pass through. Must it pass

through several stages or only one or two. The greater the number of gatekeepers it is more likely that an innovation will be turned down.

- **Susceptibility to successive modification:** If an innovation itself can be modified as conditions or technology changes it stands more chance of adoption.

- **Gate way capacity:** The adoption of one innovation or the technological policy is likely to lead to the capacity of an organisation to take up additional effort in continuing with innovation process.

- **Gate way innovators:** This refers to the fact that some innovations, even small changes in an organisation's structure, can pave the way for additional innovations.

According to the factor analysis (Table 3), the probability based on the rotated factor matrix for factor 1, of the variables terminality, status-quo compatibility, susceptibility to modification, communicability, point of margin, perceived relative advantage, and risk and uncertainty are 0.69619, 0.68512, 0.66145, 0.65286, 0.49645, 0.42143, 0.41068 and 0.30835 respectively. Similarly for factor 2, the probability based on rotated factors matrix of the variables cost, ROI, gate keepers, commitment, complexity , gateway capacity and scientific status are 0.74120, 0.73621, 0.54371, 0.51773, 0.45537 and 0.43356 respectively. Similarly for factor 3, the probability based on rotated factor matrix of the variables, interpersonal relations, gateway innovators, efficiency and publicness vs privateness are 0.63253, 0.47153, 0.43968 and 0.42081 respectively.

In the factor analysis, the nineteen factors such as cost of return on investment, efficiency, risk and uncertainty, communicability, compatibility, complexity, scientific status, perceived relative advantage, point of origin terminality, status

Table 3: Rotated Factor Matrix

Variables	*Factor 1*	*Factor 2*	*Factor 3*
VAR 00011	.69619	-.01738	.17905
VAR00012	.68512	.06311	-.19083
VAR00006	.66145	.0 6209	-.53594
VAR 00017	.65286	-.08839	.16068
VAR 00005	.49645	.19830	-.18322
VAR 00010	.42143	.14942	.34000
VAR 00009	.41068	-.18241	.14864
VAR00004	.30835	-.30259	.06503
VAR00001	.03090	.74120	.45339
VAR00002	.03197	.73621`	.40089
VAR 00016	-.40920	.59371	.44533
VAR000013	.11440	.51773	.07847
VAR00007	-.12412	-.49544	.44387
VAR00008	.37028	.43356	.04416
VAR00014	.06714	.13836	-.63253
VAR00019	.02243	.23589	.47153
VA00003	.20907	.10456	.43968
VAR 00015	.02524	.12472	.42081

quo ante, commitment, interpersonal relations, publicness vs. privateness, gate keepers, susceptibility to successive modification, gate way capacity and gate way innovators are reduced to three factors based on factor analysis. They are :

(i) Process related factors.

(ii) Procedure related factors

(iii) People related factors

Conclusion

Planned change is essential to make effective implementation. Planning makes change goal and result oriented. Innovation process involves changing the existing system in new ways and through methods of doing the task that result in higher output, cost effectiveness and increased value. Improving the function or reducing the cost through new methods would result in higher value. Value analysis will lead to cost effectiveness. Developing a vision, orienting and motivating people toward attaining the vision forms the basis for change accomplishment and the outcome of productivity and return. Further researches may be carried out to determine the relationship between innovation and performance.

References

Kharbande V.P. (2002), "Facilitating Indian Small and Medium Enterprises" **Current Science.**

Kumar. S., **Total Quality Management,** Laxshmi Publications (P) Ltd., New Delhi.

Nagarajan, R.S. and A.A. Arivalayan (2005), **Total Quality Management,** New Age International Publications, New Delhi.

Racul Schumann, Downa Prestwood, Alwin Tong John Vansto (2003) **Innovation,** Mcgraw Hill Inc, New Delhi.

2

Innovation and Research in Small and Medium Enterprises

Ezhilarasan, M and Selvalakshmi, M

Abstract

To succeed in the era of globalisation and to manage change more effectively, Small and Medium enterprises need to innovate, develop, market and integrate new technology. The prospects of SMEs would be widened if they are provided with a more innovation friendly environment with improved conditions for the creation and development of new companies, the diffusion of new technologies, the emergence of new economic activities and at fostering the "innovation culture" in the Indian business Scenario. This must also be accompanied by a legal, regulatory and financial framework which encourages innovation rather that stifling it. Thus the prime steps for inducing innovation into the system and evolution of SME's would be (1) To foster an innovation culture (2) To establish a framework conducive to innovation (3) To better articulate research and innovation.

This paper aims at exploring the innovation culture and conducive environment prevailing in our Indian subcontinent which would nurture the growth of SMEs. It also analyses the new innovations of SMEs which rattled the market place and set themselves as role models.

Introduction

The importance of Small and Medium Scale Enterprises cannot be overlooked in any economy especially in a developing economy as that of India. The importance of the SME sector is well recognized world over from its significant contribution in gratifying various socio- economic objectives, such as higher growth of employment, output, promotion of exports and fostering entrepreneurship.

Definition of SMEs in India

In India the small and medium enterprises are not well defined. The internal group set up by the Reserve Bank of India has recently recommended that the units with investment in plant and machinery in excess of SSI limit and up to Rs. 10 crores may be treated as medium enterprises. SMEs have been defined against various criteria such as the number of workers employed, volume of output or sales, value of assets employed, and the use of energy. Organization for Economic Cooperation and Development (OECD) defines establishments with up to 19 employees as 'very small', between 20 and 99 employees as 'small, from 100 to 499 employees as medium and over 500 employees as large enterprises.

Significance of SMEs in India

The SME sector in India employs around 26 million people and is involved with the production of over 7500 industrial items with the product range varying from very simple items produced with traditional technology to high tech products. At present, the SSI sector accounts for over 90 per cent of industrial units in the country, 40 per cent of value addition in the manufacturing output and approximately 35 per cent of India's exports. The Small and Medium Enterprises also have unique advantages due to their :

- Size
- Higher labor-capital ratio
- Shorter gestation period
- Focus on relatively smaller markets
- Lower investments
- More equitable distribution of national income
- Effective mobilisation of resources of capital and skills, which might otherwise remain unutilised.

All this and more depicts the clear potential of SMEs becoming the future power centre of our country.

Innovation in India

Innovation is one of the key differentiators for the success of companies. Successful firms differentiate themselves by how well and how fast they can adapt technology to suit their business processes. But such innovation really is not an option today. Innovate or perish has become the unwritten norm of the globalised economy. With the phenomenal increase in the velocity and complexity of information innovation is not a threat, but rather an opportunity...to better serve customers.

However, statistics show that India registered a mere 354 patents in 2003, compared with Taiwan's 5,300 and Korea's 3,952. Israel, a nation-state with a population as small as that of Bangalore city, is in a steady state of innovation — a record 1,188 US patents registered in 2003. It has around 100 venture capital firms, that have been responsible for more than 120 companies being listed on Nasdaq.

The prospects of SMEs would be widened if they are provided with a more innovation friendly environment with improved conditions for the creation and development of new companies, the diffusion of new technologies, the emergence of new economic activities and at fostering the "innovation culture" in the Indian business Scenario.

We need an incubation ecosystem to compete with innovation societies. This must also be accompanied by a legal, regulatory and financial framework which encourage innovation rather that stifling it. Thus, the prime steps for inducing innovation into the system and evolution of SME's would be :

1. to foster an innovation culture
2. to establish a framework conducive to innovation
3. to better articulate research and innovation.

Innovation and speed-to-market are two effective ways for the SMEs to compete successfully against the large, publicly held companies. Creating, fostering and sustaining the right environment really are the best innovative imperatives.

Foster Innovation Culture

Katalin Eibel-Spanyi, an Associate Professor of Marketing at Eastern Connecticut State University [ECSU] suggests eight rules to foster innovative culture in SMEs.

They are as follows:

1. **Foster Market orientation:** In many markets, the customer is no longer just the king, but has become the dictator. Therefore understanding the needs and wants of customers has become a fundamental aspect of satisfying customers. SMEs will have to find means to collect and disseminate and implement strategies in response to their information. They also need to be creative in their interaction with other companies and leverage their links to opinion leaders, universities, and industry associations to source market intelligence.

2. **Think beyond the product:** Customers no longer make purchasing decisions based mainly on product features.

Instead they are looking for responsiveness, service and the overall experience. The move towards providing customers with total solutions is particularly noticeable in industries characterised by complex and high-value products and services, where SMEs frequently play a dominant role. These are industries such as telecommunications, computer technology, aerospace, transportation networks and medical devices.

3. **Learn to Forget:** Innovation will increasingly require not only new technology and products or services, but new ways to organise and deliver value. Clinging to old models may have significant negative impact on the new ideas and thoughts. That is why it is important to have selective organisational memory and to learn to forget.

4. **Reach out**: With the effect of globalisation and technological revolution which has caused "the death of distances", no longer can a firm afford to look exclusively within its boundaries for breakthrough ideas. The information flow across continents should facilitate the SMEs to reach out for newness.

5. **Cultivate a learning organization** : The extent of a firm's learning orientation is comprised of four distinct components; commitment to learning, shared vision, open-mindedness, and inter-organisational knowledge sharing. The characteristic of promoting the value of curiosity, a habit of reaching out for ideas and help, and the display of a mixture of confidence and humility can create a highly collaborative culture within SMEs.

6. **Bid and Collaborate:** SMEs need to nurture relationships with government, universities and associations in order to access funding for innovation, data on emerging trends, and develop broader network of

contacts. This would enable them to take advantage of public funds available to foster innovation and bidding on such funding.

7. **Dabble with Weird ideas:** Thinking outside the box, or promoting lateral thinking among the team is a sure way to foster innovation. For example, weird ideas such as 'rewarding both success and failure and punishing inaction' and 'using job interviews to get new ideas - not to screen candidates' are both intriguing concepts that apply equally to SMEs.

8. **Rethink:** Fostering and sustaining innovation requires that SMEs continuously rethink everything. Not just products, but business processes, technology and organisation. Not just rethink, but reconfigure, re-sequence, relocate, reduce, reassign, and retool which requires challenging conventional wisdom.

Establish a Framework Conducive to Innovation

Intrepreneurship is a strategy for stimulating innovation by making better use of entrepreneurial talent. When effectively promoted and channeled, intrepreneurship not only fosters innovation, it also helps employees with good ideas to better channel the resources of a corporation to develop more successful products. Some of the greatest business leaders of the past century made their early mark in business as intrapreneurs. Former General Electric chairman Jack Welch made a name for himself by building GE's engineering plastics business as if he were starting his own company. Lew Lehr, former chairman of 3M, similarly built his career on his intrapreneurial pursuit of 3M's expansion into the healthcare industry.

A conducive environment for innovation can be facilitated by the legal, regulatory and financial support provided by the Government. In India, the National Innovation Foundation, run by the Council of Scientific and Industrial Research, is a government initiative with similar intent — fostering innovation and creativity in S&T with an ultimate go-to-market proposition, as is the department of science and technology's Tifac.

Several low-key private sector initiatives, like the KReSIT, IIT, Mumbai & Madras and Indiaco, India's largest private sector incubator, to name a few, are places where this is being done, albeit on a much smaller scale. Nasscom, on its part, has recognised its own role in facilitating innovation under a recent Innovation Initiative Programme for its SME constituency and has achieved initial success. However, all told, there is a group of about 100-200 incubates with these guardian organisations, when the actual need and potential for a country this size is 100 times that.

Better Articulate Research and Innovation

China has an Innovation Fund for small technology based firms to promote technological innovation amongst SME units. The SME agency of Japan supports the innovation activities of SME's through various products and services. Direct subsidies are also given by Government of Japan for R&D activities of SME's in Japan. However, in India, the much-publicized Indian government and MIT Media Lab Asia project to facilitate the invention, refinement and deployment of innovations to benefit all sectors of Indian society, however, never replicated its American success (Computer Clubhouse Network and Lances).

The need to support initiatives in development and application of frontier technologies like Nano Technology, Development of new materials, Genetics, Biotechnology, Chip Manufacturing, Communications Technology, Mobile Computing, Robotics, Energy saving and development of new sources of energy etc. has to be recognised by the Government. Handholding and facilitation services, space in industrial sheds and flatted factories provided on concessional rates may enable the SME's to think BIG.

The innovation agenda therefore has to be set through participative processes. Pumping in research funds into public R&D institutions will not help much in the development of SMEs. Public -private partnerships would be more beneficial.

In the words of **Zeitz (CEO of Puma)**, "But if you want to change the industry and do something completely new and innovate, research is a bad tool because all you will get fed back is perception today and not tomorrow." So, adequate support to implement the proposed ideas is far more important to encourage Innovation in SME's.

Conclusion

One who is enterprising is taking a big leap from being a job seeker to a job giver. People behind SME's therefore will have to reward for this difference they make. Some of the people just think, some just start, some get going, and some sustain. Only very few are successful. In the era of global markets, innovation on an ongoing basis is the true reason not for growth but for the very survival of Small and Medium Scale Enterprises.

References

Govindarajan, Vijay, and Chris Trimble (2005), **Ten Rules for Strategic Innovators: From Idea to Execution**, Harvard Business School Press, New York.

Shapiro, Stephen M. (2001), *24/7* **Innovation: A Blueprint for Surviving and Thriving in an Age of Change,** McGraw-Hill, New Delhi.

www.sssedonline.org.

www.aside.in/blog/innovation/

www.dsir.gov.in

www.nifindia.org/news

www.refresher.com

3

Innovative Waste Management: A Case of Agro–Based Industry

Rathakrishnan, L Saravanan Naidu, A

Abstract

During the past many decades unprecedent and powerful changes have transformed the economic landscape in the world. One change among them is the role of agriculture, which was earlier viewed as subsistence. But now this sector has developed substantially due to its versatality. But still there are many gaps, which have to be filled. One among them is the generation of waste, which at present is not properly managed. Many Agro-based industries in India are not practicing waste management techniques. The waste is waste if untreated, but if it is modified in some other form, it is a potential resource or a wealth in various capacities. This paper tries to trace the avenues of managing waste in agro based industry through introducing innovative practices in this sector.

Introduction

The importance of agriculture in the overall development of human beings is an accepted fact, which cannot be ignored. Human civilisation matured as a result of agricultural practices from time immemorial. Agriculture as an art has changed over a period of time. Now it is an important sector of the economy of many developed as well as developing countries.

India is predominantly an agricultural country where agriculture plays an important role as it provides food security, generates employment, helps in alleviating poverty, contributes significantly to the exports of the country. It is estimated that around 65 percent of the work force is connected with this sector. Over a period of time there has been a decline in the share of agriculture to the GDP. It was around 52 per cent in 1950s, which has came down to 26 percent at present, but still agriculture is the single largest contributor to the GDP. The development of the industries in one way or the other depends upon agriculture, which provides the raw materials and also at the same time generates demand for consumer goods. This type of industry comes under the broad area, agro-based industrial sector.

Agro-based industries are of two types, namely those industries which process raw materials obtained from agriculture and those associated sectors like animal husbandry, forestry, logging, fishery etc. and on the other hand there are industries, which produce inputs for the agricultural processing and allied industries. Agro-based industries, in general are not re-cycling their waste material. They simply dump the waste on the open yard or adapt 'no care policy'. Industrialists do not know the wealth behind the waste material. Practicing an innovation method of usage of waste may bring a little more profit to the food processing agro-based industry.

Growth of Agro-based Industry

The agro-based industry in general and the food processing industry in particular have started to register a positive trend of progress. As these industries require a very less fixed capital and a large working capital in comparison with other industries they have wider scope for progress. The total market of the value-added food products is estimated at about Rs. 2,500 to Rs. 3,000 billion. Besides this, there are many positives for these industries as the Government of India has also accorded high priority to them by extending the needed incentives to encourage value addition and trade.

The agro-based industry has employed around 1.6 million workers directly and it is projected that it will provide to 37 million both direct and indirect employment by the end of 2025. Today India is one of the largest producers of milk, fruits, cashew nuts, coconuts and tea, second largest producer of wheat, sugar, vegetables, and fish, third largest producer of rice and tobacco, and seventh largest producer of grains in the world. India has a very large marine product and processing potential with different fish resources along the stretch of 28,000 km of rivers and millions of hectares of reservoirs and brackish water. India's livestock population is one of the largest in the world with 50 per cent of worlds buffaloes and 20 per cent of cattle's, however only about one per cent of the total meat production is converted to value added products. The present situation offers enormous potential for export of agro-based industry.

Table 1 shows the growth and employment status of the agro-based industrial units in India over a period of two decades. First during the post-reform period, in the unorganised sector there was a fairly high annual growth rate of the agro based industry, which registered 6.7 per cent whereas the non-agro-based industries witnessed a steep decline of 7.9 per cent over the same period.

Table 1: Growth of Agro-based Industry and Employment (1984–85/2000-01)

NIC Code	*Description*	*Enterprises*		*Employment*	
		1984-85/ 1994-95	*1994-95/ 2000-01*	*1984-85/ 1994-95*	*1994-95/ 2000-01*
	A. Unorganised Manufacturing				
20 – 21	Food products	-3.1	2.5	-1.5	2.0
22	Beverages etc.	0.4	8.5	0.9	6.3
	Food processing	-1.9	5.0	-0.8	3.5
23 to 25	Cotton-Wool-Jute Textile	-7.7	-0.1	-6.7	-0.7
26	Textile products	-11.4	24.0	-5.9	15.5
27	Wood and its products	-0.7	1.7	0.9	1.6
28	Paper and its products	2.5	4.9	3.4	4.7
29	Leather and its products	-8.8	-2.4	-4.0	-3.1
	Non-food processing	-5.8	7.8	-3.6	5.2
	Total agro-based	-4.4	6.7	-2.6	4.6
30-39	Total non-agro-based	0.4	-7.9	2.6	-4.3
	All industries	-3.0	2.7	-1.1	1.9

NIC Code	Description	Enterprises		Employment	
		1984-85 / 1994-95	1994-95 / 2000-01	1984-85 / 1994-95	1994-95 / 2000-01
	B. Organised Manufacturing*				
20-21	Food products	1.9	1.6	2.0	0.9
22	Beverages etc.	1.6	-14.6	5.5	-1.3
	Food processing	1.8	-2.0	3.1	0.1
23 to 25	Cotton-Wool-Jute Textile	2.3	-3.6	-1.8	-2.7
26	Textile products	6.6	2.8	11.5	6.3
27	Wood and its products	-0.04	2.7	-0.8	0.5
28	Paper and its products	1.6	3.3	0.7	-2.0
29	Leather and its products	7.3	3.4	6.5	-1.8
	Non-food processing	2.8	0.4	0.1	-0.9
	Total agro-based	2.3	-0.8	1.4	-0.4
30-39	Total non-agro-based	2.6	2.7	1.1	0.8
	All industries	2.5	1.0	1.3	0.1

NIC Code	*Description*	*Enterprises*		*Employment*	
		1984-85 / 1994-95	*1994-95 / 2000-01*	*1984-85 / 1994-95*	*1994-95 / 2000-01*
	C. All Manufacturing				
20-21	Food products	-3.0	2.5	-1.1	1.9
22	Beverages etc.	0.4	8.4	1.5	5.2
	Food processing	-1.9	4.9	-0.3	3.0
23 to 25	Cotton-Wool-Jute Textile	-7.6	-0.1	-5.7	-1.1
26	Textile products	-11.4	23.9	-5.2	14.8
27	Wood and its products	-0.7	1.7	0.8	1.6
28	Paper and its products	2.5	4.8	2.5	3.0
29	Leather and its products	-8.7	-2.4	-2.8	-2.8
	Non-food processing	-5.8	7.8	-3.2	4.6
	Total agro-based	-4.4	6.7	-2.2	4.0
30-39	Total non-agro-based	0.5	-7.8	2.3	-3.3
	All industries	-3.0	2.7	-0.8	1.6

Sources: 1. Government of India, 1989; 1998 (a) and Unit level data (for 2000-01) on CD- ROM, supplied by National Sample Survey Organisation, New Delhi.

2. Government of India, Annual Survey of Industries, various issues.

* Latest available data is for the year 1999-2000.

In the case of the organised sector there was a reversal in the growth of the agro-based industry, which registered a negative growth rate of 0.8 per cent. In contrast, the non-agro-based industry had a positive growth rate of 2.7 per cent.

Table 1 clearly shows that there are wide variations in trends between the growth rates in unorganised and the organised segments of agro-based industry during the post reforms period, which only shows that the Indian industry is in the significant process of structural transformation, where the unorganised sector, which is predominantly small and tiny industrial units have an upper hand over their counterparts that is the organised sector.

The employment scenario is also very similar to the trend of growth of industry discussed above, which only shows that there is a direct link between the growth of the enterprise with the employment generaticn.

Table 2 depicts the growth performance of agro-food processing industries during the post economic liberalisation period (1992-2001). The table reveals that the production of rice has increased by 27.77 per cent, whereas the number of rice mills has only increased by 6.18 per cent. The number of flour mills has increased at the rate of 17.8 per cent and production of wheat by 25.50 per cent. The installed capacity of fruits and vegetable processing have increased from 9.5 lakh tonnes to 21.10 lakh tonnes and the production of processed fruit and vegetables also has gone up from 3.5 lakh tonnes to 9.9 lakh tonnes during this period. The increase in the installed capacity of fruits and vegetables processing is far less when compared to the production of fruits and vegetable in the country. After the reform period the number of FPO – licensed units in the country has increased by 33.4 per cent, production of milk by 44.6 per cent, production of processed milk products by 45.45 per cent and the production of marine products by 39.53 per cent. Table

Table 2: Growth of Agro-food Processing Industry in India During 1992-2001

Year	*Number of modern rice mills*	*Production of rice (million tones)*	*Number of roller flour mills*	*Production of wheat (million tones)*	*Production of fruit and vegetable products (lakh tones)*
1992	32969	72.86	696	57.21	3.5
1993	32969	80.3	702	59.84	4.69
1994	33557	81.81	750	65.77	5.5
1995	34113	76.98	800	62.1	6.78
1996	34685	81.74	812	69.35	8.5
1997	34688	82.53	812	66.35	9.6
1998	34688	86.08	820	71.29	9.1
1999	35088	89.68	820	76.37	9.4
2000	35088	84.87	820	68.76	9.8
2001	35000 (6.18)	93.1 (27.77)	820 (17.8)	71.8 (25.50)	9.9 (182.85)

Year	*Installed capacity of fruits and vegetable processing (lakh tones)*	*Number of licensed units under FPO*	*Production of milk (million tones)*	*Production of processed milk products (lakh tones)*	*Production of marine products (lakh tones)*
1992	9.5	4057	58.5	2.20	43
1993	11.8	4132	61.2	2.29	46
1994	12.6	4270	63.5	2.49	47
1995	14.02	4368	65	2.61	49
1996	17.5	4674	68	2.76	53
1997	19.1	4932	71	2.85	53
1998	20.04	5112	74.5	3.01	56
1999	20.6	5198	74.5	3.07	56
2000	21	5293	78	3.16	56
2001	21.10 (122.10)	5413 (33.4)	84.6 (44.6)	3.20 (45.45)	60 (39.53)

Source: Annual Reports, Ministry of Food Processing Industry, Govt. of India (various issues)
Note: Figures within the parentheses indicate the percentage change during the ten-year period.

2 clearly shows that after the liberalisation period there is a steep increase in the production as well as installed capacity of all the agro-based food processing industry in India.

Waste Generation in the Agro-based Industry

Agro-based Industrial sector is a versatile area bringing many industries under its fold. In this broad sector each industry has a certain type of waste stream associated with it, which is either treated in-house or disposed off at a cost.

Among the various agro-based industries, rice processing industry is regarded as the largest industry in India in terms of rice mills and rice production. There are about 1, 38,000 units comprising about 91.28 thousand hullers, 4.54 thousand shellers and 8.38 thousand hullers-cum-shellers and 35.08 thousand modern rice mills. All these units are producing rice to the tune of 93.1 million tonnes per annum. The main by-products of rice milling industry are husk, bran, germs and brokens which comprise nearly 20-25 per cent, 5-7per cent, 1-2 per cent and 2-3 per cent of the total rice milled respectively.

The next important agro based industry is fruit and vegetable processing sector. The installed capacity of fruit and vegetable processing industry has increased from 11.08 lakh tonnes in 1993 to 23.28 lakh tonnes in 2004. The total production of fruit and vegetable processing products in 2004 was 10.72 lakh tonnes. The utilisation of fruits and vegetables for processing in the organised & unorganised sectors is estimated to be around two per cent of the total production. It is very sad to note that nearly 30 per cent of fruits and vegetables are wasted. It is estimated that the quantum of fruits and vegetables wasted in India is equal to the annual consumption of the United Kingdom.

Waste in these industries is generated during canning and preparation of juices, squashes, jams, jellies, and dried products. The major wastes are in the form of peelings, coring, seeds, stones, rinds, skin, trimmings, over ripe and defective materials, which are being left over. Disposal of this waste material becomes difficult and poses serious problems to the environment.

Innovative Waste Management Options for Agro-based Industry

Waste Management in Rice Processing Industry

As we know that the major waste, or in other words by-products, of rice milling industry are husk, bran, germs broken, straw, which can be effectively used in many ways so as to convert the waste into wealth.

For example, the rice bran is an important raw material for solvent extraction industry. It is estimated that on an average rice bran contains about 16 per cent oil. So, bran can be efficiently used for extracting edible oil.

The rice husk can be utilised for generating power and steam. It is observed that one kilogram of rice husk can generate 2.5 to 2.8 kg. of steam at 11 kg/cm^2 pressure which is equivalent to 0.33 kg of fuel oil. The steam, which is generated can be utilised for boiling the paddy and the power can be used for the operation of rice mills. (Varshney 1987).

The rice husk ash can be used to extract sodium silicate. It is noted that it has a high silica content of about 80 per cent, which makes it an economical source for producing sodium silicate. As we know that sodium silicate is a chemical used in the production of soaps, detergents and silica gel, which can be easily produced at a very low cost by using rice husk ash.

Rice husk ash when mixed with lime shell generates a good quality cement due to the presence of silica in it, which is a cheap alternative to the ever increasing price of ordinary cement.

Fine quality veneer and boards for roofing houses, at a very low cost can be made with the rice husk, a by-product of the rice processing industry.

In general, the agricultural waste like cereal, straw, plantation waste etc. can be used to produce mushroom, which is very much in demand worldwide.

Waste Management in Fruit and Vegetable Processing Industry

The waste from banana as such is of high significance. The fibre of the banana tree is a sustainable resource to manufacture paper, fabrics and ropes etc. The banana peels can

Table 3

The possible by-product from fruit wastes are given below.

Fruit	*Waste %*	*Nature of Waste*	*By-products*
Apple	20-30	Pomace	Juice, wine, vinegar, pectin, cattle feed.
Citrus			
1. Orange	50	Peels, seeds and pulp	Essential oil, pectin, cattle feed, peel candy
2. Lime	60	Peels, seeds and pulp	Essential oil, pectin, cattle feed, peel candy
Grapes	20-30	Steams	Cream of tartar
		Pomace	Tartaric acid, cattle feed, jelly
		Seeds	Edible oil
		Skins	Food colourants
* Guava	40-45	Pomace, peels and seeds	Jam, cheese, toffee, biscuits
Mango	40-60		
-Peel	12-15	Peel and pulp	Pectin, cattle feed, alcohol.

Fruit	*Waste %*	*Nature of Waste*	*By-products*
-Pulper waste	5-10	Fibre	Uline, vinegar, juice
-Kernel	15-20	Hull and Kernel	Fat tannins, starch.
** Pineapple	30-60	Mill juice	Bromellin, wine, sugar, syrup, citric acid, waxes, sterols, cattle feed.
		Core	Conserve bulking agent.
		Peels	Vinegar
		Stem	Bromellin, starch
		Crown	Cattle feed
		Leaves	Cattle feed, fibre, fabrics, paper
		Effluents	Single cell protein oxalic acid, Biogas gum.
*** Peaches Apricots and cherries	-	Piths, Kernels	Oil, stock feed

Source: Anand and Mani (1997)
* Chadha (1993)
** Joseph and Mahadeviah (1988)
*** Anon (1998)

be converted into fuel as they contain 11 percent alcohol. And even biogas can be produced with the help of banana peels is the cheapest source of energy for our future. In addition these wastes are effective sources of fertilizer and also animal feed.

Suggestions for Effective Management of Waste in Agro-based Industry

I. General Waste Management Suggestions

- The economical way of managing waste in agro-based industry is to convert the waste into animal feed,

- Composting of waste is another alternative,

- The waste can be either utilised as fuel directly or can be converted to methane by anaerobic digestion, and

- 50 to 60 per cent of water consumed in Agro-based industry can be reused so that the cost of water needed for processing will be lower.

II. Administrative and Regulatory Suggestions

- As most of the agro-based industries are small scale units, which generate small quantity of waste it is not economical for them to treat waste individually. So, there should be a common plant for waste / by-product recovery and treatment,

- A linkage mechanism should exist between the agro-based industrial units with regard to the dissemination of information in respect to waste because "Waste of one industry is raw material for the other", and

- The government should provide some incentives to the industries which are willing to implement waste management techniques. These may be in the form of financial incentive or the technical know how abcut the latest waste management practices.

III. Human Resource Suggestions

- The industry should provide employees with training in waste reduction techniques and practices,

- The employees should be encouraged to contribute some valuable suggestions regarding changes in design and techniques for waste reduction in the industry; and

- There should be involvement of the employees in implementing waste reduction measures in the industry.

Conclusion

To sum up, agro-based industry in India continues to enjoy a prominent place in the development of the economy. Due to the versatility of this sector the waste is also increasing day by day. Though many waste management techniques have been developed their affordability and practice depend upon the willingness of the industries to convert the waste into wealth. Hence, the agro-industry entrepreneurs should come forward to utilise the waste by adapting innovative measures suggested.

References

Chadha G.K. and P.P. Sahu (2003) "Small Scale Agro- Industry in India: Low Productivity is its Achilles Heel", **Indian Journal of Agricultural Economics,** 58 (3): 522-526.

Bharti D.K., L.S. Gangwar and Sendeep Kumar (2004), "Food Processing Industry in India: An Economic Analysis", **Agricultural Economics Research Review,** 17 (2): 191-192.

Varshney A.C. (1987), "Rural Industrial Waste", **Rural Waste Management,** Associated Publishing Company, New Delhi: 205.

Kalsi Harsimrat and S.S. Dhawan (2001), "Potential of by products Recovery from Fruit Waste: A Review", **Beverage and Food World,** 28 (5): 5.

Anand, J.C. and Maini, S.B. (1997), "Utilization of Fruit and Vegetable Wastes", **Indian Food Packer,** 51 (2): 45-63.

Chadha, M. (1993), **Nutritional Evaluation and Utilisation of Guava,** unpublished M.Sc. Thesis, CCS HAV, Hisar.

Joseph, G. and Mahadeviah, M. (1988) "Utilisation of Waste from Pineapple Processing Industry", **Indian Food Packer,** 42 (1): 46-58.

Anonymous (1998), "By Products from Food Processing Waste", **Yojana,** 39: 75.

4

Quality Circle in Small and Medium Enterprises

Rathakrishnan, L Uma, P

Abstract

Small and Medium Enterprises (SMEs) have significantly contributed to the economic development, particularly in production, exports, employment generation, innovation and the overall growth of the country. The growth of SME sector and its contribution to the economy is well recognised in India. In the modern world consumers have become more and more conscious of quality and standardisation of product. Quality and competitive pricing alone can give SMEs an edge over their rivals. It is now accepted that quality is everyone's responsibility. It is in this context that the SMEs in India have recently started applying quality practices. This paper is an attempt to explain quality improvements through quality circle activity and its importance in small and medium enterprises.

Introduction

Small and Medium Enterprises (SMEs) are considered the engine of economic growth and promoting sustainable growth. They account for a major share of industrial production and exports. Quality in small and medium enterprises is becoming a vital component in giving them a competitive edge. Hence, understanding quality aspect and the initiatives through quality circle has become imperative for small entrepreneurs.

Quality is conformance to the requirement for perfection. Quality can be referred to (i) a specific characteristic of an object; for example the hardness of Ice combined with melting characteristics; (ii) the achievement or excellence of an object; for example good quality ice; (iii) it may be related to quality of an object. It is the quality of ice – that is ice ness; and (iv) the meaning of excellence itself. It is nothing but a feeling of extraordinary.

The first meaning is technical, the second one is practical, the third is artistic and the fourth is metaphysical. All four meanings together bring the quality, which is synonymous with 'good or the best'. Some thing might be good because it is useful, because it is beautiful, or simply because it exists.

Quality requires continuous improvement. It is the essence of managing an Institution. Total quality management is a philosophy that involves everyone in an organisation involved in a continual effort to improve quality and achieve excellence.

Quality Circle for Total Quality Management

Quality circle is a small group of members who voluntarily meet regularly for about an hour every week to identify, analyse and resolve problems, leading to improvement in their total performance and enrichment of their work life. In Industry it is a volunteer group composed of workers who meet together to discuss workplace improvement, and make presentations to management of their ideas.

A quality circle is a participatory management technique. It helps employees in solving problems related to their own jobs. Joel E. Ross and William C. Ross define a quality circle as "a small group of employees doing similar or related work who meet regularly to identify, analyse, and solve product-quality and production problems and to improve general operations".

A circle is a voluntary group of workers who meet regularly to discuss problems and present to the management of their ideas. Quality circle was started in Japan in 1962. Kaoura Ishikawa has been credited with creating quality circles as another method of improving quality. The movement in Japan was coordinated by the Japanese union of Scientists and Engineers (JUSE). Ishikawa, who believed in tapping the creative potential of workers innovated the quality circle movement to give Japanese industry the creative edge.

Characteristics of Quality Circle

Quality circle concept is attributed with three major variables, namely

(a) Quality circle is a form of participation management;

(b) Quality circle is a human resource development technique; and

(c) Quality circle is a problem solving technique.

As such it is a forum of employees who come together and evolve innovative techniques or ideas to be implemented by the management in a consensus method. Hence, it is participatory. In the process the quality circle enhances the characteristics of human resources. Eventually, all these developments lead to the solution of the local problems of employees or the problems related to the environment of the management. Thus, it solves twin problems, namely employees' grievances are addressed and the sustainable growth of the firm in terms of cost and profitability is ensured.

The Structure of the Quality Circle

The quality circle is a relatively autonomous unit, usually led by a supervisor or a senior worker and organised as a work unit. Employees who participate in the quality circles will be given training in formal problem-solving methods - such as brainstorming, pareto analysis, and cause-and-effect diagrams. All these methods can be used either to solve specific or general company problems. After completing an analysis, they often present their findings to the management and then execute implementation of approved project. Quality circle projects are selected on a wide range of application areas. Broadly the areas can be classified into two namely, (i) cost aspect and (ii) employees' benefit.

Employees are motivated by their participation in making such improvements. Quality circles can help a small business to reduce costs, increase productivity, and improve employee morale. Other potential benefits that may be realised by a small business include greater operational efficiency, reduced absenteeism, improved employee health and safety, and an overall better working climate. Quality circle is the best group work for meeting the goal of designating quality into a product.

The interest of manufacturers in quality circles was sparked by dramatic improvements in the quality and economic competitiveness of Japanese goods in the post-World War II. The emphasis of Japanese quality circles was on preventing defects from occurring rather than inspecting products for defects following a manufacturing process. Japanese quality circles also attempted to minimise the scrap and downtime that resulted from part and product defects. The quality circle movement was evolved to accomplish the broader goals of cost reduction, productivity improvement, employee involvement, and problem-solving activities.

Characteristics of Quality Circle

The quality circle has seven major characteristics, namely small in group, workers homogeneous group, voluntary circle, regular/periodic meeting - at least once in a week, resolve issues related to work problems, tries to improve performance and finally it enriches the work life.

1. Small Group of Employees

The optimum number of members in any quality circle is about to 10. The active participation of member can be possible with optimum size of members.

2. Workers are from the Same Discipline

Workers are from the same discipline or doing similar type of work: A homogenous group is always a pre-requisite for the success of the quality circle.

3. Quality Circle is Voluntary

Members' decision join in the quality circles is voluntary. No pressure is exerted on them to join or not to join the quality circle.

4. Meets Regularly Every Week

The members of quality circles should meet regularly once in a week for an hour after their work or during working hours to discuss the problems related to their work.

5. Quality Circle Identifies, Analyse and Resolves Work Related Problems

Workers, in a work place know best what problems are blocking achievement of good quality, productivity and optimum performance and also how those problems could be solved.

6. Improves Total Performance

The Members resolve the work related problems leading to improvement in their total performance. As the members identify and analyse the problems related to work place, they can easily resolve the work related or product related problems leading to improvement in their total performance.

7. Enriches Work Life

Quality circle enriches the work life of the workers. The objectives of Quality Circles are multi-faced. As the members identify and analyse the problems related to work place, they can easily resolve the work related or product related problems leading to improvement in their total performance.

Steps Involved in Problem Solving

Step 1: Identify the Problem

The first step is to identify the problem and to state the problem accurately; for example lack of communication. Start the Cause and Effect Diagram with an arrow pointing from left to right towards the problem:-

Step 2: Determine the Main Causes (using Fish bone Diagram)

A problem is caused by various factors. These factors can be categories according to the resources of production such as man, machine, material and method like:-

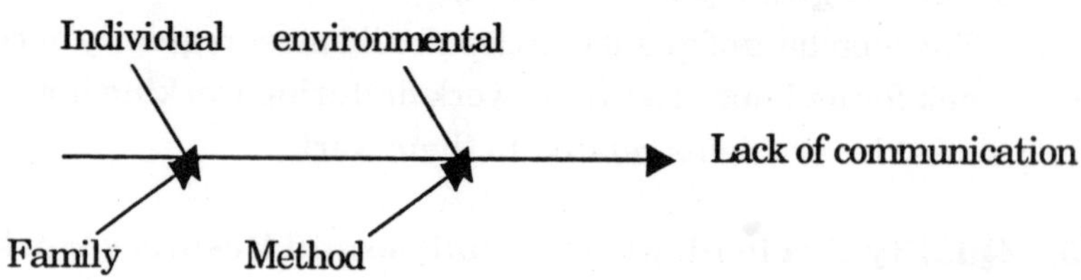

Step 3: Pareto Analysis: - (Go for vital issues)

Pareto analysis provides the mechanism to control and direct effort by fact, not by emotion. It helps to clearly establish top priorities and to identify both profitable and unprofitable targets. Pareto analysis is useful to:

- Priorities problems, goals, and objectives
- Identify root causes
- Select and define key quality improvement programmes
- Address the Vital Few and the Trivial Many causes of nonconformance

This is also known as 80/20 rule which means 80 per cent of the problem are caused by vital-few while 20 per cent alone are caused by trivial-many problem.

Requirements for Successful Quality Circles in SMEs

The small and Medium Enterprise owners should be comfortable with a participative management approach. It is also important that the small business owners learn this quality circle and its importance. They should be committed in implementing quality circle projects. They should ensure cooperation from the employees through creating awareness about quality circles and their benefits. The support of middle managers for the quality circle programme is also equally important.

The small business owners must be willing and able to commit the time and resources needed to train the employees who would participate in the programme, particularly the quality circle leaders and facilitators. It may even be necessary to hire outside facilitators if the time and expertise do not exist in-house. Some small businesses can get external resource persons to establish a steering committee to provide direction and guidance for quality circle activities. Even if all these requirements are met, the small business will only benefit from quality circles, if employee participation is voluntary.

Employees should be given training input for the selection of problems to be addressed. The small business owners must give time for the quality circles to achieve desired results. In some cases it may take more than a year for expectations to be realised.

Successful quality circles results in lots of benefits for small businesses. For example, management becomes aware of employee ideas, and employee recognises the need for innovation within the company.

Quality circles also serve to facilitate communication and increase commitment among both workers and management. Employee satisfaction increases through participation in decision-making; such involvement may also improve the ability to recruit and retain qualified employees by the small business owners.

Small companies find that quality circles strengthen team work and prepare employees for change. Quality circles can improve overall competitiveness of a small business by reducing costs, improving quality, and promoting innovation.

Basic Principles of an Effective Quality Circle

(1) Creating logo and Name: The team needs an identity through team's name, flag, banner, logo, behavioral norms to facilitate team work.

(2) Setting priority for identifying the problem: The team should identify problems of immediate need and then proceed with higher level need.

(3) Walk then run: Team should start with worthwhile but easy problems. Support should be given for analysis and solution.

(4) Team members should be given equal responsibility: Every one in the team is equal. Team members should be trained to gather information, participate, take minutes of the meeting, and involve in problem solving.

(5) Active listening: Team members need to be trained in empathatic listening. They should improve their questioning ability. It enhances their self esteem, encourages co-operation and help identifying problems.

(6) It is very difficult to make people attend the meeting. Meeting should be conducted at fixed timings. Adequate preparation is required for the meeting.

(7) Structure group and individual work: It is very important to decide group and individual work. Then the task should be allocated to individuals.

Impact of Quality Circle on Workers

The quality circle not only helps to increase the productivity but also helps the workers in many respects. It could bring in a change of attitude, self improvement, develop team spirit and finally it improves organisational culture.

Change Attitude

A major breakthrough in the quality circle is a change in attitude among workers. It is a positive attitude from "I don't care" to "I do care". It also helps in continuous improvement in quality of work life through humanization of working atmosphere.

Self Development:

The quality circle also influences self development. It will bring out the 'hidden Potential' of the people. The workers involved in this circle get to learn additional skills. Hence, there is a possibility to develop individual talents.

Development of Team Spirit

The concept of oneness to collective spirit may spur the workers through the habit of working to-gether or as a team rather than individually. They could also say that "I could not do but we did it". Above all it eliminate inter-departmental conflicts.

Improved Organisational Culture

Total quality circle may develop a positive working environment. Here total involvement of people at all levels is possible. Finally, it will act as an instrument for higher motivation.

Conclusion

Formulation of Quality circle enables the employees to improve their personality. It improves their individual self respect. It helps them to change some of their personality characteristics. It increases mutual respect. Employees can understand the difficulty faced by others. Quality circle changes the negative attitude. It reduces the conflict stemming from the working environment. Workers can understand why many problems cannot be solved quickly and it gives workers a better understanding of the importance of quality. Industries should create awareness among workers and take initiative to formulate quality circle.

References

Deepa Sharma (2004), "Family Quality Circles", **Indian Journal of Training and Development,** XXX1V (2).

Gupta, S.R. (1994), Quality Circles: **Progress Through Participation,** Tata Mcraw-Hill Book Company: (195-198).

Robert F., Wickman, Robert S. S. Doyle (1993), **Break Through Quality Improvement for Leaders Who Want Result,** Tata Mcraw-Hill Book Company, New Delhi: 195-198.

Sridhara Bhat, K. (2004), **Total Quality Management,** Himalaya Publishing House, New Delhi: 328-330.

Sundara Raju, S.M. (1995), **Total Quality Management,** Tata Mcraw-Hil, New Delhi: 16-18.

Vijaya Banu C. (2007), "The Effectiveness of Quality Circles at BHEL- A Study", **ICFAI Journal of Management Research, V1** (3).

5

Quality Management Systems in Dairy Industry

Sriram, K

Abstract

Changing life styles, urbanisation and demand from consumers for safe, hygienic, quality convenience foods are transforming the food processing sector from the traditional small scale production into a modern one to meet the varied tastes and needs of consumers. Though India is one of the largest producers of food in the world through abundant availability of wide varieties of crops, fruits and vegetables, livestock and sea food, due to various constraints only meager percentage is converted in food processing which has a very good market potential. Total Quality Management, a philosophy aimed at delighting the customer by ensuring quality by involving every one in the business process, is the most appropriate approach as it will provide the food processing industries with required quality to compete with global players in the post WTO regime. The application of TQM principles in the emerging, promising, growth oriented food processing sector will bring to light the remarkable improvement made by the dairy sector, as it has the largest growth potential and clearly one of the most largest market. Few examples from practicing dairies are given to substantiate the benefits that have been accrued due to TQM.

Introduction

Total Quality Management (TOM), a philosophy propagated by Edward Deming, a world renowned quality guru, uses the principles of organisation and wide quality systems to prevent the defects occurring at the source by extensive use of statistics by involving everyone in the quality programme working in teams to continuously improve the whole process, system, people to produce quality products to ensure total customer satisfaction.

India has progressed from being an agriculture deficit to agriculture surplus country due to implementation of white and green revolutions initiated by the government under various plan periods. Today the country is proud to be rated as the largest producer of food in the world in products like wheat, rice, fruits and vegetables, grains, pulses and in animal based products like milk, meat and poultry.

Food industry is one of the most important industries as it affects human beings in their everyday life. It is therefore, imperative and critical for the industry to produce products with the highest quality and safety.

Recent outbreaks of food borne diseases, some of which have proved fatal as the one that happened in China due to poor quality of milk implies that food processors should place their priority in safety, hygiene, and quality in a consistent manner.

TQM can play a vital role in promising these results. The guideline issued by the Ministry of Food Processing and the incentives offered for implementing TQM in food processing sector bears testimony to the importance of TQM.

This paper examines the Quality Management Systems (QMS) adopted by the food processing industries to compete with global players in the post WTO regime and shows how TQM can enhance the country's product acceptance by overseas buyers.

As the food processing industry is highly diverse in nature, it is not possible to analyse the implementation and benefits of TQM in all sectors. This paper is limited to milk and milk products as the dairy sector is a vital segment which has shown remarkable growth and is still poised for further growth in terms of volume and value addition.

Overview

Dairying provides a livelihood to millions of farmers and is a source of additional income for rural people. It enables women to contribute to the economic and social development of the villages.

During the 60's it was a common sight to see surplus milk being freely given to poor and needy and the balance thrown as waste as there was no way to scientifically preserve the milk or there was little knowledge about making milk related products in a bulk manner.

Reserving the milk sector to small scale and marginal farmers prevented its growth due to their unwillingness to adopt new technologies and better practices and many capable private enterprises not having the vision to see this sector as a prospective business venture.

The white revolution initiated by the government made India progress significantly in the dairy sector and the cooperative movement added further impetus to its growth. Today India is the largest producer of milk in the world. Dairy sector contributes 6.3 per cent to the country's GDP and employs nearly 1.6 million people.

Milk and milk products like instant milk foods, malted foods, condensed milk cheese have an estimated 70 billion US dollar market potential. However, the share of export market is a meager 1.5 per cent mainly due to low value addition, which is currently at 8 per cent compared to 20 per cent in China, 45 per cent in Philippines and a whoopping 188 per cent in the U.K.

TQM is one way to address this problem as it identifies the value added activities and helps in eliminating non-value added activities and will be the most appropriate tool for the Indian dairy industry to boost its sale in the international market.

TQM Application at Various Levels

Farmers

Though TQM is not technically understood, our farmers have started evincing keen interest in one or the other quality management systems due to :

(a) Customers rejecting non-conforming products,

(b) Pressure from producers for more value addition,

(c) Compulsion to adopt continuous supply to existing producer,

(d) Higher profits and more healthy products, and

(e) Awareness of the benefits of TQM practised by the producers.

By Implementing TQM the farmers can achieve :

(a) Premium for their produce.

(b) Security of supplies.

(c) Cost savings.

(d) Recognition.

(e) More healthy farming environment and ability to do forward planning. More importantly they learn better animal health management. Ongoing inspection allows them to evaluate their own operations. TQM helps farmers learn and understand better daily dairy process management, documentation of safe and wholesome milk production. They also learn their areas of weakness and ways to improve and achieve their measurable goals.

Dairies

Many dairies wrongly assumed that implementing information technology could enhance their routine operations and as such computerised their units without realising that IT is only an enabler for TQM, which can bring improvements only in the long run.

TQM can help dairies gain a better understanding of the entire operation chain and identify the processes that affect the quality and safety of milk products. As the variations in the processes of milk and milk products production are very huge knowledge to detect and control such variation at the source by TQM will ensure product quality.

Regardless of the herd size, TQM simplifies dairy work life by clearly defining the quality goals, ways to achieve and ensure customer satisfaction by improved product quality.

Many dairies are confused between milk quality and safety and consider both as same . Milk or milk product can be safe but not necessarily of good quality. Processors should understands safety as an integral part of quality.

Food product quality involves making sure that the product is safe at the same time attractive to customer by retaining the natural flavour, mouthful, colour and texture.

Quality Management Systems (QMS)

Many dairies implement one or the combination of the following QMS and believe that they have a safe and quality product.

(a) ISO – 9000

(b) ISO 14000.

(c) Hazard Analysis Critical Control Point (HACCP)

(d) Good Manufacturing Practices (GMP)

(e) Good Laboratory Practices (GLP)

Most of these systems are only documentation of the various processes or procedures and help only in detecting and reporting the variations after it's occurrence, whereas TQM by employing problem solving tools identifies the root causes and ensure the elimination of the causes of variations at the source level itself.

By integrating other QMS with TQM, the organisation can certainly gain additional benefits and increases the accountability, productivity, responsiveness which would result in improved financial performance through cost reduction.

Also as the variation level is very high in milk and milk product processing the use of statistical analysis, which is the main tool of TQM, must become handy for the dairy quality programme.

TQM Successes on Dairies

To understand the significance of TQM a few examples from the dairies are given to show how beneficial this approach is to enhance the overall performance.

Amul : Anand Milk Union Limited

Amul is a very successful cooperative organisation. The a cooperative movement is formed for eliminating middlemen and to enable farmers to get due returns on their investments and efforts. Amul is a classic example of an organisations success by effective TQM implementation. The motto of the Amul is delighting customers by offering products of high quality focusing on their customer needs which is the very foundation of TQM concept. Amul started practicing TQM from 1995 and adopted the following TQM principles.

1. formulation and implementation communicated to allthrough. The process of policy deployment = Hoshin Kanri, of strategy.

2. They concentrated on value addition.

3. Formed quality circles involving dealers and encouraged their participation

4. Farmers and employees were given training on self leadership.

5. Farmers were given training in cooperation, that made them set quality goals and trained them to view challenges as opportunities.

6. Integration of their procurement, processing and distribution functions by employing Information Technology.

7. Coordination amongst the entire value chain is the other notable feature.

8. True to TQM philosophy of improvement on continual basis they Automated the entire milk collection process. Dairy information and services kiosk through which everyone in the system can get details pertaining to their area of operation. They established an enterprisewide integrated application system to improve the efficiency and effectiveness of the distribution side of the supply chain which is generally the important but weak link.

9. As part of the TQM programme Amul implemented
   (a) Training of rural masses in quality of milk supply.
   (b) Networking the entire activity chain to have continuous information flow.
   (c) Simplifying of the complexity in the milk collection process.
   (d) Empowerment of rural people in self development.
   (e) Participation by all and open communication.
   (f) Transparency and trust amongst the villagers in the system.

No doubt the slogan of Amul "Taste of India" is a true reflection of management commitment for delighting the customer, by offering products as per their needs by following TQM principles of continuous improvement, team work, education and training, empowerment and involvement of all and supplier partnership.

By practicing TQM Amul has made remarkable improvements in every sphere and carved a niche not only in India but in the entire entire dairy world for the quality products and customer service. Amul has also implemented other QMS programmes like ISO, HACCP and EMS

Hassan Dairy

Hassan dairy operating in Karnataka also practices TQM philosophy with a firm belief in cooperative social responsibility. They practice Kaizen 5-S house keeping principles and extensively use the cross functional team suggestions to ensure participation and implement improvement projects. They concentrate more on energy conservation and based on employees suggestion replaced a firewood boiler with multi-fuel using agricultural waste like rice husk, coffee waste, coconut shells etc. They also have ISO, HACCP & EMS in place.

Mysore Dairy

Like it's counterpart in Hassan this dairy also uses Kaizen 5-S principles and cross functional teams for improvement projects. Based on employees suggestions they have implemented more than 20 projects for energy conservation. They also have ISO, HACCP & EMS in place.

Others

Some dairies in the U.S use flow charts to describe the breeding and conception process, as the reproductive programme is a very complicated but vital one. Monitoring and keeping records has resulted in a positive change in the work process and improvement in the reproductive program.

In six Californian dairies it was found that the primary concern has been about antibiotic residues and food borne bacteria in milk. By implementing TQM they were able to gain a full understanding of the entire production process, reasons for variations and improved the testing methods.

In another dairy, which had bulk milk tank for collection from farmers to be accepted after sampling and testing, a common practice followed to detect and ensure low somatic (body tissue) and bacteria count, has incorporated information about herd management. The farmer should key in feed supplies and drug treatment given to their animals to ensure non procurement of milk from herds undergoing treatment.

Conclusion

TQM has many similarities with strategic management, both requiring top management commitment, long term fundamental change process, orientation towards customers, future and continuous improvement. In India nearly 60 per cent of the quality of food is lost due to lack of storage, transportation and supply chain problems due to which the farmers get only 30 per cent of what the customer pays for the product compared to 70 per cent of what a farmer gets in U.S. TQM by integrating the entire value chain, enables the dairies to identify the critical areas for improvement by describing the causes. As the philosophy involves everyone responsible for the final quality by total customer focus the performance in all areas is bound to improve. Also other QMS programmes can be integrated with TQM structure as they will render additional support and benefits. However, TQM should be implemented with total commitment and true spirit to be successful. To be effective, TQM should not be viewed as separate from good leadership and management practices. Everyone must have quality in their mind focusing on customer and continuous improvement and the processes and systems should become a way of life.

References

Andrea Frazeur, AG (1998), "Quality and Safety Conditions for Customer Satisfaction in the Whole Meat Chain", **Innovation News,** Cacilin Hernandix.

Ursula Rickert, Grehard Schiefer, University of Bon, Chair for BusinessManagement: 7 (2).

Anon (1999), **Dairies Adopt TQM to Improve Milk Quality, Food Safety:News and Information Outreach,** University of California, Agriculture and Natural Resources.

Anon (2006), "TQM Quidelines for Food Processing Industries", www. mofpi.nic.in.

Anon (2007), "Total Quality Management: Lisa Lop", www.Qualityassurance.com article id 552, issue id 44.

Zoller C (2001), "Using TQM to Organize Labour and Work", **Buckeye Dairy News,** 4 (1).

www.maf.gov.nz/ (rural-nz)/sustainable/resorce use.

www.amul.com, Chaimans address in1999, e-experience of amul.

6

Total Quality Management in Facilitating Effective Performance of Small and Medium Enterprises

Rajasekar, N and Thillai Raja, P

Abstract

Total Quality Management (TQM), has become one of the most frequently discussed topics in current business parilance. Because of the competitive pressures created by Japanese companies, quality became a competitive weapon in 1980s in most industries. Competitive pressures of the 1980s and 1990s have been felt most strongly in the major industries that are dominated by very large firms. The main assumption is that quality is as important for small businesses as it is for large corporations. One reason is that some small companies have been competing directly with foreign firms for a long time; some have suffered the same consequences as large companies, while others have prospered in the competition. A second reason is that many large firms rely on a number of small companies for parts and services they use in producing their products. Third, competition in the economy seems to be intensifying, and new conditions emerge to which small firms have to adapt. Quality and productivity seem to be the indispensable main ingredients in a small firm's struggle for survival in these new conditions. In most cases a customer may have a general idea about a product's design and quality, but most consumers know nothing about the product specifications—and often do not care. TQM has evolved from the ideas of many quality experts and practices of very successful companies. This paper aims at linking the key concepts of TQM as applicable to the small and medium enterpries focusing on the principles and practices.

Introduction

Total Quality Management (TQM) is a management style based upon producing quality product or service as defined by the customer. TQM is defined as a quality-centered, customer-focused, fact-based, team-driven, senior-management-led process to achieve an organisation's strategic imperative through continous process improvement. TQM principles are also known as total quality improvement, world class quality, continous quality improvement, total service quality and total quality leadership.

The word "total" in Total Quality Management means that everyone in the organisation must be involved in the continous improvement effort, the word "quality" shows a concern for customer satisfaction, and the word "management" refers to the people and processes needed for quality.

Total Quality Management is not a programme; it is a systematic, integrated, and organisational way-of-life directed at the continous improvement of an organisation. It is not a management fad; it is a proven management style used successfully for decades in organisations around the world. TQM is not an end in itself; it is a means to an organisational end. Total Quality Management must not be the primary focus of an organisation; it should merely be the means to achieve organisational goals.

Small and Medium Business Enterprises: An Overview

In the globalised and industrialised world small and medium business has been experiencing fast growth over the past decades. About 84 per cent of all U.S. companies have less than 50 employees, because these small to medium-sized companies must continuously improve or die, implementing quality programme is critical. Smaller company may not realise the huge returns of a large company, but that does not reduce the impact of a quality programmes return on investment.

Internationally, empirical research into the rate and success of implementation of quality initiatives in SMEs is largely considered to be inadequate (Ramsey 1998; Kuratko, Goodale & Hornsby, 2001). Literature in this area is more often conceptual than empirical, and where empirical, it sometimes suffers from methodological limitations (such as unclear or inconsistent definitions of what constitutes an SME or what is TQM). Of the limited research available, it appears that SMEs have been very slow to implement formal quality models, and where they have, the outcomes are inconclusive (Husband & Mandal 1999).

Research pointing to the effectiveness (or otherwise) of quality initiatives in SMEs is important to the continued development and competitiveness of small business. Every small and medium business enterprise must satisfy customers, stakeholders and employees to survive. Day-to-day details often divert attention from what is good for the company. Conflicts in priorities and contention for resources combine to form a huge barrier to organisational excellence. Smaller businesses also have a narrow buffer to shelter customers from error and waste. In a small business, quality planning and business planning are synonymous. The best time to start a quality programme is during the initial planning for the business when designing quality into product and service delivery. Integrating quality into an existing company culture is more difficult, but no less critical. Smaller businesses have certain advantages over larger ones:

- Small businesses can move more quickly because innovative ideas are approved and developed at a faster pace.
- Communication channels are shorter and simpler.
- Fewer bureaucratic procedures need to be overcome in getting ideas to market.
- Employees acquire decision-making skills faster by exercising the authority that has been granted to them.
- Employees tend to form a close-knit effective work team.

These advantages are an important springboard for management in starting a quality programme. A truly integrated quality system is based on three principles: customer focus, process improvement and total involvement. Customer focus encompasses both the external and internal customer's needs. Process improvement is the lifeblood of an organisation wishing to sustain growth. Total involvement is the vehicle through which the company realises the daily activities that act on the first two principles.

These elements are taken from the Malcolm Baldrige National Quality Award performance excellence criteria. Though other models can successfully help small-business leaders segment their processes into measurable and stable components, small- to medium-sized businesses compete along with *Fortune* 100 businesses for recognition under these criteria. The Baldrige website even offers a free tool to help companies of any size assess their initial quality positions. One of the first things managers are instructed to do during business planning activities is a SWOT (strengths, weaknesses, opportunities and threats) analysis. The Baldrige self-assessment tool is an excellent complement to the traditional SWOT exercise.

There have been many studies identifying what composes TQM (GAO 1991; Easton 1993; Saraph **et al.** 1989; DDI 1993; Mann and Kehoe 1994, Plimpton **et al,** 1996; Black and Porter 1996; and Shin **et al.** 1998). Through these studies they have produced different results, there seems to be some common elements that are critical to TQM success. These elements include strong top management leadership and commitment, customer focus, employee involvement and empowerment, a focus on continuous improvement, supplier partnerships, and the recognition of quality as a strategic issue in business planning (Shin. **et al.** 1998). The use of SPSS and statistical tools in various segments of the organisation from product idea to product delivery has also been deemed essential to effective TQM implementation. The obvious flaws in TQM implementation or the five deadly diseases that must be eliminated from an organisation before TQM implementation are: Bottom-line management, Evaluation using organised by-the-members performance appraisals, Emphasis on short-term gains, Lack of consistency of purpose and Mobility of the work force.

Basic Principles of TQM Implementation

Based on the experiences learned by various companies implementing TQM as reported in the literature, there are some principles of practices that are instrumental to the success of TQM implementation (Department of Defence 1990 and Moore 1990):

1. Quality is everyone's business

2. Customer emphasis quality
3. Quality must be built into the product
4. TQM requires management commitment and involvement at all levels
5. TQM accomplishment involves continual training
6. Leadership is substituted for slogans and exhortations
7. Long-term emphasis on measurable process and productivity improvement
8. Understand the current process before improvement begins
9. Cross-functional orientation and teamwork
10. Effective use of statistical methods and quality control tools
11. Constant process, product, and service improvement
12. Incentive TQM involvement
13. Information sharing
14. Eliminate communication barriers
15. Suppliers must have a TQM philosophy

With the effective conceptualisation of the above said principles, total quality management can be effectively imbibed in small and medium enterprises for facilitating their effectiveness and thus enhancing the competitiveness in the globalised economy.

Productivity improvement techniques can be applied effectively in enterprises of any size, from one-person companies to corporations with thousands of staff. The majority of the techniques were first seen in mass production operations but the benefits they can yield in SME is not to be underestimated. Indeed the absence in SMEs of many of the rigidities commonly found in large companies make it easier for them to reap the benefits of productivity improvement techniques.

Various companies may deter SMEs from implementing TQM due to cost; employee resistance to change; personnel resource; specialized knowledge: and activities not standardised. A well-structured TQM system comprises the following components that are to be adopted by the SMEs in order to facilitate their competitiveness in the globalised scenario.

JIDOKA

Aimed at describing the man machine interface such that people remain free to exercise judgment while machines serve their purpose. The following three principles are central to the jidoka way of working:

- Don't make defects
- Don't pass on defects
- Don't accept defects

The jidoka system shows faith in the worker as a thinker and allows all workers the right to stop the line on which they are working.

HEIJUNKA

Is a key operating concept of JID manufacturing system. In practice it involves load leveling and line balancing. The underlying rule is an even workload for all employees.

JUST-IN-TIME

The American production and inventory control society (APICS) defines just-in- time (JIT) as: "A philosophy of manufacturing based on planned elimination of all waste and continuous improvement of productivity". The basic aim of JIT in SME is to:

- Reduce low time
- Minimize inventory
- Reduce defects rate to zero and
- Accomplish all of the above at minimum cost

- **KANBAN**

The word kanban literally means visible record. In the kanban system, flow is controlled by the use of cards. When implemented correctly in SMEs, JIT and KANBAN can result in reduced inventory and higher efficiency in a manufacturing system.

KAIZEN

Imai (1986) defines total quality control as organised kaizen activities involving everyone in a company-managers and workers-in a totally integrated efforts towards improving performance at every level. Kaizen is a Japanese word meaning gradual never-ending improvement. Kaizen approach proceeds in the following steps

- Define the area of improvement
- Analyse and select the appropriate problem
- Identity its causes
- Plan counter measures
- Implement counter measures
- Confirm the result
- Standardise

The various techniques used in facilitating kaizen include the following:

Zero defects, just-in-time, kanban, total preventive maintenance, 5s, suggestions schemes, robotics, productive improvement, eliminating waste, PDCA (plan, do, check, action cycle) quality circle.

The following principles are recognized as essential for continuous improvement

- Traceability
- Design of experiments
- top- in -time
- Root cause detection (who, what, where, when, why, how, how much,)

THE 5 S's

The concept was developed by Osada in the early 1980 and is used to establish and maintain all aspects of quality in an organisation.

The 5's stand for five Japanese words

- Seiri (proper arrangement) sorting out
- Seiton (orderliness) tidying up
- Seiso (cleanliness) neatness
- Seiketsu (standardising), housekeeping
- Shitsuke (discipline), obedience

All five of the five 5's can be accomplished with little or no capital investment whilst the financial returns from the resulting productivity improvements-in the form (for example, improved storage facilities can be quickly realised) and will offset any cost involved.

The basic concept of continuous improvement highlighted in this chapter is fundamental to the improvement of productivity. That they have their roots in Japanese management techniques and have been proven in large organisations such as Toyota and Kawasaki should not be a barrier to the SMEs. Companies of any size can apply these techniques to realise the benefits.

The productivity improvement tools highlighted in this chapter are all low cost; indeed some incur no direct cost at all. They are about working smarter rather than harder. In particular 5's principles are easy to apply and do not require major capital investment other than training, and they should quickly identify possible areas for further productivity improvement drives.

A gradual implementation of selected tools and techniques should lead to reduction in production waste and improve the morale of employees involved as they see the immediate visual impact of the productivity improvement ideas.

The challenge for the SMEs is to overcome barriers to the adoption of productivity tools and to understand and implement some of the productivity improvement tools and techniques identified in this paper. The application of such tools should mean that SMEs could become and remain preferred suppliers in the ever-developing agile supply chains of which they are key elements.

In addition to the said principles and concepts of TQM, more quality control tools and techniques are also available to identify, analyse, and to solve the different business related problems, mostly manufacturing oriented.

Total Quality Management (TQM) Tools

Total quality management (TQM) tools help small and medium organisations to identify, analyse and assess qualitative and quantitative data that is relevant to their business. These tools can identify procedures, ideas, statistics, cause and effect concerns and other issues relevant to their organisations. Each of which can be examined and used to enhance the effectiveness, efficiency, standardisation and overall quality of procedures, products or work environment, in accordance with ISO 9000 standards (SQ 2004).

According to Quality America, Inc. (ReVelle 2003) the number of TQM tools is close to 100 and come in various forms, such as brainstorming, focus groups, check lists, charts and graphs, diagrams and other analysis tools. In a different vein, manuals and standards are TQM tools as well, as they give direction and best practice guidelines to you and/or your staff.

TQM tools illustrate and aid in the assimilation of complicated information such as:

- identification of your target audience
- positive and negative forces affecting business
- assessment of customer needs
- competition analysis
- market analysis
- brainstorming ideas
- productivity changes
- various statistics
- staff duties and work flow analysis
- statement of purpose
- financial analysis
- model creation
- business structure
- logistics analysis

The list goes on, though essentially TQM tools can be used in any situation, for any number of reasons, and can be extremely effective if used properly.

The following are some of the most common TQM tools in use today. Each is used for, and identifies specific information in a specific manner. It should be noted that tools should be used in conjunction with other tools to understand the full scope of the issue being analysed or illustrated. Simply using one tool may inhibit your understanding of the data provided, or may close you off to further possibilities.

Pie Charts and Bar Graphs

This is used to identify and compare data units as they relate to one issue or the whole, such as budgets, vault space available, extent of funds, etc.

Histograms

To illustrate and examine various data element in order to make decisions regarding them and effective when comparing statistical, survey, or questionnaire results are used.

Fig.1: Histogram

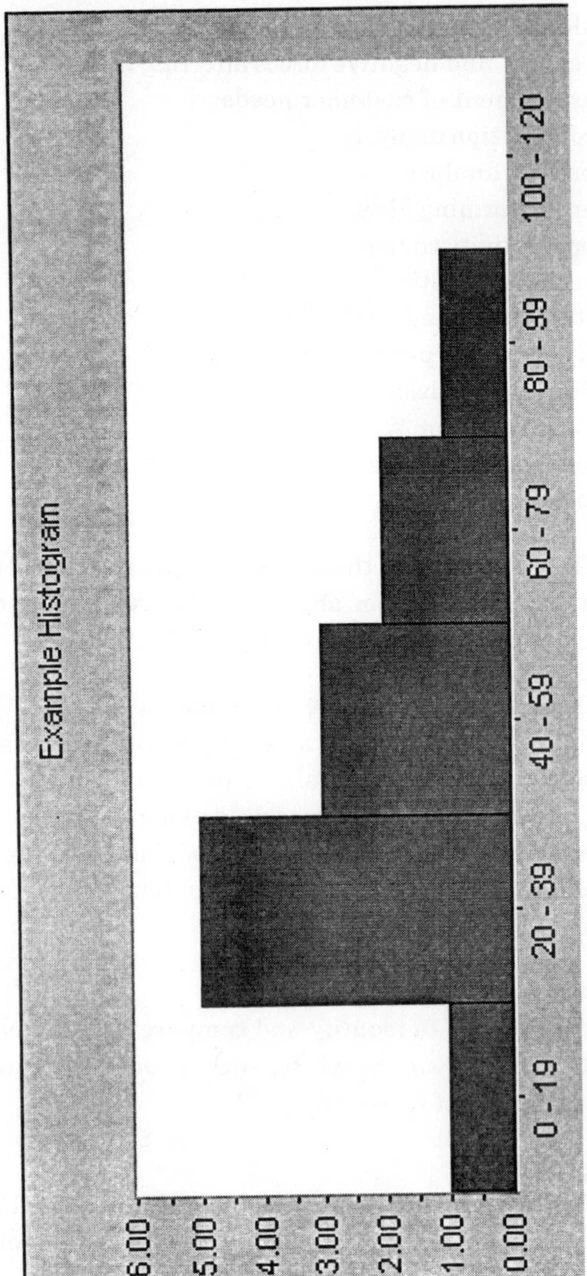

Source: SkyMark(2004), http://www.skymark.com/resources/tools/histogram.

Fig. 2: Run Chart

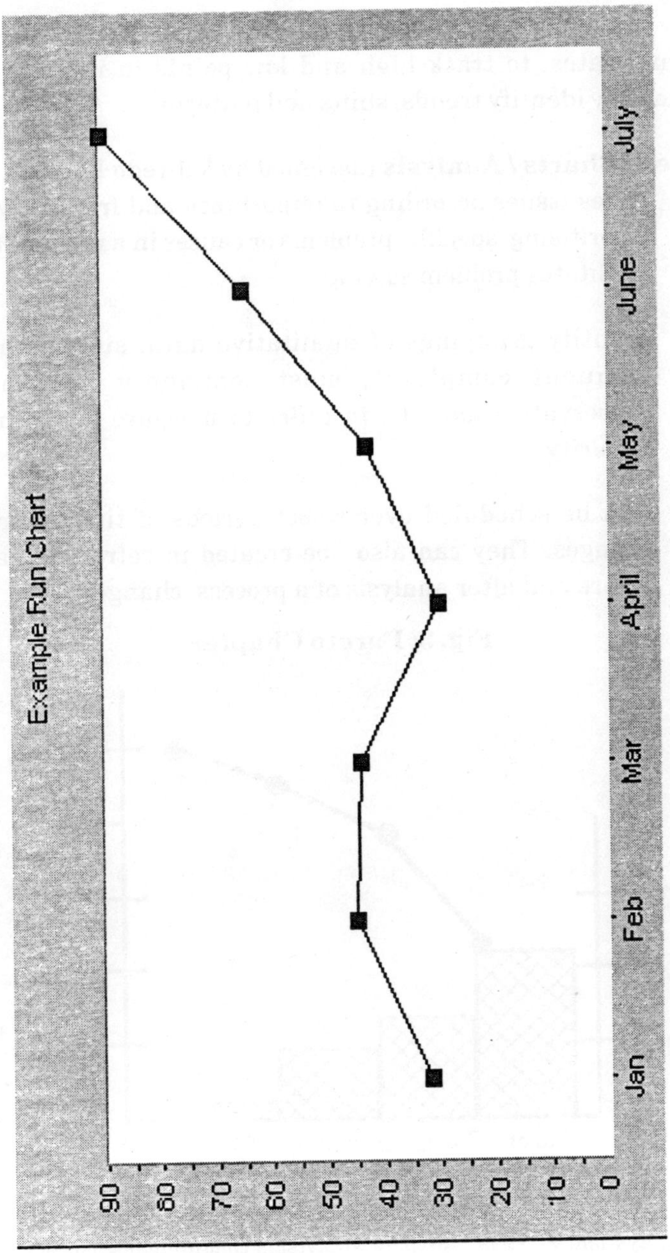

Source: SkyMark (2004)., http://www.skymark.com/resources/tools/run_chart

Run Chart

Follows a process over a specific period of time, such as accrual rates, to track high and low points in its run, and ultimately identify trends, shifts and patterns.

Pareto Charts / Analysis (designed by Vilfredo Pareto)

- Rates issues according to importance and frequency, by prioritising specific problems or causes in a manner that facilitates problem solving.

- Identify groupings of qualitative data, such as most frequent complaint, most commonly purchased preservation aid, etc. in order to measure which have Priority.

- Can be scheduled over select periods of time to track changes. They can also be created in retrospect, as a before and after analysis of a process change.

Fig. 3: Pareto Chapter

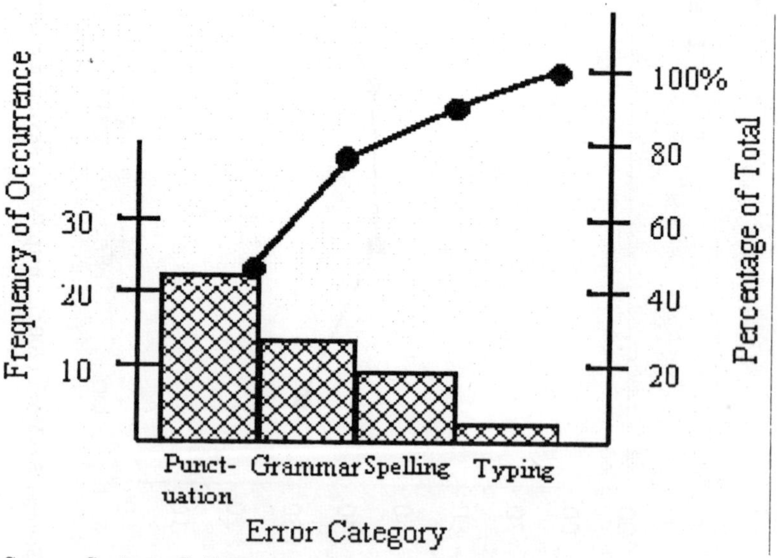

Source: Systma, S (1999)., http://www.sytsma.com/tqmtools/pareto2.gif

Fig4: fishbone Diagram

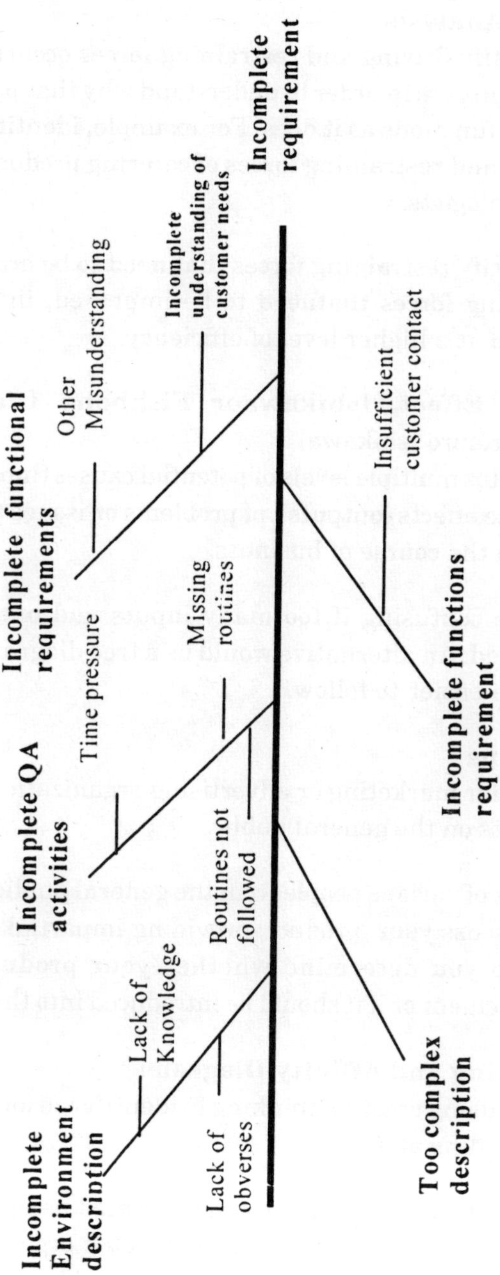

Source: International Software Consulting Network. (2004)., http://www.iscn.at/select_newspaper/measurement/telenor_fig4.gif

Force Field Analysis

- To identify driving and restraining forces occurring in a chosen process in order to understand why that particular process functions as it does. For example, identifying the driving and restraining forces of catering predominantly to genealogists.

- To identify restraining forces that need to be eradicated, or driving forces thatneed to be improved, in order to function at a higher level of efficiency.

Cause and Effect, Ishikawaor Fishbone Diagrams (designed by Kauro Ishikawa)

- Illustrates multiple levels of potential causes (inputs), and ultimate effects (outputs), of problems or issues that may arise in the course of business.

- May be confusing if too many inputs and outputs are identified. An alternative would be a tree diagram, which is much easier to follow.

Focus Groups

- Useful for marketing or advertising organizations to test products on the general public.

- Consist of various people from the general public who use and discuss your product, providing impartial feedback to help you determine whether your product needs improvement or if it should be introduced into the market.

Brainstorming and Affinity Diagrams

- Teams using creative thinking to identify various aspects surrounding an issue.

- An affinity diagram, which can be created using anything from enabling software to post-it notes organised on a wall, is a tool to organise brainstorming ideas.

Tree Diagram

- To identify the various tasks involved in and the full scope of a project.

- To identify hierarchies, whether of personnel, business structure, or priorities.

- To identify inputs and outputs of a project, procedure, process, etc.

Flowcharts and Modeling Diagrams

- Assist in the definition and analysis of each step in a process by illustrating it in a clear and comprehensive manner.

- Identify areas where workflow may be blocked, or diverted, and where workflow is fluid.

Fig. 5 : Flow Chart

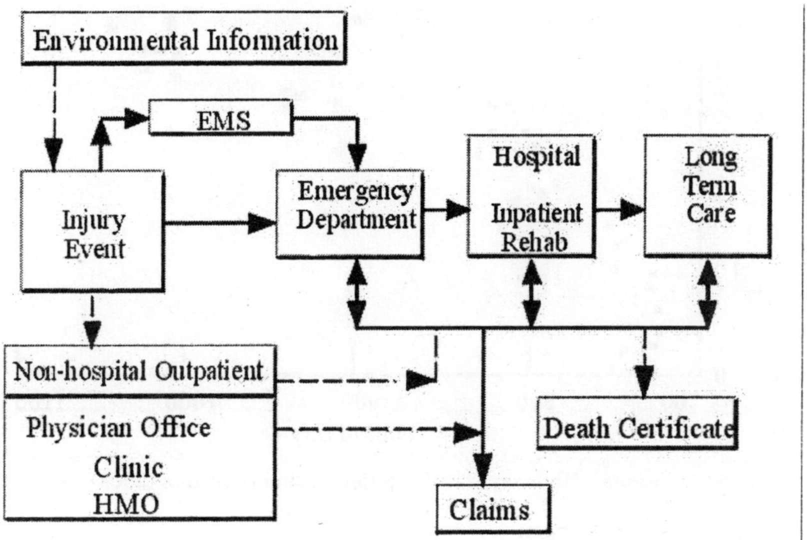

Source: Yeadon Energy Systems. (2004)., http://www. yeadoninc. com/ diagram

- Identify where steps need to be added or removed to improve efficiency and create standardized workflow.

Scatter Diagram

- To illustrate and validate hunches
- To discover cause and effect relationships, as well as bonds and correlations, between two variables
- To chart the positive and negative direction of relationships

Fig. 6

Scatter Diagram

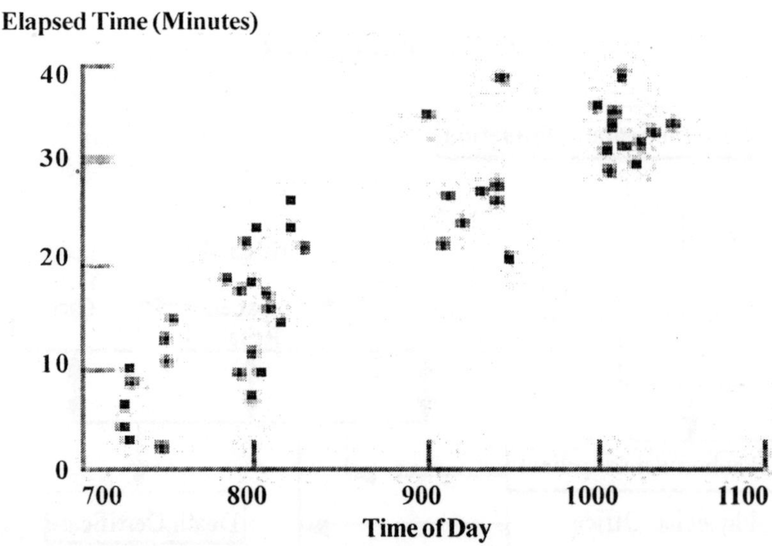

Source: National Highway Traffic Safety Administration (2004).

Relations Diagram

To understand the relationships between various factors, issues, events, etc. so as to understand their importance in the overall organisational view.

PDCA

- The Plan-Do-Check-Act style of management where each project or procedure is planned according to needs and outcome, it is then tested, examined for efficiency and effectiveness, and then acted upon if anything in the process needs to be altered.

- This is a cyclical style to be iterated until the process is perfected.

All of these TQM tools can be easily created and examined by using various types of computer software (Pollock 2003) or by simply mapping them out on paper. They can also be easily integrated into team meetings, organisational newsletters, marketing reports, and for various other data analysis needs. Proper integration and use of these tools will ultimately assist in processing data such as identifying collecting policies, enhancing work flow such as mapping acquisition procedures, ensuring client satisfaction by surveying their needs and analysing them accordingly, and creating an overall high level of quality in all areas of small and medium enterprises.

Conclusion

As discussed, small and medium-sized enterprises in developing countries have major obstacles in marketing their products - whether competing against foreign imports in their domestic markets, or gaining access to international markets. A number of factors bear on this - finance and investment issues, international trading regulations, and agricultural subsidies in developed countries etc. - many of which are largely beyond the power of the SMEs and their governments to influence. There is, however, one critical factor that SMEs can themselves do much to improve - the quality of their products. Delivering products with a level of quality that meets customer requirements is essential to business success. Indeed, in the fierce competition of today's markets, the level of quality needs to exceed what customers already expect, and at a competitive price.

Achieving this quality will involve the entire company - and often suppliers and customers as well. It requires good management systems and practices throughout the organisation, from having a vision of the future of the company to maintaining a safe and healthy workplace. It means having well-trained and motivated employees, standardised work procedures, and effective production control. It means ensuring the quality of incoming supplies, and operating a fast and efficient after-sales service. Above all, it requires the active participation of senior management. In short, every function in the company, and every member of staff can and must support quality, hence the name Total Quality Management (TQM). Implementing TQM throughout the enterprise for the full range of management activities - from managing company policy to keeping the workplace clean and tidy, adopting TQM principles and practices to formulate and to prepare well-structured implementation plans in small and medium business enterprises lay the foundation path towards effectiveness and thus improves the competitiveness of SMEs in the globalised economy.

References

Samuel Kho (2002), **TQM and Integrated Approach,** Crest Publishing House, New Delhi.

Joel E. Ross(2000), **TQM - Text Cases and Readings,** Deep & Deep Publication, New Delhi.

Sharma D.D (2003), **TQM Principles, Practice and Cases,** Sultan Chand and Sons, New Delhi.

Anschuliz, Eric. E. (1996), **TQM America,** Synergy Books International, Malaysia.

Mainuddin Afza (2005), "Superior Subordinates Relationship and Satisfaction in India", **Small Business Enterprises**, Vikalpa, 30(3).

Ghobadian, A. And D. Gallear (1996), "Total Quality Management in SMEs Omega", **TheInternational Journal of Management Science,** 24 (1): 83 -106

Imai, MASAAKI (1986), **KAIZEN: Key to Japan's Competitive Success,** McGraw Hill- New York.

Gunther, J., Hawkins, F. (1999), **Making TQM Work: Quality Tools for Human Service Organizations,** Springer Publishing Company, New York.

Narasimhan, T., Trotter, E. (1999), "The Application of TQM Tools in a Strategic Business Plan", **Center for Quality of Management Journal, 8 (3).** http://cqmextra. cqm. org/ cqmjournal.nsf/reprints/rp10700

Pollock R. (2003). Online Resources on, **Quality Management &Performance Excellence**, from http://www. gslis. utexas. edu/~rpollock/tqm.html

ReVelle, J. (2003), **TQM Tools & Tool Kits**, from http:// www.qualityamerica.com/knowledgecente/articles/ revelletqmtools.html

Simply Quality (2004), "What are ISO 9000 and ISO 9001", **Easy Navigation and Understanding of the ISO 9000 and 9001 Standards on Total Quality Management.** http:// www.isoeasy.org/).

SkyMark, (2004), **Classic Tools.**, Ecyclopaedic Reference Site for Various Quality Control Charts and TQM Tools, with descriptions and examples of each.

Sytsma S., Manley K. (1999), **The Quality Tools Cookbook.**, Encyclopaedic reference site for commonly used TQM tools, describing use and creation of the specific tool, http:// www.sytsma.com/tqmtools/tqmtoolmenu.html.

7

Role and Relevance of Private Branding in Small and Medium Enterprises

Ezhilarasan, M and Sangeetha, D

Abstract

India is a land of villages. Villages are the backbone of India. The strength of India is the rural industrial sector. The Indian rural industry is small and unorganised in nature. As the areas of operations of the rural industries are widely dispersed and the Indian rural market is illiterate, the small and medium level entrepreneurs are mostly ignorant of the modern business practices and concepts. They are more conservative and traditional in their approach. There is a vast growth in the concept and practice in the marketing field. Gone are the days wherein the market was manufacturer-oriented. This is a consumer-oriented era. This shift in the orientation has necessitated many marketing practices, which were hitherto not think of. With the advent of the consumer-oriented marketing concept, there came an issue of the branding of products. It is found very difficult by the manufacturer to take his product to the far stretched rural consumer. Further, the consumer also finds it difficult to fetch the more popular branded products. As a solution for this situation many organisations are going in for outsourcing their manufacturing processes. Mostly, these outsourced suppliers for the branded manufacturer are in the SME sector. Instead of being an outsourcer/supplier for a branded manufacturer, these SME people may think of catering to the market in their own private brand.

Introduction

In today's highly competitive global market trend, with its overwhelming selection of similar and frequently identical goods and services, if a brand cannot differentiate itself from other brands, and the goods and services it is meant to promote from those of the competitors, then it is useless and thereby worthless. Inversely, the stronger the differentiation power of a brand is, the greater is its effectiveness and therefore its value both for its owner and for consumers. Only a brand with a strong differentiation power can serve as a focal point, which promotes an enterprise's products and services and, develops their reputation thereby attracts and maintains consumer loyalty, the essential reason for justifying the investment of time, money and effort required to develop a successful brand.

Liberalisation and globalisation present new and potentially lucrative opportunities for some but also threaten the survival of others. However, by the same token, they are faced with the threat of higher competition and the loss of market shares. Moreover, many formerly differentiated products are becoming commodities with the consequence of falling profit margins. Branded products are not exempt from this trend.

The undesirable impact of these global trends is forcing managers to carefully consider how they will act to protect their businesses. They are trying to defend their market shares and shield their products from becoming commodities while maintaining profitability.

Branding is a difficult and potentially expensive undertaking, often producing uncertain results. Therefore, especially when designed for SMEs in developing countries, effectiveness and efficiency become a major concern for programme planners and implementers.

Effectiveness must be defined in terms of the rate of achievement of the "goal" of branding programmes. In other words, the extent to which the programme can create a symbol that is associated with a message prompting the consumer to respond favourably. Efficiency is achieved when this is done with a minimum expansion of resources.

In order to create a differentiated offer, branding programmes must be based on a business strategy. That is, a branding programme needs to give a business the tools to differentiate a product by defining a strategy, in other words, by positioning the product to meet the needs and wants of a segment. A message should then and only then, be prepared and linked to a symbol. Building branding programmes on a business strategy will also improve the effectiveness and efficiency of communications, as it will enable the business to communicate a clear message to a target segment.

It is here the necessity of private brands is felt advantageous. While the SMEs can try to be a manufacturer alone the way in which they can face the competition would be more competitive and fierce. On the other hand, when the SMEs try out with private brands they can enjoy better positioning. The true value of private label programmes now goes well beyond gross margins and shelf presence.

Meaning of Brand

Although the term "brand" is sometimes used as a synonym for a "trademark", in commercial circles the term "brand" is frequently used in a much wider sense to refer to a combination of tangible and intangible elements, such as a trademark, design, logo and trade dress, and the concept, image and reputation which those elements transmit with respect to specified products and/or services.

Although, strictly speaking, a brand is composed of the sum of its individual parts, the brand ultimately exists independently of and its value is greater than the mere sum of those parts. In fact, the value-added of a brand is precisely the concrete and direct result of the synergy that is created among its component parts.

Brands today are generally recognized as a key asset for creating value for a business. Any "enterprise", in the wide sense of that term, be it for-profit, not-for-profit, small, medium-sized or large, even a country or geographical region, can develop a brand image. Perhaps many entrepreneurs do not yet understand or are not truly convinced that a brand image can be a powerful tool for promoting and marketing goods and services.

Meaning of Branding

Branding refers to the process of building an image of an organisation's brand or trademark or logo in the mind of its target market. A brand image is developed through an effective branding strategy, which, as already stated, should constitute an integral part of any business plan. A successful brand cannot be created, developed and maintained in a vacuum. For a successful marketing strategy, the organisation's product or service must fit into its target market in terms of price, quality and service. If the organisation is a small and medium enterprise (SME), it has to meet a very tight budget and schedule for branding.

Meaning of Private Brand and Private Branding

Private Brand is a special case in which the retailer has his own label or brand on the product rather then that of the manufacturer. Private branding is when a distribution channel member (usually a retailer), buys from a manufacturer and puts its own name on the product. Hence, private brand is sometimes also called Retailer Brand or Own Brand.

Thus, Private Branding would mean the situation in which the retailer is in the process of extending its good-will as the image to the product it is dealing as a private brand.

Advantages of Private Branding

Private branding paves way for many advantages to both the retailer and the manufacturer.

The advantages to the retailer
Private label allow retailers

- to design for their specific target market – as the brand is chosen by the retailer with the target customer hood in mind.
- more freedom and flexibility in pricing – the retailer has more autonomy in fixing the price.
- more control over product attributes and quality – as the product is made as per the orders of the retailer.
- increased channel control, improving flexibly to be responsive to trend cycles – as the retailer has closer touch with the target market
- increased product differentiation – as the product is made to order by the retailer with the target market in mind.
- higher margins (or lower selling price) – as various components of marketing overheads is not incurred such as transportation, advertising and promotional costs.

The advantages to the manufacturer
Private label allow maufacturers

- reduced promotional costs – as the retailer renders a brandname the manufacturer is relieved of various costs of promotion.

- stability of sales volume (at least while the contract is operative) – as the retailer makes orders for the product based on the target market requirements.

Private Branding and the SME

Developing a private brand image is not an out-of-reach venture for small and medium-sized enterprises. It does require time, effort and commitment, and certainly some financial resources, but not as much as might be expected. Moreover, experience and knowledge of the market, a creative and flexible approach to problem solving, enthusiasm about one's products or services, and the courage to take risks are just as important factors in developing a powerful private brand image, and these are common attributes of most successful small and medium-sized entrepreneurs.

Business Challenges for SME Private Branding

The process of private branding does have many business challenges to be faced.

- Accessing Market Trends – general market trends are always fluctuating,

- Addressing cost component with creative planning – the costing pattern of the manufacturer brand would be different from that of the private brand,

- Design co-ordination – the SME's specifications might be different from that of the manufacturer's,

- Production monitoring – the SME's specifications might be different from that of the manufacturer's,

- Product life-cycle management – as the product is in the mind-set of the SME, the manufacturer might find it difficult,
- Quality management – the SME's specifications might be different from that of the manufacturer's, and
- Logistic planning – as transport schedules are to be based on SME orders.

Core Competencies to be Developed

These challenges necessitate some core competencies to be developed for effective private brand management among the SMEs.

- Strategic Direction – the SME should possess the ability to frame sound vision, mission, objectives and goals,
- Brand Management – strong knowledge in managing brands,
- Trend Management – ability to identify fades, fashions and trends of the target market,
- Project Management – overall project management ability,
- Technical design skills – as private brand is the child of the SME,
- Product costing skills – since private branded SMEs are totally buying the product from the manufacturer and selling it in their own brand,
- Pricing optimisation – since private branded SMEs are totally buying the product from the manufacturer and selling it in their own brand,
- Customer insight – as private brand is the child of the SMEs,

- Demand forecasting – ability to identify fads, fashions and trends of the target market, and
- Logistics efficiency – as transport schedules are to be based on SMEs orders

Indicators of Insufficiency

The indicators of insufficiency may be as follows.

- Inaccurate forecasting – ability to identify fads, fashions and trends of the target market,
- Low percent of private branded merchandise – as the SMEs might not have the full confidence in the private brand other manufacturer brands may also be dealt,
- Low assortment productivity – as the SMEs might not have the full confidence,
- Poor brand perception – as a result of the inability to identify the target market mind-set,
- Inefficient sourcing – as a result of the inability to identify the target manufacturer mind-set,
- Quality problems – as the product is not directly manufactured by the SMEs, and
- Missed market trends – as a result of the inability of the SMEs to identify the target market.

The resultant impact of these indicators would include increase in overheads, reduction in sales, lesser profit margins, and lower customer satisfaction, leading to high customer switch-over and lower customer loyalty.

Overcoming the Insufficiency

In order to manage the process of private branding in an effective way there should be some mechanism to identify and eliminate some elements that could lead to insufficiency.

- Demand planning – the SMEs should be able to identify the target market requirements;
- Balance of private label business – the SMEs should be able to identify the target market requirements accurately and balance between the private brand and the manufacturer brand;
- Customer insights – the SMEs should have means to assess the target market mind-set;
- Integrated planning calendar – the SMEs should perfectly plan the various marketing activities;
- Ability to track production process – the SMEs should be able to influence the production schedule of the manufacturer;
- End to end logistics tracking – the SMEs should be able to track the entire transportation problem;
- Design collaboration – the SMEs should be able to incorporate the target market requirement into the product;
- Trend interpretation/ monitoring – the SMEs should possess knowledge on various indices of trend analysis; and
- Coherent brand management – the SMEs should be able to maintain a brand management policy which is polarised with the vision. Three essential core competencies seem more compelling in managing the process.
- Trend optimisation,
- Efficient product development and
- Life-cycle Management.

Guidelines for Achievement of Private Brand Efficiency

There are some guidelines for the achievement

- Brand Strategy Support
- Customer Experience Enhancement
- Process Integration
- Efficient use of Technology
- Alignment of Skills & Requirements
- Clearly Defined Objectives & Metrics

Trend optimisation and efficient product development combine to reduce markdown expense and optimise inventory ownership. Shifting unit volume from markdown to full price creates significant revenue opportunity.

Factors Responsible for Success of Private Brand

Many factors go into making a successful private brand. There is no single miracle formula. Private brand development is as much a science as it is an art. Nevertheless, to be successful, a private brand must at least be clear, specific and credible in terms of its message, its differentiation power, and the quality it symbolises. It should be attractive and appropriate in relation to the goods and services, which the private brand embodies.

Among the various factors that determine a private brand's success, one of the most important ones is the private brand's differentiation power. The private brand must have a "point of difference" as far as the target group of consumers is concerned.

This point of difference must be:

1. Recognisable (in terms of the good and/or services marketed);

2. Desirable (in terms of the quality and value of the goods and/or services offered);

3. Credible (in terms of reliability); and

4. Properly communicated (in terms of how the message is formulated and to whom it is targeted).

Conclusion

Only a private brand with a strong differentiation power can serve as a focal point to promote a SMEs products and services, develop their reputation and thereby attract and maintain consumer loyalty, the essential reasons for justifying the investment of time, money and effort required to develop a successful brand.

Reference

http://en.wikipedia. Org/wiki/Private label

8

Patent Rights for Invention: National and International Trade Fair and Missions

Rajasekaran, N

Abstract

Knowledge Economy is gaining momentum in today's emerging globalised scenario. An idea which strikes a mind first becomes an intellectual property, which needs to be protected like any other tangible asset. Innovation is the output of prolonged research or experience. The patent right is a scientific method of commercialising an invention, which may be a new product or new method or new procedure which saves resources. The inventor if goes for patent right, safeguards his future against exploitation by Giants. Patent rights registration is a pre-requisite to commercialise inventions. In India there is a patent Act. Similarly at global level WTO prescribes rules and regulation for patenting. However, it is hard for underdeveloped and developing nations, as they have to pay to the developed countries to use the technology. Even though the inventions were done much earlier, only those with registered patent rights can claim benefits. Only after the patent registration, new products are exhibited in the national and international trade fairs. Trade fairs are the medium through which new products are brought to the knowledge of end users. Demonstrations provide a clear cut idea about the products. Negotiations for commercialising new product is facilitated in trade fairs and exhibitions, as different stake holders converge at a single place.

Introduction

Inventions of yester years are being commercialised today in a much sophisticated manner, to make living more comfortable and rational. Protecting inventions right is scientifically termed as either Patent Rights or Intellectual Property Rights. The benefits of patented inventions are enjoyed by the inventors, commercialists, consumers and the whole nation. In India we have Patent Act which provides a scientific mechanism for registration, assignment, sale, leasing, and commercialisation of inventions. The under-developed and developing nations face exploitation from the developed nations. Countries like India are suffering from international trade because much of their agricultural products are not patented. The technical service fee collected from the underdeveloped countries by the developed countries make the products much costlier in the international market leading to the price incompetitivness for the products coming out of such countries. Only after patenting and safeguarding, the inventors usually bring their inventions to the trade fairs. In this way the inventors and industrialists partner with each other to execute and commercialise a new and innovative business idea. From the above details we can realise the importance the patent right.

Inventions

An invention is a new thing that someone has made. Computer was an invention when it was first made. New things made and created are called inventions. Invention is the output of prolonged research or experience.

World Trade Organisation (WTO)

WTO is based in Geneva, Switzerland and it was established on 1st January 1995. The functions of WTO are:

- Administering and implementing the multilateral and plurilateral trade agreements which together make up the WTO,
- Seeking to resolve trade disputes,
- Overseeing national trade policies,
- Acting as a forum for multilateral trade negotiation, and
- Cooperating with other international institutions involved in global economic policy making.

Intellectual Property Rights (IPR)

India ratified the agreement establishing the World Trade Organisation (WTO). This agreement, inter-alia, contains an agreement on Trade Related Aspects of Intellectual Property Rights (TRIPS), which came into force from 1st January 1995. The agreement provides for norms and standards in respect to the following areas of intellectual property rights.

- Copy Rights,
- Trade Marks,
- Industrial Design,
- Design Patent, and
- Patents

Copy Right: It is exclusive right granted or conferred by the Government on the creator of a work to exclude others reproducing it, adapting it, distributing it to the public, performing it in public or displaying it in public. It protects only the concrete form of expression in a work. To be a valid, a copy righted work must have originality and possess a modicum of creativity.

Trade Mark: It may be (a) a word, slogan, design, picture or any other symbol used to identify and distinguish goods and (b) any identifying symbol, including a word, design, or shape of a product, container that qualifies for legal status as a trade mark, trade name or trade dress.

Industrial Design: Obligations envisaged in respect of industrial designs are independently created designs that are new or original and shall be protected. Individual Governments have been given an option to exclude from protection, designs, dictated by technical and functional considerations as against aesthetic consideration, which constitutes the coverage of industrial design.

Design Patent: A government grant of exclusive rights in a novel, non-obvious and ornamental industrial design. A design patent right confers the right to exclude others from making, using, or selling designs that closely resemble the patent design. A design covers ornamental aspects of design.

Patent: The term patent originated from the Latin word 'patere', which means to lay open or make available for public inspection. A patent is a set of exclusive rights (the inventor or assignee) for a fixed period of time in exchange for the regulated, public disclosure of certain details of a device, method, process or composition of matter, which is new, inventive and useful or industrially applicable. The exclusive right granted to the patentee in most countries is the right to prevent or exclude others from making, selling, offering to sell or importing the claimed invention.

Development of Patent

Although there is evidence suggesting that something like patent was used among ancient Greek cities, patents in the modern sense originated in Italy in 1474. At that time the Republic of Venice issued a decree by which new and inventive devices, once they had been put into practice, had to be communicated to the Republic in order to obtain legal protection against potential infringers. England followed with the statute of Monopolies in 1623 under King James I, which declared a patent could only be granted for 'project for new invention'. During the reign of Queen Anne (1702-1714), the lawyer of English court developed the requirement that a written description of invention must be submitted. These developments, which were in place during the colonial period, formed the basis for the patent law of modern English and United States law. In the United States, during the colonial period and Articles of confederation years (1778-1789), several states adopted patent system of their own.

Obtaining a Patent

A patent is obtained by filling a written application at the relevant patent office. That application will contain a specification detailing the invention and the protection claimed, together with forms relating to the procedural aspects of obtaining a patent. Once a patent application has been filed, a patent office examines that application for compliance with the requirements of the relevant patent law. If the application does not comply with all the requirements, the objections are communicated to the applicant or his representative, who can then respond to those objections to overcome them and obtain the grant of a patent.

Patent Prosecution

It describes the interaction between applicant or his representative, and a patent office with regard to a patent or an application for a patent.

Patent Attorneys and Patent Agent

In some jurisdictions only authorised parishioners can act before the patent office. Authorisation is usually obtained by passing examinations set by the appropriate patent office thereby proving that the representative is competent in the relevant laws and process. Due to the complex nature of patent obtaining procedure, it is generally considered advisable to employ a professional representative or agent when applying for a patent.

List of Patent Office

World Intellectual Property Organization (WIPO) has maintained a list of patent offices which located in various countries. They are

- African Regional Intellectual Property Organisation (ARIPO)
- Canadian Intellectual Property Office (CIPO)
- Eurasian Patent Organisation (EAPO)
- German Patent Office (DPMA)
- Indian Patent Office (IPO)
- Ip Australia
- Japan Patent Office (JPO)
- Irish Patent Office
- State Intellectual Property Office of China
- Intellectual Property Office of Singapore
- Intellectual Property Office of Philippines
- United Kingdom Patent Office

- United States Patent and Trade Mark Office (USPTO)
- World Intellectual Property Organisation (WIPO)

The Indian Patent Office

It is administrated by the office of the controller general of patents, designs, and trade marks (CGPDTM), located at Mumbai. This is the subordinate office of the Indian Government that administers its Intellectual property (IP) laws. The CGPDTM has mainly five administrative sections.

- Patents
- Designs
- Trade Mark
- Geographical Indications
- Patent Information System

The Head office of the patent is located at Kolkata and its branches are located at Chennai, New Delhi, and Mumbai, while the CGPDTM office is located at Mumbai, the Trade Marks Registry is at Mumbai with its branches located in Kolkatta. The office of the patent information system is at Nagpur. The controller of General supervises the working of the patent act the designs act, and the trade marks act. In order to protect the geographical indications of a goods a geographical indication registry has been established in Chennai to administer the geographical indications of goods (Registration and Protection) Act 1999 under the CGPDTM. Indian patent office has around 135 examiners, 50 assistant controllers, 5 deputy controllers, 1 joint controller, 1 senior joint controller operating from the four branches.

Trade Fair

Only after the patent registration, new products are exhibited in the national and international trade fairs. Trade fairs are the medium through which new products are brought to the knowledge of end users. Demonstrations etc., provide a clear cut idea about the products.

National and International Trade Fair

The trade fairs are conducted at national and international levels. Trade shows are often conducted in the following places; namely, Bangalore, Bangkok, Beijing, Frankfurt, Jakata, Kulalumpur, Karachi, London, Mumbai, New Delhi, New York, Paris, Shanghai, Sharja, Singapore, Malaysia and other places.

Trade Fair Missions

The aims of trade fair missions are

* To create awareness for future oriented goods and services,
* to help the society to increase the standard of living through commercialising the new products and to introduce services,
* to act as a starting point for newer investment as they act as sparkplug.
* The GDP of various countries get enhanced through newer investment originating from trade fairs.

Conclusion

We need better patenting laws across the globe to safeguard the original inventors. So that the inventor who has registered patent rights can claim benefits. Otherwise his invention will be exploited by others. So, we must create awareness and popularise the terms and concepts among the inventors, industrialist, customers and general public.

9

WTO on Small and Medium Enterprises with Special Reference to Patenting Rights

Balasubramaniyan, R

Abstract

India's industrial economy encompasses organised as well as unorganised large and medium industries and small scales industries. The village and small industries (VSI) constitute an important segment of the economy. The VSI sector is divided into eight sub-sectors such as Khadi village industries, handlooms, sericulture, handicrafts, coir, small industries, and power looms. Small industries are significantly labour intensive. They always provide wider employment opportunities for the people of India. The SSI sector contributes 40 per cent of national production and 35 per cent of national exports. The composition of exports shows largest shares of SSIs are hosiery and garments (29 per cent), food products (21.4 per cent), and leather products (18 per cent). Our country has about 35.31 lakh SSI units, providing employment to more than 200 lakh persons. This sector is the second largest employer of Indian work force after agriculture (GOI 2005). The aim of the global producers is to offer various products with good quality at low cost to achieve maximum efficiency. Globalisation of developing countries will improve the allocative efficiency of resources, reduce the capital output ratio and increases the inflow of the capital and updated technology into the country. This paper highlights the impact of WTO on SMEs with special reference to patenting rights. This paper concludes that globalisation and patent law provide lot of scope for furthering economic growth of developing countries, particularly India.

Introduction

India's industrial economy encompasses organised as well as unorganised large and medium industries and small scale industries. The village and small industries (VSIs) constitute an important segment of the economy. The VSI sector is divided into eight sub-sectors, such as khadi, village industries, handlooms, sericulture, handicrafts, coir, small industries and power looms. Small industries are significantly labour intensive. It always provides wider employment opportunities for increasing population of India. The SSI sector contributes 40 per cent of national production and 35 per cent of national exports. The composition of exports shows that the largest shares of SSIs are in the industry groups of hosiery and garments (29 percent), food products (21 per cent), and leather products (18 per cent). The fixed investment in this sector has been reckoned at Rs. 84, 329 crores. Our country boasts of about 35.31 lakh SSI units providing employment to more than 200 lakh persons. This sector is the secon ' largest employer of Indian Work force after agriculture (GOI, 2005).

The aim of the global producers is to offer various products with good quality at low cost to achieve maximum efficiency. Globalisation of developing countries will improve the allocative efficiency of resources, reduce the capital output ratio and increase the inflow of the capital and updated technology into the country. But what constitutes globalisation?

The term globalisation has six parameters namely;

(a) Reduction of Trade barriers.

(b) Allowing free flow of goods and services across national frontiers.

(c) Permitting free flow of capital among nation states.

(d) Delimiting the free flow of technology.

(e) Creation of good environment for free movement of labour is allowed among the countries of the world.

(f) Envisaging more trade, investment, employment and income growth among the nations leading to economic and political prosperity.

Basic Conceptualisation of SME's

As per Government of India notification S.No. 1288, dated December 24, 1999, an industrial undertaking in which the investment in plant and machinery, whether held on ownership terms or on lease / hire purchase basis that does not exceed Rs.1 crore is regarded as a small scale industry.

An ancillary unit has been defined as an industrial undertaking which is engaged in the manufacture of parts components, sub-assemblies, tools, etc., and whose investment in plant and machinery does not exceed Rs. one crore.

The manufacturing enterprise is treated as a Tiny Unit in which investment in plant and machinery does not exceed Rs.25 lakhs, irrespective of the location of the Unit. A women entrepreneurs enterprise (WEE) is termed as an SSI Unit / industry managed by one or more women entrepreneur in proprietary concerns or in which she / they individually or jointly have a share capital of not less than 51 per cent as share holders

/ partners / members of co-operative society. An industry related service / business enterprise with an investment up to Rs.10 lakhs in fixed assets excluding land and building is treated as Small Scale Service and Business Enterprise (SSSBE). A unit with an obligation to export at least 30 per cent of its annual production by the end of the third year of commencement of productions and having an investment ceiling of Rs. 1 crore is termed as an export oriented SSI unit. Medium enterprises are those units with an investment in plant and machinery up to Rs.10 crore.

The Emergence of WTO

The International trade was not very smooth during 1940's, when there were many restrictions imposed by different countries with a view to protecting their domestic industry. After the end of the Second World War it was felt that the artificial restrictions imposed on international trade be removed and thus GATT was born. In 1948, some 23 countries, including India, formed General Agreement on Tariffs and Trade (GATT) as an international body with headquarters in Geneva, Switzerland to pursue the objective of free trade in order to encourage growth and development of all member countries. The main objective of GATT was to ensure healthy competition in commodity trade through the removal of trade barriers. It was after the formation of GATT that the average import tariffs in the world were reduced substantially at lower levels which enabled remarkable growth in world trade. Since the inception of GATT, eight rounds of negotiations on trade matters have been held.

The first round was held at Havana in 1947, the second at Annecy in France (1949), the third at Torquay in Britain (1950-51), the 4th, 5th and 6th were held in Geneva (1955-67) and the 7th round in Tokyo (1973-79). The 8th round of Multi-lateral Trade Negotiations, popularly known as Uruguay round covered 7 years (1986-93) and took place at Punta del Este in Uruguay.

There was a deadlock on certain critical areas such as agriculture, textiles, TRIPS and anti-dumping measures when agreement could not be reached. To break this deadlock, Arthur Dunkel, Director General of GATT brought a document and presented it before the member countries for possible settlement.

The WTO came into existence on 1-1-1995 with headquarters in Geneva, Switzerland. The Uruguay round negotiations on December 15, 1993 and the Marrakesh Declaration, Morocco on 15th April 1994 finally paved the way for. The emergence of WTO. It has 149 members including China. China joined the WTO in December 2001. The basic objectives of WTO are to ensure global free trade, expand production, remove tariff barriers and optimal use of world's resources. It acknowledges the need for special concern for LDC's. So far five conferences have been held. The first one was held in Singapore (1996), second one at Geneva (1998), third one in Seattle (1999), fourth one in Doha (2001) and last one at Cancun, Mexico (2003).

The Impact of WTO on SME's

Small and Medium Enterprises (SME's) have emerged as an engine of growth in several developed and developing economies of the world. SMEs are a key component in economic life, not only because of their number and variety but because of their involvement in every aspect of the economy, their contribution to regional development, the complementary role they play in support of the large sector. SMEs could be termed as seed – bed of industrial growth.

In India, SME's have emerged as a vibrant and dynamic component of Indian economy by virtue of their significant contribution to GDP, industrial production and exports. As on March 2005 there were 11.36 million SME's in the country, which are providing direct employment to around 28.29 million persons (RBI 2005). These numbers are exclusive of the units in the unregistered sector, which constitutes about 85 per cent of the tiny and small scale enterprises. Considering its potentiality and ability, the SMEs sector has been assigned a target of 12 per cent annual growth and additional employment of 4.4 million estimated during the 10th plan period.

After the implementation of WTO norms in our country, the protected environment for SMEs is gradually vanishing. SSIs are now facing increased competition from the MNCs and survival of the fittest has become the buzzword in the Indian industrial sector today. In the WTO regime, reservations may have to be withdrawn, preferential purchase and other support measures will not be available and thus SSIs have to compete not only with large units within the country, but also with cheap imported products. SSIs are losing their markets to cheap imported products. Consequently, a very large number of SSI units are becoming sick or have closed down.

Thus, the SSIs, which accounts for 40 per cent of manufacturing output, 50 per cent of employment and over 33 per cent of exports is in jeopardy. Further, the entry of multinationals in ordinary consumer goods like ice cream, agarbatti, food processing, mineral water etc., are also adversely affecting the SSI sector since these were the traditional areas of this sector. For instance, in soft drinks, the entry of powerful Coca Cola and Pepsi have eliminated practically all small units engaged in the manufacture of local "Koli Soda". In the name of WTO, MNC's continue to swallow SMEs and eliminate them from the market (Appa Rao 2005). The impact of WTO on SMEs in India is presented in Table 1. It reveals clearly the nature of agreement, scope and cover, age and nature of impact on SMEs

Table 2 captures the performance of small scale industries during 1994-95 to 2004-05. It clearly shows that in the year 1994-95, the total number of units was (79.60 lakh) and it had increased to 131.38 lakh in 2004-05. There is a significant rise in the employment generation and exports of SSI sector. For instance, in 1994-95, the 'total employment generated in SSI sector was 191.40 lakh and it has now increased to 245.25 lakh in 2004 – 05.

Table 1: Impact of WTO Agreements on SME's Sector in India

No	*Agree-ment*	*Scope and Coverage*	*Nature of Impact on SMEs*	*Range of Impact*
1	ATC	Textiles and clothing : All export quotas to be phased out by 2005, open competition for developed country markets	Producers will now have to compete on price and quality without any concessions	Segments in textiles and clothing which are below international standards of scale and // technology
2	TRIMS	Foreign investment : Member countries prohibited from imposing special requirements, such as export commitments, on foreign investors, non-discrimination between foreign and domestic firms post-establishment	Increased flow of foreign investment opens up new markets for SSI, however this agreement per se will not have much impact on investment flows	SSI sector that can compete on price and quality against imported components

No	*Agreement*	*Scope and Coverage*	*Nature of Impact on SMEs*	*Range of Impact*
3	TRIPS	Intellectual Property : Member countries committed to granting product patent rights, enforcement of anti-piracy, copyright Infringement and counterfeit laws	Costs will increase because of Royalties, patents on traditional technologies in other countries can undermine these activities	Pharmaceuticals, including products based on traditional knowledge
4	SPS	Activities involving health and hygiene : Member countries can subject imports to domestic standards	Constraints on exports of Indian products despite price competitiveness	Food products, other plant and animal products
5	TBT	All Activities : Member countries can subject imports to domestic technical requirements	Constraints on exports of Indian products despite price competitiveness	Electrical and electronic goods, various household goods

Source: GOI Report on Small Scale Industrial Sector

Table 2: Performance of Small Scale Industries during 1994-95 to 2004-05

Year	Number of Units (in lakhs)			Production (Rs.in crores)		Employ -ment (in lakhs)	Exports At current prices (Rs. in lakhs)
	Registered	Unregistered	Total	At current prices	At 1993-94 Constant prices		
1	2	3	4	5	6	7	8
1994-95	11.61	67.99	79.60	122,210.00	109,116.00	191.40	29,068.00
1995-96	11.57	71.27	82.84	148,290.00	121,649.00	197.93	36,270.00
1996-97	11.99	74.22	86.21	168,413.00	135,380.00	205.86	39,248.00
1997-98	12.04	77.67	89.71	189,178.00	147,824.00	213.16	44,442.00
1998-99	12.00	81.36	93.36	212,901.00	159,407.00	220.15	48,979.00
1999-00	12.32	84.83	97.15	234.255.00	170,709.00	229.10	54,200.00

Year	*Number of Units (in lakhs)*			*Production (Rs.in crores)*		*Employ -ment (In lakhs)*	*Exports At current prices (Rs. in lakhs)*
	Registered	*Unregistered*	*Total*	*At current prices*	*At 1993-94 Constant prices*		
2000-01	13.10	88.00	101.10	161,289.00	184,428.00	239.09	69,797.00
2001-02	13.75	91.46	105.21	282,270.00	195,613.00	249.09	71,244.00
2002-03	14.68	95.42	110.10	311,993.00	210,636.00	261.38	86,013.00
2003-04	15.54	99.68	115.22	357,733.00	226,392.00	273.14	NA
2004-05	16.38	115.00	131.38	399,020.00	245,747.00	245.75	NA

Source: Ministry of Small Scale Industries, Govt. of India, 2005.

The Impact of Patenting Rights

India enjoys the proud privilege of having the third largest pool of scientific and technical human resources in the World. The country has emerged as BPO for IT and IT related services. In spite of being the leading light in the age old wisdom in a number of spheres of human endeavor we have not patented our innovations. The awareness among our technical experts to apply for and get the patents registered for their innovations remains wanting. Table 3 presents the patents applied for by different countries, R and D spent, and HDI Rank in 2005. A number of countries, which are comparable in size to our states, have acquired large number of patents. Table 3 shows that there is a correlation between R & D and patenting right. For instance, USA spends 2.7 per cent R & D of G.D.P and filed patent rights to the tune of 45,452, followed by Japan R & D (3.1 per cent) and patent rights (24, 800), Germany R & D (2.5 per cent) and patent rights (15, 981) and India R & D (0.8 percent) and patent rights (675) in 2005.

Table 3: Cross Country Patent Rights and Research andDevelopment Expenditure in 2005

Country	*R & D Expenditure (% of GDP)*	*HDI Rank / (in 2005)*	*Patent Application filed (in 2005)*
Sweden	4.3	6	3,236
Finland	3.5	13	1,884
Japan	3.1	11	24,800
USA	2.7	10	44,452
Germany	2.5	20	15,981
Korea	2.5	28	4,422
China	1.2	85	2,501
Russian Fed.	1.2	62	NA
Brazil	1.0	63	275
India	0.8	127	675

Source: Human Development Report, 2005.

India has over 3000 institutions (IIT's, IIM's, Universities and colleges) engaged in higher education and research in the fields of Science and Technology. With such a background, the number of applications filed for patent registration in India during the year 2005 has been pathetically low at 675. Most of our experts in the fields of science and technology make handsome contributions with their innovative approaches. However, they do not venture to apply for registration and get their innovations patented. This may lead to a situation where our innovations get patented by someone else and we may have to pay royalty charges for our own innovations. The farmers in Israel, ably guided by the scientific community have introduced a number of innovations and made the dessert blossom, Japan and Singapore with no natural resources worth mentioning, with their innovative approaches, have emerged prosperous into the league of developed nations of the World. These countries have patented their innovations in time to make progress (Mahalingam 2005).

Conclusion

With the advent of WTO regime, we need to prepare our SMEs for the global competition with cost effective production and efficient management. It is obvious that benefits to developing countries like India, in terms of increasing their exports will occur only after the elimination of exports subsidies and substantial domestic support in the developed countries. The WTO has a direct impact on all economic activities including the development and promotion of SMEs. The umbrella of WTO is likely to create some far reaching implications for the SMEs in India, with particular reference to their competitive ability and integration with global markets. The SMEs in India are facing lot of problems due to the unorganised nature, lack of data and information, use of low level of technology, and poor infrastructure. Their capital bases are poor and do not possess the expertise of modern management practices. Globalisation and patent law provide a lot of scope for furthering economic growth. But unfortunately, our labourers engaged in the shop floors, process industries, dairy farms, poultry farms, etc have failed to live up to their reputation to patent their innovation.

The students of law have to be trained and empowered to handle applications for patent registration and disputes relating to patent law. Globalisation has necessitated important structural changes in the SSI in order to keep them competitive. Following measures are to be taken in this regard.

1. To withstand competition from products of MNC's, the quality of the products produced by our SSI units should be improved and should be made available at competitive prices.
2. The SSI should discard old technologies and adopt modern technologies.
3. The SSI should give on the job training to the employees to improve quality of workers.
4. More credit facilities should be created for SSI to sustain under competitive conditions.
5. Around 675 items reserved for SSIs would now open for MNC's (Competition) market in India. This has to be phased out gradually to protect our SSIs.

References

AppRao **et al.** (2005), "Implications of WTO on Small and Medium Enterprises –Opportunities, Challenges and Responses", **88th Indian Economic Association**:44-61.

Avvai Kothai, T.K. (2005), "The World Trade Organisation and SSIs in India", **Kisan World**, 32 (7): 25-26.

Mahalingam, N (2005), "Innovations in Science and Technology", **Kisan World,** 31(7): 3-4.

Neela Mukherjee (2000), **WTO and Indias Trade Policy in Services,** Vikas Publishing House, New Delhi.

Ramana, A. (2001), "Indias Policy on IPR's and Agriculture", **Economic and Political Weekly,** 26 (51): 1576.

Vibha Mathur, (2002), **Indian Economy and WTO Challenges and Strategies**, New Century Publications, New Delhi.

Part – II
Technology Intervention for Enhancing Competitiveness

10

Technology Revolution: Boon or Ban for Small and Medium Enterprise Development

Dayanandan,

"…. in the realm of technology, the change from simple and traditionalised techniques towards the application of scientific knowledge"

(Smelser 1968:126)

Abstract

This paper emphasises the need for technological revolution, essential for economic development. Although technological revolution resulted in some problem in SMEs its contribution to this sector is immense. These insignificant problems can be rectified in different ways and means. Participatory technology development is the one method through which technology intervention can be achieved more effectively.

Introduction

The importance of Small and Medium enterprises (SMEs) in any economy need not be exaggerated. They serve the following purposes.

- They provide the basis for creation and promotion of entrepreneurial capabilities; they are the breeding ground for entrepreneurship and mopping up latent and unutilised resources like hoarded wealth and ideal entrepreneurial ability.
- They serve as middlemen in facilitating and consolidating linkages between the different sectors of the economy and between rural and urban establishments;
- They promote balanced regional development by regional dispersal of industries;
- They are labour intensive and have tremendous employment creation capability
- They possess the qualifications necessary for fair and equitable distribution of national wealth;
- They are important instruments for poverty alleviation and eradication and they bring about pro- poor growth through, among others, women empowerment; and
- They have relatively bigger input to an economy's value and/or GDP.

Globalisation provides lot of avenues for the development of SMEs. Globalisation is not a political conquest, but economic partnership. This concept of togetherness and localisation is named globalisation. It does not discriminate on the basis of rich or poor but it does discriminate between the skilled and unskilled. In other words it is building up a society of merit.

Thus, it provides opportunities for all types of entrepreneurs, which is one of the necessities for the sustainable development of any country.

Modernisation, development and industrialisation have sometimes been treated as synonymous concepts. This is not to suggest that the benefits of heavy industry have been universally applauded. There has in fact been a long tradition of trying to improve living standards by other means, such as by improved agricultural production, enhancement of small and medium enterprises and alternative technology. Recently these efforts have been encouraged by the decline of heavy industry in some countries such as Britain, and by an increased recognition of the appalling environmental effects of rapid industrialisation in India. Nevertheless, the view that development is impossible without industrialisation remains a potent one, linking together Marxist and classical economic theory with most neoclassical and development economics. Economic development and the eradication of poverty tend to be connected inextricably with industrialisation especially small and medium enterprises.

'Economies of scale are the basic idea behind the development of mass production. The likely occurrence of economies of scale' varies from one place to another, and from one product to another. It has already been noted that in some countries industrialised agriculture is less efficient than labour-intensive, peasant farming. Similarly, for some non-agricultural products small production units may be more efficient. It needs to be borne in mind that GNP may reflect the increased per capita income from industrial production more accurately than the per capita income from agriculture, because non-agricultural commodities are more likely to be marketed through 'official' channels. Another much studied model of flexible production has emerged in the Emilia Romagna region of Italy, where over the last 25 years small firms have established a competitive position in world markets in shoes, leather goods, furniture, and musical instruments and in the machinery used to make these products. The fundamental idea is that clusters of mainly small and medium sized firms can gain economies of scale and economies of scope by increased flexibility and inter-firm co-operation.

"The Italian experience of flexible specialisation is based on the development of a cluster of small firms, spatially concentrated and sectorally specialised, developing forward and backward linkages such as exchange of goods, information and people, and supported by local government institutions" (Kiely 1998:148).

Technology is an essential aspect of human activity – and, hence SMEs development. Think of the millions of poor people who make their livelihood in low-income countries especially India in small – scale enterprises and again try to imaging these without a technological input. At a different level, think of what facilitates the process of globalisation. The answer is firstly information technology, with its fast, reliable communication, and secondly transport, which has grown ever cheaper with technological development. Finally, for all human activity we have to harness energy – as heat, light, sound, electricity and to make things move – which many argue is the most fundamental technological activity of all. According to Gordon Wilson and Richard Heeks, "Technology is a purposeful, practical activity that involves the application of knowledge by organisations of human beings and their interaction with hardware". It denotes the necessarily for of innovative technology to improve productivity. In addition to this, technological capability is also an essential condition.

Technological Capability

According to Trindade, technological capability is the ability to manage the technological function of an enterprise

(Trindade 1991). Thus knowing how to marshal and organise or manage the different 'types' of knowledge for technological development is an other key area, one which usually goes under the name of technological capability. There are different levels of knowing how to manage knowledge for technological development. Wilson (1996) distinguishes between 'management as coping' on a day-to-day basis, which equates with an enterprise's routine production capability, and strategic management, which is the ability to make strategic choices about the enterprise function. This distinction, while useful, should however, be considered as representing opposite ends of a technological capability spectrum for enterprises in low income countries, with a range of capabilities at different levels in between which are as follows (From 'day – to – day coping' to 'strategic management').

Production (or coping) Capability

Routine management of production, that is the ability of an enterprise to produce and sell products at the given levels of efficiency and given inputs, including the ability to operate hardware, manage finances, and organisational management.

Formal and Informal Linkage Capability

The ability of the enterprise to mange interactions and information sharing between enterprises, suppliers and contractors, buyers and sellers and service providers (such as maintenance and repair) and other support institutions.

Minor (small) Change Capability

The ability of the enterprise to adapt and improve products and processes, including small changes to existing production processes, products and markets and marketing strategy.

Major (big) Change Capability

The ability of the enterprise to implement new or different production processes and/or products and markets or marketing strategy, or make significant changes to them.

Strategic Management Capability

It refers to the stock of capabilities of an enterprise which results in the ability to gather and respond to information, to use existing resources and invest in new resources (internal and external) to make major or minor changes to the enterprise function (products, production processes, markets and marketing strategy).

Most enterprises within the informal sector of low-income countries are stuck at the initial levels of capability identified as above that is they rarely move beyond a production or coping capability (Platt & Wilson 1999). Enabling them to move towards higher levels is one of the key challenges facing pro-poor interventions for technology development. This is a challenge, moreover, that has to recognise that the major source of learning among such enterprises is 'by doing' or by various informal mechanisms, such as from previous employment, a family member or a friend.

Information Technology (IT) and SMEs Development

As everyone is aware, IT is the recent outcome of technology revolution. It is considered a vital ingredient for the development of any field especially in small and medium enterprises. Information technology can be defined as 'electronic means of capturing, processing, storing, and communicating information'. IT (also known as ICT; information and communication technology) is based on digital information held as 1s and 0s, and comprises computer hardware, software and networks. It is not the only technology that deals with information. Others include:

- 'Intermediate' technology - based largely on analogue information held as electromagnetic waves such as radio, television and telephone.

- 'Literate' technology - based on information held as the written such as books and newspapers.

- 'Organic' technology - based solely on the human body, such as the brain and sound waves.

On the basis of these one can build a systemic model for the operation of a small enterprise in efficient manner shown as below.

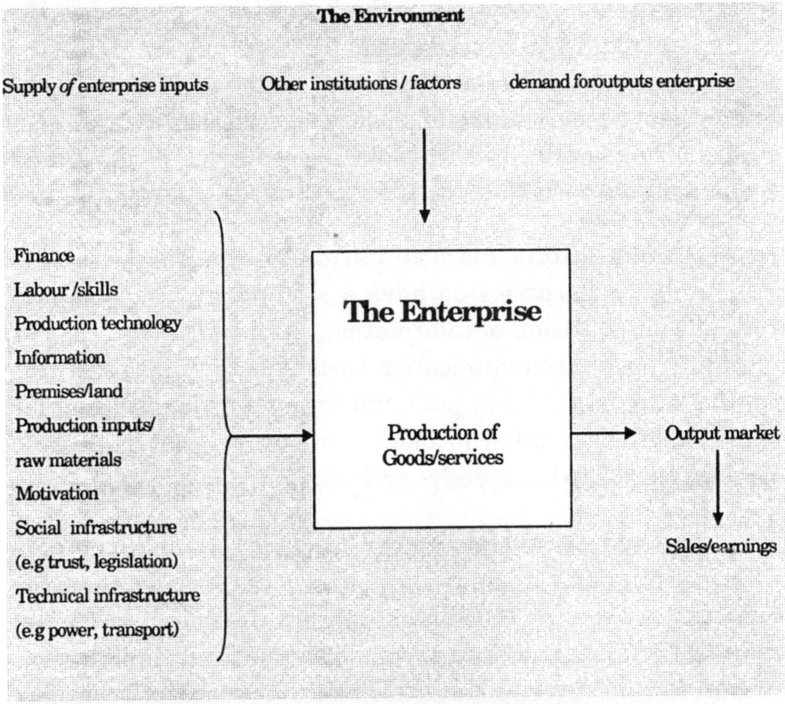

Source: Gordon Wilson and Richard Heeks, 'Technology, Poverty and Development'

Role of IT on SMEs

As an Output and as a Production Technology

Some enterprises produce either tangible (computers, networks, components) or intangible (software, Web pages) IT as an output. Other entrepreneurs, such as designers and publishers, produce heavily information-based outputs. Both use IT as a production technology, and both form part of a nation's 'information economy'. Such enterprises are becoming increasingly vital to low-income countries, and represent a beneficial application of IT in terms of income, skill and export generation.

As an Information Processing Technology

All enterprises need to process the information that arises from both inside and outside the enterprise. However, the processing requirement of most small enterprises for processing formal information is relatively limited and it can frequently be met by paper-based methods. Also, given the relatively high IT costs and low labour costs in developing countries, IT can reduce the processing costs.

As an Information Communication Technology

Small enterprises do have a significant need for both receipt and provision of information. Add in the fact that IT normally lowers communication costs substantially, and this can be seen as the main potential area for IT application for small enterprises in low income countries. Now let us analyse its role relation to both receipt and transmission of information.

As noted, IT cannot be understood without understanding information, and developing a small enterprise requires information about several different things. It needs information relating to supply, such as the availability and sources of finance, labour, technology, raw materials, and other enterprise inputs. It needs information about demand, including market demand such as location, price, size and quality. It also needs information about other environmental factors, such as competitors and laws.

Turning raw data into this kind of usable information is a staged process (the 'information chain') for which we use a '4As' model as below.

For the information chain to function, environmental components must be present. These include resources (money, skills, and technical infrastructure), embedded/social resources (trust, motivation, knowledge, power) and other relevant raw data.

Receiving and applying information are central aspects the acquisition and generation of knowledge. Also, in turn, knowledge generates information. Globalisation demands such (IT) great flows of information and processing of information that they simply could not take place without IT. As stated in the World Bank Report, "This new technology greatly facilitates the acquisition and absorption of knowledge, offering developing countries unprecedented opportunities to enhance educational systems, improve policy formation and execution, and widen the range of opportunities for business and the poor" (World Bank 1999:9).

IT can also play a positive role by allowing information and knowledge to be more widely disseminated. It could be used to transmit information from entrepreneurs to donor and government agencies. The main use for IT, though, has been to transmit marketing information about small enterprise products and services to potential customers; typically via the Web to Western export markets (World Bank 1999 and, Hegener 1998). However, there are far more rose-tinted vignettes of claimed success with IT than there are long-term analytical studies by independent researchers.

Technology as the Problem

There was a reaction also to the 'technology as solution' view. It would be wrong, however, to suggest that it has even today been superseded. Every new, generic technological development always seems to bring with it the same grand claim. In the same way the technological revolution also will affect the development of SMEs. It is dangerous to allocate ideological views to particular time slots in history and, in a real sense, the view of technology as solution has always competed with the reaction – technology as problem. As David Dickson observed

"Throughout history man has been warned that he was creating forces he would be unable to control, that the planet would demand total obedience of the human race... that to place one's faith in science and technology was to make a pact, like Faust with the devil" (Dickson 1974:15).

Far – reaching criticisms of technology were made in similar vein in Small is Beautiful, the influential book written by the unorthodox British economist. E.F Schumacher (1973) subtitled a study of economics as if people mattered. The book could just as easily have substituted the word 'technology' for 'economics'. Schumacher's view of modern technology was no less forceful than those of other critics. According to him ".......we can say that the modern world has been shaped by technology. It tumbles from crisis to crisis; on all sides there are prophesies of disaster and, indeed, visible signs of breakdown" (Schumacher 1973:122). But Small is Beautiful was also a call to action and from his fundamental critique stemmed Schumacher's enquiry into 'whether it is possible to have something better – a technology with a human face' (ibid.).

In the positive side as analysed above, IT could play a vital role in SMEs. But IT has also been associated in some cases with negative impacts. These have included job losses, increased stress, reduced flexibility, centralised control and surveillance and impoverished communications (Heeks 1998). Recent technology development also was caused a serious problem in the world like, environment pollution, terrorism, changing culture and increase the production cost of SMEs as well.

Conclusion

Though technology revolution resulted in some problems in SMEs, the proportion of positive impact is immense. The significant weak issues can be rectified by different ways and means. Participatory Technology Development (PTD) has been promoted in recent years by the Intermediate Technology Development Group (ITDG), and draws heavily on the general arguments in favour of participatory approaches to development interventions. By involving the participation of small entrepreneurs in technology development, one learns crucially about his social, cultural and economic contexts, and this makes any interventions more effective. It also enables technology interventions to build on what is already there (and hence encourages the adaptive behaviour argued for above), rather than introduce something completely new. This, among other things, requires teachers of technology to become learners themselves – in order to discover what is already there and about context. Such behavioural and institutional changes represent a considerable challenge for those who work in R&D or other agencies that promote technology development, which is a corner stone for SMEs development.

References

Anon (1999), **"World Development Report 1999-2000: Entering the 21st Century: The Changing development Landscape'**, Oxford University Press, New York.

Dayanandan R (2000), **Sustainable Development: Opportunities & Challenges**, Serials Publications, New Delhi.

Dickson D (1974), **Alternative Technology and the Politics of Technical Change, Fortana/** Collins, Glasgow.

Gordon Wilson and Richard Heeks (2000), 'Technology, Poverty and Development' in **Poverty and Development into 21st Century**, Tim Allen and Alan Thomas (Eds), Oxford University Press, Oxford.

Heeks R (1998), **Management Information and Management Information Systems,** School of Oriental and African Studies, University of London, London.

Joanna Chataway and Tim Allen (2000), 'Industrialisation and Development: Prospects and Dilemmas' in **Poverty and Development in to 21st Century**, Tim Allen and Alan Thomas (Eds), Oxford University Press, Oxford.

Khanka S.S (2000)., **Entrepreneurial Development**, S. Chand & Company Ltd., New Delhi.

Kiely R (1998), **Industrialisation and Development: A Comparative Analysis**, UCL Press, London.

Platt L.J. & Wilson G.A (1999), "Technology Development and the Poor/marginalised: Context, Intervention and Participation", **Technovation,** 19 (6/7): 393-40.

Schumacher E.F (1973)., **Small is Beautiful: A Study of Economics as if People Mattered**, Blond and Briggs, London.

Trindade S., A.S. Bhalla A.S (Eds.) (1991), **Small and Medium Enterprises: Technology Policies and Options,** Intermediate Technology Publications, London.

Wilson G.A (1996), "From day-to-day Coping to Strategic Management: Developing Technological Capability Among Small-scale Enterprises in Zimbabwe", **International Journal of Technology Management**: 488-99.

Zaid Negash (2006), 'The Dynamics of Micro and Small Enterprises: The Case of Mekelle, Ethiopia", **Micro Finance Development Review,** 5(1).

11

Building ICT Capabilities for Enhancing Competitiveness of Indian SMEs: Issues, Practices and Lessons

Rathakrishnan, L Sriraman, V.P

Abstract

The borderless world exposes SMEs to many challenges that affect their businesses both domestically and internationally. ICT enables improved business process efficiency and productivity. Businesses can reduce operational costs by decreasing material, procurement and transaction costs, resulting in lower prices for intermediate and finished goods, and they can also use more and better information to improve the value of their output. ICT can also facilitate global connectivity, resulting in new ways of creating and delivering products and services on a global scale. New business models and market configurations enabled by ICT, including business process outsourcing and value chain integration provide the SMEs with access to new markets and new sources of competitive advantage, to drive income growth. SMEs should realise that the economy and business are shifting towards a new world configuration of digital information and knowledge-based work. Therefore, SMEs should view the adoption of ICT as inevitable. SMEs should also look upon ICT as a tool to stay alive and be able to compete on a level playing field with their foreign counter part. SMEs need to embrace the state-of-art technologies to penetrate non-traditional markets and remain competitive in the face of increasing challenges posed by globalisation, liberalisation and technological advances. The present paper discusses some of the basic issues in the adoption of ICT tools by Indian SMEs. It also cites a number of cases where the adoption of ICT has given ample benefits.

Introduction

The importance of Small and Medium Enterprises (SMEs) in any economy cannot be overlooked as they form a major chunk in the economic activity of any nation. They play a key role in industrialisation of developing countries like India. They have unique advantages owing to their size, namely labour-capital ratio; shorter gestation period; smaller markets; lower investments; a more equitable distribution of national income; effective mobilisation of resources of capital and skills which might otherwise remain unutilised; and stimulate the growth of industrial entrepreneurship.

In India, SMEs (also known as Small Scale Industries - SSI) account for around 95 per cent of the industrial units, 40 per cent of the value added in the manufacturing sector output, 34 per cent of exports and provide direct employment to 273.97 lakh persons in around 115.22 lakh SSI units. It has been estimated that a million rupees of investment in fixed assets in the small scale sector produces 4.62 million worth of goods or services with an approximate value addition of ten percentage points. The SSI sector in India contributes to about 7 per cent of India's GDP.

Today, SMEs in India are grappling with the fast changes at the market place that is transiting from a controlled economy to a free market set-up. SMEs being the important members within the supply chain are also exposed to the competitive pressures either directly from the market place or indirectly passed on from their higher ups in the chain. Considering the strategic role played by SMEs, it is essential to examine how they can improve their performance in international markets and how they can enhance their export competitiveness. While several studies demonstrate the importance of technological advantage in international trade, the last decade of twentieth century has witnessed technological transformations mainly led by information and communication technology (ICT). Worldwide ICT is helping SME exporters overcome the digital divide and grab superior business opportunities

ICT for Small Business or SMEs

ICT means Information and Communication Technology. It is an electronic means of handling digital data. Better quality information; information that is more CARTA: more complete, accurate, relevant, timely and more appropriately presented, is critical to two activities in any business including the small business:

- Decision making
- Learning

Without poor quality information, poor decisions are made and learning does not occur. This is true everywhere in the world, but is a major problem in developing countries, because they are so information-poor and because their information infrastructure is poorly developed. This information poverty affects SMEs in developing countries that the entrepreneurs either fail to make decisions or make the wrong decisions. It means that entrepreneurs either fail to learn or learn the wrong things or learn from others' experiences. That has a direct effect that they waste money, waste time, lose out on income and, often go out of business. Information poverty makes entrepreneurs isolated, uncertain and risk-averse.

Researches show that entrepreneurs mainly lack information in three key areas; namely **Demand:** information on new and existing customers; **Finance:** information on how to get more finance for the business; and **Skills:** information on how to get more/better skills for the business.

The vast majority – at least 90 per cent and probably more in all Developing Countries SMEs do not currently use ICTs for reasons such as:

- Lack of money.
- Lack of skills or knowledge.
- Lack of technological infrastructure, e.g. electricity, telecommunications.
- Lack of other information chain resources namely: (a) **Data Resources** (they need relevant data to be available in the first place), (b) **Economic Resources** (they need the money, the skills, and the technology in order to access the data), (c) **Social Resources** (they need the motivation, confidence and knowledge to access, assess and apply the data, and they must trust the source) and (d) **Action Resources** (they must be able to act on the decisions made with the information. This will require enterprise inputs (e.g. money, skills, technology, raw materials) plus resources like empowerment).
- Lack of 'critical mass': not enough local people/organisations use computers/email or provide Web content or are able to buy via e-commerce.

Building the ICT Capability

Productivity gains from the use of information technologies involve improved control within individual production processes, smoother integration of individual production process, and better control in the acquisition of inputs and the disposition of outputs. Communication technologies play some of these same roles, but are also particularly important in coordination, e.g. relaying detailed information about inventories and scheduling throughout a distribution system. The productivity gains from ICT are realised through cost-reduction, with reduction in material inputs, labour, and capital. In addition, ICT use may make it possible to produce more with higher quality with the same levels of inputs, i.e. productivity advances that are independent of changes in input use.

Developing nations do not have the option of ignoring ICTs because industrialised countries are in the midst of organisational transitions that involve higher ICT use. To the extent that developing nations hope to develop export markets for their manufactured outputs, particularly those that are intermediate goods or that are linked to increasingly ICT-intensive retailing activities, the systems that manufacturers employ must increasingly be compatible with the emerging new industrial models based on more intense ICT use.

Examples of these developments include the growing emphasis on international quality standards with high levels of information content, the specification of product design using computer aided design and manufacturing, and the coordination of product delivery (including "just in time" and "sales driven" production) using high levels of ICT.

ICT for SMEs gives the relevant business issues in the information society and help them find new business opportunities. With this tool they could, for example, learn how to improve business process efficiency and productivity or understand how to reduce operational costs by decreasing material, procurement and transaction costs, resulting in lower prices for intermediate and finished goods. Finally they should also understand how to use more and better information to improve the value of their output. Firms in emerging economies have several competitive advantages, such as low wages, that they could not exploit without the use of recent ICT evolution.

The use of Information and Communication Technologies (ICT) is not a panacea for all development problems and that there are several obstacles that make it difficult for SMEs in the developing countries to adopt ICT and particularly Internet business tools. But detailed analysis of experience around the world reveals ample evidence that, used in the right way and for the right purposes, ICT can have a dramatic impact on achieving specific social and economic development goals as well as play a key role in broader national development strategies [Digital Opportunity Initiative, 2001]. One of the greatest impacts of ICT is the mobilisation of worldwide knowledge and expertise [World Bank, 1996] and their knowledge transfer to the sectors of developing economies.

Successful Cases

Carpet Industry

The carpet industry is one of the most rapidly growing traditional industries in India. This is a handicraft and cottage industry that provides jobs right at the doorstep of more than 100,000 workers, belonging to the economically backward class of society. In the global carpet scenerio, the market share of Indian carpets is expanding rapidly. Jaipur and its adjacent districts are the major manufacturing clusters in Rajasthan that share a substantial part (15%) of total carpet manufacturing from India. In fact, Rajasthan carpets industry is more quality sensitive, hence designs are critical elements of competitiveness. Rajasthan carpet Industry grew till 1995, but saturation in designs and increasing cost made it difficult for it to compete.

This traditional industry has been facing with declining demand due to the saturation of the qualitative output, and the development and implementation of an ICT platform has enhanced the competitiveness. Given the current scenario of the carpet manufacturing industry in India, Rajasthan Carpet Industry has been facing stiff competition from other clusters such as Bhadhoi and Panipat, which are primarily mechanised and have a high domestic market share. Also, at the global level, the export markets are flooded with cheaper produce from China and synthetics. The use of ICT platform has the power to transform the traditional industry.

PLC Consultation Ltd. offered a viable design solution by providing computer based designing system for carpets in 1998. In Rajasthan, Saraswati Carpets and K.P. & Company were the pioneers in implementing this technology to create a new range of designs. To make the technology available to all manufacturers, Rajasthan Carpet and Woolen Development Society, Jaipur set up a Carpet Designing Centre in 2000. This society makes designs available at affordable prices, thereby facilitating technology adoption. The results of this technology implementation were remarkable in terms of revenue and other operational aspects. In a short period of four years the revenue grew more than five fold. Enhancing the competitiveness has been the major positive effect of ICT adoption in the Rajasthan carpet industry. Both software creators and the government agencies played a catalyst role in supporting the technology adoption process.

National Dairy Development Board, Anand

We see how IT-based machines at milk collection centers are used in cooperatives to measure butterfat content of milk, test the quality of milk, and make prompt payments to farmers. This has resulted in the removal of incentives to those who added water to milk, reduced time for payments from 10 days to less than five minutes, and has thus instilled confidence among farmers in the cooperative set up. The importance of speed of operations should be emphasised, because 600 milk collection centers receive milk from 60,000 farmers daily. On an average, if the saving in time per farmer were 10 minutes every day, it would amount to a huge saving to the tune of 10,000 hours per day! The deployment of technology was considered instrumental to realise such savings.

PEOPLink

PEOPLink, a non-profit organisation formed in 1995, employs a grassroots strategy to help artisans in over 22 less developed countries use the internet to reach world markets. Working at the local community level, PEOPLink has opened doors for many aspiring artists the world over by providing them with access to a variety of modern technologies, including digital imaging and internet technologies. This project focuses on improving the distribution networks of low-income artisans worldwide by using digital imaging, electronic mail, and web pages to market craft products. The lessons learnt from this includes, very poor people can be introduced to e-commerce without providing all of the components of the electronic infrastructure (computers, access to ISP, image capturing device, etc.). PEOPLink partnered with New Delhi based Tara Projects, which has been working with the local artisans on a variety of alternative production and marketing techniques since 1970s, to help modernise its operations.

TARA (Trade Alternative Reform Action)

Is actively engaged in the production and marketing of handicrafts based on fair trade principles. It is also taking up community development and capacity building activities to uplift the neediest among the crafts-persons at the grass-roots. After providing training to non-profit organisations in 1998, PEOPLink helped Tara Projects create a website and introduced local craftsmen/women to digital imaging. Tara Projects quickly embraced the Internet and e-commerce, resulting in a 20 per cent increase in sales, which led to over USD 1 million per year. Tara Projects attributes approximately 10 per cent of that increase directly to the website. With PEOPLink's help the company was also able to significantly reduce the overall marketing and production costs, allowing them to reach new markets more rapidly.

SARI (Sustainable Access in Rural India)

The SARI project of DHAN foundation has been taken up with the objective of proving that there exists a viable market for information and communication services in rural poor areas which can be tapped using innovative technologies and business models. The project intends to setup 100 internet kiosks in rural areas in Madurai district to test this hypothesis.

Jan Mitra or a "friend of the public"

Is part of Government of India - UNDP project on "Improving Citizens' Access to Information" which commenced activities in 2001. This project was formulated in recognition of the need for a more open regime with freer access to information with a view to empowering citizens.

M.S. Swaminathan Research Foundation (MSSRF)

It recent development being, to harness the tools of the space age for rural development through a totally interactive satellite network, the **Indian Space Research Organisation (ISRO)** has joined hands with the MSSRF. The ISRO-MSSRF village resource centre (VRC) project is scheduled for launch at Thiruvayaru, Tamil Nadu.

The network consists of four nodes, the central one being located at the MSSRF premises in Chennai. Each node is capable of sending up to 384 Kbps of data and receiving 1.5 Mbps. Given this capability, full video and audio interactivity will be possible between the two nodes. The project seeks to promote a single-window delivery of need-based services in the areas of education, health, nutrition, weather, environment, agriculture and livelihood. These centres will handle both generic and dynamic information to empower rural communities through spatial information infrastructure, including broadband, Internet, telephone and fax. This will again greatly enhance building the ICT capability for rural entrepreneurs and SMEs.

Conclusion

In spite of all the challenges to the development of sustainable, effective and competitive SME clusters, there are enough positive signals, which indicate that the usage of ICT and the cluster approach could become an effective way for promoting SMEs development in India. In summary, ICTs do not offer an immediate solution to many of the problems the SMEs in developing countries face. At the same time, developing countries cannot afford to ignore the role of ICTs in their plans for industrialisation or the improvement of public infrastructure. It is therefore essential for Indian SMEs to absorb appropriate Information and Communication Technology (ICT) tools to leverage business advantage. Effective utilisation of an information and decision support system will provide SMEs a disciplined business environment to operate in, where decisions concerning supply and demand are fully supported by facts. This approach would also help in maximizing business value and enhancing growth and competitiveness.

References

Census (2001), Govt. of India, New Delhi.

Edward Steinmueller And Maria-Ines Bastos, "Information and Communication Technologies: Growth, Competitiveness, and Policy for Developing Nations" **Global Forum On Industry,** Perspectives For 2000 And Beyond, **UNIDO.**

Is "Survival Of The Fittest" A Tautology? - Don-lindsay-archive.

http://www.peoplink.org

http://www.tenet.res.in/rural/sari.html

http:// www.iconnect-online.org
www.developmentgateway.org
www.dsir.nic.in

12

Promotion of Small and Medium Enterprises in the Information Technology Sector: Venture Capital Schemes

Geetha, R

Abstract

The Indian software industries have come a long way in the past few years. Projects executed by Indian software companies have moved up the value chain from low level programming to re-engineering, systems integration, tools and utilities into intellectual property regime. Advent of internet has created greater opportunities for Indian software industry to come out with world class tools, utilities, products and service. More and more companies are shifting towards IT products or services, which offer exponential growth. Indian venture capital industry consists of offshore and domestic funds. With reference to the venture capital especially for the IT sector, this paper is prepared with the following objectives, namely to trace out the venture capital schemes for the promotion of SMEs and to present suggestions for the development of SMEs in the information technology sector. The analysis is based on both primary and secondary data. The Primary data had been collected from fifty computer centers of Madurai and Virudhnagar districts during the year 2005. Secondary data was collected from newspapers, journals and websites. The results presented in the paper would enable the existing and prospective entrepreneurs to solve the problems of this sector and to produce highly qualified professionals who are the need of the day.

Introduction

The industrial sector in general and the SMEs in particular are exposed to an international competitive environment after globalisation and liberalisation. A separate industrial policy was announced, which eliminated various controls on the industrial sector and provided greater role for the small and medium enterprises. SIDBI was set up as the principal institution for the promotion, financing and development of the SSI sector and for coordinating the activities of other institutions engaged in similar activities. SIDBI has also encouraged the growth of venture capital industry for hi-tech SME units in India by promoting state and regional level funds and setting up an All India Venture Capital Fund.

SMEs cover a wide spectrum of items that contribute substantially in the overall economic growth of the country. The contribution of SMEs in the total exports is 34 per cent and it also creates 20 million job opportunities. The SMEs in India produce a large number and a wide variety of items with associated technology ranging from traditional to state of the art. Information technology is not an exception to this.

The Indian software industry has come a long way in the past few years. Projects executed by Indian software companies have moved up the value chain from low level programming to re-engineering, systems integration, tools and utilities into intellectual property regime. Advent of internet has created greater opportunities for Indian software industry to come out with world class tools, utilities, products and services. More and more companies are shifting towards IT products or services, which offer exponential growth. These institutions rely heavily on knowledge workers and hence are non-asset based. Banks and other financial institutions are not ready to fund these non-asset based projects. Hence, the IT companies are in need of a partner who understands the business environment and is ready to share risk equally during the initial and growth stage. Venture capital is intended to play this role. In this paper the venture capital funds in general, venture capital schemes specially introduced for the IT sector by the recommendations of National IT task force and functioning of such schemes are presented. A study based on the primary data collected from the entrepreneurs of computer centers is also given. On the basis of the findings, suggestions have been made to these entrepreneurs to develop their business.

Venture Capital Fund

Venture capital refers to the commitment of capital as shareholding, for the formulation and setting up of small firms specialising in new ideas or new technologies. These venture capitals provide not only finance but also help in getting the skill needed, in designing the marketing strategy and organise and manage it.

Definition of a Venture Capital Company

A financing institution, which joins an entrepreneur as a co-promoter in a project and shares the risks and rewards of the enterprise, is a venture capital company. At the different stages of a project the venture capital companies render the needed assistance. At the development stage the venture capitalists provide the seed capital to translate an idea into business proposition. In the implementation stage the venture capitals provide the required start up finance to manufacture a product or to provide a service. Then to develop the marketing infrastructure, the venture capital institutions provide the required finance. Finally it also provides the necessary finance to expand the business at a rapid pace. Usually the finance is provided after analysing all the stages of a project and deciding the stage in which they need the required finance. Rarely they provide finance for all the four stages. After the successful completion of these stages the new firm is listed on a stock exchange and at this point the venture capitalists disinvest their shareholdings through the available exit routes. Indian venture capital industry consists of offshore and domestic funds. The offshore venture capital funds usually invest a minimum of one million US dollar and cater to established players with large requirements. Domestic venture capital funds usually cater to small and medium scale new or young hi-tech enterprises considering the key success factors.

In March 2000 the Department of Science and Technology was formed. On the basis of the then Prime Minister's speech in the 88th Science congress the following five proposals were put forth.

1. A dedicated Innovation Financing Fund of Rs.50 crore to be used for sponsoring time bound research to add value to grass root innovations.

2. A special 100 crore micro venture fund and venture promotion fund should be formed.

3. Small innovation patent systems should be introduced.

4. Technological innovations focused specially on women, - most of the activities in which women are working are traditional and the technologies are also old. To encourage women competitions may be announced with attractive prizes for innovative ideas.

All these recommendations are focused on agricultural sector, rural development and innovative ideas. Information Technology is an innovative sector, in which what was new yesterday will become obsolete today. Information technology industry, in the long run has a high propensity for generation of internal resources obviating the need for external financing. Therefore, in the IT sector finance is required only during the initial start-up phase until the company stabilises its operations. For the initial funding software companies do not have visible and quantifiable market. The assets of IT companies could not be submitted as collateral securities due to unconventional risks involved and high tech obsolescence triggered by unexpected innovations. Hence, the IT sector could not use the normal process of borrowings and long-term loans from banks and other financial institutions. But the IT companies are in need of long term funds for the expansion of software facilities within the country and abroad, acquisition of companies abroad and development of new products. They require short-term finance to meet the working capital requirements to bridge any short-term cash flow deficit. To meet these requirements along with the traditional types of financing such as bonds, debentures, and preference shares and promoters' funds some more long term financing instruments can be used. The new schemes are:

1. Venture capital funds and private equity.
2. Working capital and project finance.
3. Public issue.
4. Overseas listing like global depository receipts.
5. Loans from available resources.

Recommendations of the IT Action Plan – Part I

As per the notification in the Gazette of India, Extraordinary, Part-I, Section I, No. 160 dated 1-7-1998, following policies of the IT Action Plan, Part–1 of the National Task force were implemented.

- The banks were allowed to invest in the form of equity in dedicated venture capital funds meant for IT industry.

- Banks and other financial institutions like ICICI, IDBI, UTI and SBI could set up joint ventures with Indian or foreign companies for setting up of at least four different venture capital dedicated funds of a corpus of not less than Rs. 50 crores each to cater to the credit need of the industry.

- Venture capitalists could be allowed to set off losses in one invested company and profit in another invested company during the block of years for the purpose of income tax.

- The computer software companies of India or their subsidiaries abroad were allowed to issue sweat equity. Sweat equity means equity allotted to promoter–directors, whole–time directors or employees for providing any know–how, intellectual property or value addition to the company.

The IT Action Plan Part -11

To promote hardware development, manufacture and export certain policies were laid down for the IT hardware ventures. They are

- IT products sector is included under the priority sector. IT industry is given the status of infrastructure industry in order to be globally competitive and be able to tap funds globally.

- Venture capital: The banks are allowed to invest in the form of equity in dedicated venture capital funds meant for IT industry.

- Banks like ICICI and TDICICI are allowed to set up joint ventures with Indian or foreign companies for setting up at least two different venture capitals dedicated funds of a corpus of not less than Rs.100 crores each to cater the credit need of the hardware industry.

- Venture capitalists will be allowed to set off losses in one invested company and profit in another invested company for the purpose of income tax.

- All IT products and related services will be considered eligible for exemption under the income tax act for Venture Capital investment. IT product means IT products including IT software of services.

To remove the bottlenecks in the growth of venture capital funds, which is crucial in the high growth of the IT industry following measures were taken by the government.

- Income Tax Act section 10 (23D) is applicable to Venture Capital funds, which was previously applicable for mutual funds only.

- Under Sec 10 (23F) of the Income tax act the eligible investments were only equity and now quasi-equity and loans were also added.

- Rule 2 (d) of the income tax act 1962 was modified to remove the time-bound investment schedules. It was ordained that VCF should invest 80 per cent of the corpus in 4 years.

- SEBI guidelines were changed to permit mutual funds to invest five per cent of the corpus in Venture Capital Funds.

- OTCEI helped small companies to raise money from the public and also helped Venture Capital Funds to exit from the small companies.

- Company's bill was enacted to enable the companies to buy-back the shares of healthy companies from the venture capital funds.

- Limited Partnership Act was passed to facilitate the formation of Venture Capital Funds. Managers and investors to VCF constituted the partnership, which was of limited life. Investors to the fund were called limited partners and managers who manage the fund were called general partners. General partners receive a salary and management fee. The liability of the limited partners was limited to the extent of the investment in the fund.

- Fifty per cent tax exemption was provided for investments in VCF.

- PF Act was changed to allow them to invest five per cent of the corpus in VCFs private sector; insurance companies should be asked to support VCFs.

Many additional policy recommendations are made by NASSCOM with specific reference to the raising of VCF. The VCF brings more money to the portfolio companies as they provide specialised industry experts and connections. Venture capital financing could be in the form of:

- Relatively small amount of capital provided to an entrepreneur to prove a concept.

- Finance provided to companies that have expanded their initial capital

- Finance provided to companies that have expanded their initial capital and require funds for sales and manufacturing.

- Working capital for the initial expansion of the company that is producing and shipping but may not be showing profit.

- Funds provided for the major growth of the company whose sales are increasing and that are break-even or profitable.

- Financing for a company expecting to go for public issue in 6 to 12 months.
- Funds provided to enable operating management to acquire a product line or business.

In the year 1999 SIDBI Venture Capital Ltd, a wholly owned subsidiary of SIDBI was formed. It was established in order to manage Rs.100 crore venture capital funds for Software and Information Technology (NFSIT). This fund invested Rs. 75 crore in 30 IT companies. Investments were made in BPO/ ITES, Software products, Software services and internet related businesses. All were from the SMEs segment. This shows that SME IT segment is using the venture capital funds as their major source of funding. By the end of May 2006, the venture fund exited partially or completely from 11 of the IT companies and got revenues 1.8 times the investment.

Another SMEs Growth Fund was formed with a corpus of Rs.500 crore dedicated to the SMEs sector. With the main objective of meeting the long term risk capital requirement of innovative and technology oriented projects this fund was formed by SIDBI in the year 2004 for a period of 8 years. This is the largest venture capital fund dedicated to the SMEs sector. The demand for the venture capital activities in the SMEs, sector in IT and other growth sectors will enable the SMEs growth fund to be invested its entire corpus over 3 to 4 years.

Karnataka Information Technology Venture Capital Fund (KITVEN) is an IT specific. Rs.15 crore registered with Securities and Exchange Board of India (SEBI). The fund has been subscribed by SIDBI, Karnataka State Industrial Investment and Development Corporation limited (KSIIDC) and Karnataka State Financial Corporation (KSFC) in 1999. It invested Rs.12.08 crore in 13 companies. KITVEN exited from six companies with four very good exits including ECAD and recovered partial amounts in the other two companies. It has also returned 38 per cent of the money subscribed by the three institutions.

A case study related to the investment by SIDBI Venture Capitals Ltd and Karnataka IT Venture Fund is given below.

ECAD Technologies Ltd., Bangalore

ECAD Technologies Ltd., Bangalore, an early stage IT company was funded by SIDBI Venture Capitals Ltd., (Rs. Two Crore) together with Karnataka Venture Capital Fund (Rupees one crore) in March 2001. After a period of 4 years both the funds have fully divested from their investment for a consideration of Rs.7.5 crore, which means that with a profit of 150 per cent over the original investment. The controlling interest of ECAD was purchased by an Austrian company, "Austria Technologies and System Technique (AGAT&S).

The Chairman, SIDBI Venture Capitals Ltd., opined that the exit process was ideal and it improved the faith of the SVCL towards the SMEs. He also stated that SMEs contributed immensely in generating employment opportunities and also contributes by way of generating revenues, including exports to the national exchequer.

IT Education and Training

The above discussion discloses the source of finance available to the SMEs in the IT sector. The IT services include computer education and training. Computer education is inevitable for all just like the other subjects in the school level. Though the Government and the public realised the need for computer education, it is not an easy task to provide computer education for the whole population through the formal sector. To provide computer education, it is necessary to install the required systems and with other facilities needs huge investment.

The elders need only computer literacy whereas the youngsters need it for their employment opportunities. The children would like to have computer knowledge to enjoy the computer games. Hence, different categories of people go to the private computer centers to satisfy their requirements. The government and private schools approaches the private computer centers and have tie ups to provide computer education to their students at their own premises.

When computer education was introduced in India, very few centers were there to provide computer education but in the 90s the scope for IT professionals was very vast and the number of centers and the demand for computer education were at the peak in late 90s. When the Y2K problem was solved in 2000 many Indian IT professionals returned home from USA and then the introduction of Euro currency and the development in the ITES sector provided enormous job opportunities for the IT professionals. This in turn increased the demand for computer education in India.

In the private sector IT education and training is provided by very big international companies such as NIIT, APTECH and SSI, national level and regional level companies such as BDPS, RADIANT and CSC. In addition to these certain local centers are also in the market. The big centers have a network of centers and they offer uniform courses with their own syllabi and course design. The center owners have to pay a certain percentage of the fee collected to the franchiser. The local centers provide basic courses to those who are in need of computer literacy and also by the local businessmen who would like to give training to their employees. A study was conducted to trace out the profile of private computer centers and their problems.

Methods and Material Data Sources

Data were collected from 50 computer centers with a structured questionnaire. The center owners were selected among the centers situated in Madurai and Virudhunagar Districts, which have at least five years past track record. The period of the study was 2004-2005. The sample centers were 31 international, national and regional level center franchisees and the 19 centers were local centers.

Tools for Analysis

The data is described with percentage analysis. To analyse the data Garrett ranking technique was used.

Objectives of the Study

(i) To trace out the profile of the computer centers,

(ii) To analyse the factors which motivated the center owners to start a computer center,

(iii) To examine the problems faced by the center owners, and

(iv) To suggest remedies to the private sector.

Profile of Computer Centers

Marketers' Age and Education

Computers and computer education are of recent origin and therefore most of the owners of computer centers (the marketers of computer education) are the pioneers in this industry. The age of the marketers has a say on them since experience is gained with the passage of time and knowledge is obtained by education or training. People who utilise opportunities and transform knowledge into commercial value only can succeed. Those who possess academic qualifications such as M.Sc., B.Sc or Diploma in computer science or Information Technology, MCA, BE (Computer Science or Information Technology) and degrees in related fields naturally acquire computer knowledge from their curriculum. The computer centers, either franchise or local, could be started without much difficulty from the technical side. Some marketers

Table 1: Age and Educational Qualification of Owners

Centers	*Below 35 Years*			*Above 35 Years*		
	Computer Degree or Diploma	*PG or Professional Degree*	*Total*	*Computer Degree or Diploma*	*PG or Professional Degree*	*Total*
Franchise	4 (40)	6 (60)	10 (100)	10 (48)	11 (52)	21 (100)
Local	4 (44)	5 (56)	9 (100)	5 (50)	5 (50)	10 (100)
Total	8 (42)	11 (58)	19 (100)	15 (48)	16 (52)	31 (100)

Source: Primary data
Note : Figures in parentheses are percentages.

without technical kncwledge also enter into the business and manage the centers by employing technically qualified people. The details regarding age and educational qualification of the entrepreneurs are given in Table 1.

It is stated in Table 1 that in total 19 owners are less than 35 years old. Only nine out of these 19, own local centers and the others own franchise centers. Among the 31 owners of above 35 years of age, 21 owners own franchise centers and 10 are the owners of local centers.

In the less than 35 years age category, 40 per cent of the franchise owners and 44 per cent of local owners possess degree or diploma in computer. Among the owners of above 35 years age, 53 per cent of franchise owners possess post graduate degree of any discipline or professional degrees whereas in local centers 50 per cent possess such degrees. It indicates that majority of the marketers possess computer knowledge.

Motivational Factors

Educational entrepreneurs came into existence due to the technological changes and non-availability or insufficiency of formal academic facilities in certain areas. A few entrepreneurs are born but many are created. Desire or need motivate people to become entrepreneurs apart from being motivated by relatives and friends. The factors of motivation may differ from person to person. Self - employment and profitability also inspire an entrepreneur to start a business. The owners were asked to rank the motivational factors. The factors which motivated the marketers along with their ranks are given in Table 2.

It is clear from Table 2 that 50 per cent of the owners rank self employment in the first position and 20 per cent gives second rank. Possession of the required qualification gets the first rank from 14 per cent of the owners and another 14 per cent gives second place to this factor. Parental or spouse

Table 2: Motivational Factors and Ranks

Factors	Ranks Given								Total
	1	2	3	4	5	6	7	8	
1. Self Employment	25 (50)	10 (20)	7 (14)	4 (8)	2 (4)	1 (2)	1 (2)	0	50 (100)
2.Having Qualification	7 (14)	7 (14)	10 (20)	8 (16)	7 (14)	7 (14)	0	4 (8)	50 (100)
3.Parental/Spouse Motivation	2 (4)	5 (10)	7 (14)	4 (8)	4 (8)	6 (12)	11 22)	11 (22)	50 (100)
4. Motivation by Friends	6 (12)	4 (8)	4 (8)	5 (10)	4 (8)	10 (20)	8 16)	9 (18)	50 (100)

Factors	*Ranks Given*								*Total*
	1	*2*	*3*	*4*	*5*	*6*	*7*	*8*	
5. Motivation by Relatives	2 (4)	2 (4)	1 (2)	6 (12)	5 (10)	7 (14)	15 30)	12 (24)	50 (100)
6.Demand for Computer Education	7 (14)	6 (12)	8 (16)	8 (16)	8 (16)	2 (4)	6 12)	5 (10)	50 (100)
7. Easy to Start and Maintain	0	8 (16)	6 (12)	6 (12)	13 (26)	9 (18)	5 10)	3 (6)	50 (100)
8. More Profitable	1 (2)	8 (16)	7 (14)	9 (18)	7 (14)	8 (16)	4 (8)	6 (12)	50 (100)
Total	50	50	50	50	50	50	50	50	-

Source: Primary data

Note: Figures in parentheses are percentages to total.

motivation and motivation by relatives are given the first place by 4 per cent of the owners each. The factor motivation by friends gets the first rank from 12 per cent of owners. Demand for computer education gets the first place from 14 per cent of the owners and 12 per cent gives second rank. No owner gives a first rank to the factor that it is easy to start and maintain. Only 2 per cent of the owners rank profitability as their chief motivational factor whereas 16 per cent of them rank it in the second place.

The ranks given by the owners are converted into percentage position by using the following formula.

$$\text{Percent position} = \frac{100(Rij - 0.50)}{Nj}$$

Rij = Rank given for the ith factor by the jth owner.
Nj=Number of factors ranked.

The percent position of each rank obtained was converted into scores by referring to the table given by Garrett. Then for each factor the scores of individual owners were added together and divided by the total number of owners. These mean scores for all the factors were arranged in a descending order, ranks were assigned and the important factors identified. The mean score and ranks are given in Table 3.

It is revealed in Table 3 that self-employment is the topmost factor among the motivational factors. The number of unemployed as per the records of employment exchange is 1,15,000 in Virudhunagar District and 1,62,624 in Madurai District. The difficulty of getting employment motivated them to seek self-employment. Hence, this factor gains the highest rank.

The factor, which got the next highest score is the educational qualification they possess. A study by Sharma stated

Table 3: Garrett Ranking for Motivational Factors

Factors	*Total Score*	*Mean score*	*Rank*
1. Self Employment	3469	69.38	I
2. Having Qualification	2742	54.84	II
3. Demand for Computer Education	2738	54.76	III
4. More Profitable	2285	45.7	VII
5. Easy to Start & Maintain	1922	38.44	VIII
6. Motivation by Friends	2622	52.44	IV
7. Parental/Spouse Motivation	2410	48.2	VI
8. Motivation by Relatives	2414	48.28	V

Source: Primary data

that technically or professionally qualified entrepreneurs consider educational qualification as the main motivational factor. In the study area also, the educational qualification they possess and the knowledge on computers, motivated many entrepreneurs to start the centers.

Demand for computer education is the factor, which got the third position according to Garret ranking. All government departments, small scale or large-scale units and private or public organisations are being computerised, which has made computer literacy the basic job requirement. According to a NASSCOM survey, by the year 2008, the demand for computer professionals for IT and IT led industry would grow at a very high rate. Demand for computer professionals creates demand for computer education, which in turn motivated the owners to market computer education and training.

Years of being in the Business

The demand for computer professionals has shrunk by 40 per cent in the year 2000-2001 leading to a supply demand imbalance. Those who had entered the education and training industry during the boom time, without sufficient experience or technology back up vanished. Many were forced to exit. Because of these reasons many computer education centers had only a shorter life span. The life periods completed by the centers in the study area also reflect the situation. The life spans of the centers studied are given in Table 4.

Table 4: Life span of the Centers

Centers	*< 7 years*	*> 7 years*	*Total*
Franchise	19 (61)	12 (39)	31 (100)
Local	14 (74)	5 (26)	19 (100)
Total	33 (66)	17 (34)	50 (100)

Source: Primary data
Note: Figures in parentheses are percentages to total.

It is clear from Table 4 that in both types of centers the number of centers with less than seven years life was more. It was 61 per cent among the Franchise centers and 74 per cent among the local centers. Only a few centers are in existence for a long period.

Investment in the Computer Centers

The investment in centers depends upon the hardware, software and other infrastructures. Ayyamperumal, Director, CSC, opines that a minimum of 2 lakh rupees was required to start a CSC franchise in small towns. The investment was either from own funds or borrowed funds. Some of the marketers invested their own funds. On the basis of the primary data, the centers are categorised into three, depending upon the investment. The average investment in centers and the way by which the capital is raised are given in Table 5.

It is stated in Table 5 that the number of local centers having capital below six lakh rupees was 11. It was 15 in the case of franchise centers. Among the franchise centers 16 and eight local centers have an investment of more than rupees six

Table 5: Investment and Source of Capital

Investment Rs. in lakhs	*Franchise centers*			*Local centers*		
	Own	*Borrowed and Own*	*Total*	*Own*	*Borrowed and Own*	*Total*
< 6	12 (80)	3 (20)	15 (100)	9 (82)	2 (18)	11 (100)
> 6	12 (75)	4 (25)	16 (100)	6 (75)	2 (25)	8 (100)
Total	24 (77)	7 (23)	31 (100)	15(79)	4 (21)	19 (100)

Source: Primary data

Note: Figures in parentheses are percentages to total.

lakh. When the center owners were asked about the financial assistances provided by banks and about the venture capital schemes, only a few told about the bank loans and no one had the awareness of venture capital funds. Majority of the centers in all the categories are run with their own capital.

Number of Computers Installed in the Centers

The systems are the basic requirements of the computer centers. The number of courses offered depends upon the number of systems installed, which in turn depends upon the investment. The Number of systems installed in the centers is given in Table 6.

Table 6: Number of Computers in the Centers

No. of Systems	*Franchise Centers*	*Local Centers*	*Total*
<10	15 (48)	14 (74)	29 (58)
> 10	16 (52)	5 (26)	21 (42)
Total	31 (100)	19 (100)	50 (100)

Source: Primary data
Note: Figures in parentheses are percentages to total.

It is shown in Table 6 that per cent of the centers have less than 10 computers. Only 42 per cent of the centers have more than 10 computers. Among the franchise centers 52 per cent have more than 10 computers, whereas it was only 26 per cent among the local centers. Franchise centers have more number of computers than the local centers.

Nature of Systems Installed in the Computer Centers

The computers installed in the centers are branded or assembled. Though the PC market in the educational segment have grown up but only assembled PCs form a major portion. Assembled PC enjoys over 60 per cent share of the Indian PC market as compared to 17 per cent of the Indian brands and 22 per cent of MNC brands. The number of systems and nature of systems installed in franchise and local centers are shown in Table 7.

Table 7: Nature of Systems Installed and Nature of Centers

Types of Systems	*Franchise Centers*	*Local Centers*	*Total*
Fully Branded	12 (39)	3 (16)	15 (30)
Fully Assembled	5 (16)	7 (37)	12 (24)
Both the Types	14 (45)	9 (47)	23 (46)
Total	31(100)	19(100)	50(100)

Source: Primary data
Note : Figures in parentheses are percentages to total.

It is evident from Table 7 that 24 per cent of the centers in the study area installed assembled systems only. Among the franchise centers, 39 per cent have branded systems. But only 16 per cent of the local centers have fully branded systems. Assembled systems enable the marketers to install more number of systems with minimum investment.

Problems Faced by the Owners

IT education and training is a business with good prospects, and also many problems. It requires constant revision of curriculum, which in turn requires constant upgradation of systems. Improper handling of systems by the students is another problem. High rate of turnover of faculty, dropout of students and power failures are the other problems to be tackled by the owners.

The owners have ranked these problems. Ranks have been converted into scores and total score for each problem was obtained. Method of scoring used here is that the first rank is given five score and it is decreased along with the ranks. Thus the problem which is ranked in the fifth position is given one. Total scores are calculated and then ranked on the basis of

Table 8: Ranking of Problems

Centers having Problems	*I*	*II*	*III*	*IV*	*V*	*Total Score*	*Rank*
Upgrading Systems	18	12	6	7	7	177	I
Courses Becoming Obsolete	12	16	10	6	6	172	II
Turnover of Staff	8	8	10	12	12	138	III
Poor Strength and Drop - outs	4	7	14	12	12	126	V
Improper Handling of Systems by the Students	8	6	10	13	13	133	IV

Source: Primary data

total scores. The item, which secured the highest total score, is the most serious problem. The total scores and ranks are given in Table 8.

Table 8 shows that upgrading the systems was the most severe problem faced by the marketers. IT industry is a very dynamic industry. One has to keep oneself updated with the latest technology. To introduce new courses and for upgrading the systems, software is to be identified, acquired, and the course design and courseware are to be prepared. All these procedures consume much time and money. Thus, it is one of the major challenges of non-formal IT education sector.

Second rank is given to the problem courses becoming obsolete. As it is a developing field new developments are introduced daily and improved versions are to be installed, which require heavy and continuous investment. Staff turnover was the problem in the third rank, which could interrupt the working of centers. Only if the staff members are paid an attractive salary they could be retained. The attrition rate in the IT education is the highest in the total IT industry. Improper handling of the systems and poor strength and high rate of drop out of students and power failure are the least important problems as per ranking by the owners.

Suggestions

The findings showed that the IT education field suffers from the problems, which could be solved by adequate finance. Only if sufficient finance is available systems could be updated. To acquire the software it is essential to have sufficient capital. The staff could be retained only if they are paid a reasonable salary. Hence, these computer center owners should approach the available sources of finance. As per the Tamil Nadu Government's Policy 2002 IT education institutions are given 'Industry' status. The study area being a semi-urban, the small entrepreneurs do not have the awareness about the venture capital schemes. Awareness camps are to be arranged for the existing and the budding entrepreneurs to educate them about all these schemes. The local centers could come together to form a consortium or a company to approach venture capital companies for finance and expert services. If the local centers, which have a hold on the market join such other centers from different nearby places and form a company they could compete with the franchise centers. All such centers suffer from the following problems.

(i) Shortage of working capital and high staff turnover.

(ii) Shortage of funds to upgrade the hardware and software; and

(iii) Inadequate finance to introduce new courses.

Conclusion

When computer centre owners jointly form a small-scale company, getting the finance and other assistances from the venture capital companies they could solve all these problems and would enable them carry on their centers profitably. They provide employment for themselves and also to the educated youth who search for a job and could find a solution for the national problem namely unemployment.

13

Internet Trading and Small and Medium Enterprises

Parivallal, R

Abstract

The networked economy supports distributed working practices (teleworking), and distributed teams, supply chains, and even companies (remote collaboration virtual business). It also allows remote marketing (via telemarketing and web advertising) and the building of relationships with customers and trading partners at a distance. These make it possible to be really effective in e-commerce as part of a total e-business approach. The very emphasis on SMEs acknowledges that they are the largest group of businesses. They tend to create innovation, which drives our economy. Anyone who browses the internet will quickly see SMEs presence. These SMEs have either established a steady addition to their turnover through internet trading or have established a booming new trading approach that has completely changed their business. The technical arena for e-business is also changing fast. In the early stages only larger companies could afford the expensive design and programming efforts that went into trading sites. This is still true for large companies who want large and complex integrated systems for a total business solution. However, for the smaller business there are many readily usable solutions on the market that have now been tried and tested. Internet trading offers many options for all types of SMEs and the technology is now mature enough for literally anyone, even a one-person business, to exploit new opportunities

Introduction

We use the term "e-Business" because the smart business of today can exploit not only the specific online trading processes commonly described as "online transactions", but also a host of other business trading activities, which benefit from the increasingly networked economy. The networked economy supports distributed working practices (teleworking) and distributed teams, supply chains, and even companies (remote collaboration and virtual business). It also allows remote marketing (via telemarketing and web advertising), and the building of relationships with customers and trading partners at a distance. These make it possible to be really effective in e-commerce as part of a total e-business approach.

Online transaction processing may be how the new traders 'clinch' the deal, but without the support of the whole suite of e-business functions the success in online transactions, or ecommerce, may be limited. New entrants may even exploit other internet business opportunities to set up a complete new business approach before embarking on e-commerce transactions.

The very emphasis on SMEs acknowledges that they are the largest group of businesses. Statistics vary, but a general view is that more than 90 per cent of companies fall into the 'SMEs' category, with nearly 60 per cent being small businesses having less than 10 employees. Despite being smaller in size it is SMEs who tend to create the innovation, which drives our economy.

SMEs and Internet Trading

Anyone who browses the Internet will quickly see SMEs presence. While the larger companies may dominate through early exploitation and establishment of new forms of business (new business models), smaller players are already emerging in numbers. These SMEs have either established a steady addition to their turnover through internet trading, or have established a booming new trading approach that has completely changed their business.

The technical arena for e-business is also changing fast. In the early stages only larger companies could afford the expensive design and programming efforts that went into trading sites. This is still true for large companies who want large and complex integrated systems for a total business solution. However, for the smaller business there are many readily usable solutions on the market that have now been tried and tested.

The interactivity needed for web sites aiming at on-line trading is now available in different ways. SMEs can buy a (relatively) cheap solution in a box' (for the self-maintained site), or outsource development to an Internet Access Provider (IAP) or Internet Service Provider (ISP) who can manage and maintain the trading site.

The most difficult aspect of trading online has also become reasonably well organised of late - online transaction processing (securing payment online). At one time only large and well established companies could get approval from banks (and online data connections) to do credit card verification and sales validation in real time. However, a large number of 'trusted third parties' (TTPs) have appeared who accept and process online payments on behalf of smaller companies (at a charge). Internet trading offers many options for all types of SMEs and the technology is now mature enough for literally anyone, even a one-person business, to exploit new opportunities.

Dynamics of SME Business

The dynamics of SME business markets tend to be determined by four key factors:

- Suppliers
- Buyers
- Products
- Services

Any enterprise needs a strategy if it is to be successful. The normal dynamics of SME business apply in the arena of internet trading, but are added to by novel features that emanate from the new 'on-line' style of trading.

Supplier Dynamics

In any market, the competition is often the greatest from new players who see an opportunity not yet exploited by established traders. This leads to two interesting scenarios for SMEs contemplating internet trading. First, new entrants find it hard to make way because established business is in a position to fight back. However, if new players in your market are emerging via internet then traditional strategies for repelling them may not be so effective - you may have to develop an online strategy to fight back.

Next, if you are now trading online then you are taking part in a 'less well established' form of trading, even in your established market. That means there may be more 'cracks in your 'armour' and so more opportunities for new players to gain advantage. The solution is not to steer clear of internet trading, since the new competitors will appear there anyway - but to make better is than (or at least match them) at online trading.

A further source of concern in the supplier area is a shift in bargaining power. Suppliers may be innovative and so are new products and services (see later). They may compete on a cost basis. In a well-established market fluctuations may be rare, but with new players emerging on internet the scope for new services, new products, and dramatic price reduction is greatly increased. It could be argued that if an established market is being estabilised by new online activity, the first counter might be to go online and make a competitive offering.

A final recommendation here concerns integration of the supply chain. Competition from established or new players moving online will cause the development of new business relationships to consolidate a strong position. A counter strategy might be to move ahead of likely competition and consolidate the supply chain by using online methods for better integration of communications and processes. There is also scope for reducing the numbers of middlemen in the forward section of the supply chain (process streamlining).

In summary, entrants to online trading are able to reach new markets, reduce supply chain, improve process and corporate/brand image, reduce costs and differentiate their products and services against competitors.

The Buyer's Position

It is generally felt that the power of buyers is weak, unless they are large corporate whose custom represents a substantial percentage of a supplier's turnover. However, electronic trading has already seen evidence of smaller buyers combining strength (backward integration in supply chain) to improve their position against large suppliers.

In the retail scenario, the end-customer is no longer confined to a local high street or town shopping centre, and in business-to-business, there is less and less reliance on providers in the immediate vicinity (locale). This means that for products, which people will buy for delivery, the buyer's position is greatly enhanced by internet trading. So long as they are looking at branded goods where the uncertainties are reduced, they may buy on price alone.

This means that companies have to compete either on price (cheapest outlet), quality (better goods), added services (e.g. better support) or on 'lifestyle' (market image). Cost reductions are common in internet trading and are generally paid for through savings in infrastructure (reduction of expensive shop/outlet space, shortening of delivery chain, etc.), or through dramatic increase in sales throughout.

Products and Services

Since existing products and services can be differentiated on price, image, etc. (covered earlier), there is only one further issue where products and services can contribute effects to the market dynamic. That is in the area of 'substitute' products and services. In offline trading a common approach to capturing market share is to shift consumers away from established products and services to new products and services (or 'slightly' different ones but with dramatic image shift).

The emergence of online trading has created huge new opportunities for substitute products and services. The most commonly cited example of success here is probably Amazon Books (www.amazon.com). What people often fail to say about Amazon is that it is a simple substitute for the local bookshop, differentiated by ease of use (books to the door), breadth of choice (millions of titles), and cost (the best prices anywhere).

Other examples of service substitution include online auctions. The ofcited ebay (http://www.ebay.co.uk) is an extremely successful online auction house. It provides a substitute service for classified advertising and includes service enhancements (quality increase) of different kinds. For example, a vendor can offer something for sale at what he/she thinks is a good price (and can set a reserve). It may be that they have underestimated the object's value and the bids go ahead of the asking price (as often happens with, for example, collectibles).

In summary, internet trading allows cost reduction, product and service differentiation, and development of substitute services. Online trading requires businesses to completely rethink their delivery strategy and their own differentiation. The flexibility of internet trading means that dramatic changes in product and service offerings are possible with minimal loss of time or investment in marketing materials and activities.

Being Competitive

One interesting feature of internet trading is that as pressure increases in a specific market through competition (see previous) the opportunities for profit decrease quite rapidly. Areas such as IT and games, which were thought to be the most likely areas of success, have not paid dividends at the expected rate due to enormous competition. This is thought to be due to the ease of entry into IT markets (easy to engage the upstream supply chain) and the consequent proliferation of competitive vendors for undifferentiated products and services.

Traditional marketing theory suggests that a company that tries to be all things to all people will fail miserably. However, this is not necessarily true on internet. It is the case that off-line it is hard to be the cheap and easy supplier, while at the same time offering quality and service. However, since corporate identity can be manufactured and discarded easily in the virtual world, some companies exploit multiple presences in markets where they wish to capture a share of every sector. For example, it is possible to trade good drinkable wine cheaply in bulk from one web site (a no frills approach), while also trading selected wines from a site rich in information and customer support the up market (arm). These could be both supplied from a single warehouse with the only added costs being one additional web front end (to a common database and delivery management system), and unique labeling for the delivery packaging.

Whichever approach is taken it is still hard to escape the traditional strategies for competition, even on-line.

Product or Service Differentiation

This is about providing (or seeming to provide) something different or unique. As soon as a genuinely different product appears it is often copied, but there are exceptions. Others trade what appear to be similar products (to a technical eye) but have differentiated the supplier identity (lifestyle and up market approaches).

Niche Marketing

David Frieslander could not find leather covers for personal digital assistants (PDAs) anywhere in the UK or on the web. So he organised manufacture and began selling them via his web site. He made his first million quite quickly and proved that a unique product idea is still a mighty weapon on the internet. Having an unusual offering attracts attention in the news and on the internet which is a village of gossips - word soon spreads and that means free advertising.

Cost Reduction

We have talked about cost reduction already. Taking business online offers many opportunities for cost reduction and is a standard feature of competitive internet trading. If these factors can be combined the competitive advantage is greatly increased (multiplied).

Clear Targets for New Internet Traders

As with any business area, internet trading may start with a strategic view, but this must be turned into achievable objectives. Needless to say, internet trading objectives need to follow standard textbook advice and be precise, realistic and measurable. They must say exactly what is to be achieved, and how this can be done within the operational scope of the business. They must also, when put into play, be accessible to allow precise assessment of attained value (evaluation).

Remember, the strategic objective "To obtain a 10 per cent increment in sales via internet" is easily measurable - you either get 10 per cent or not. But the precision needs to be put in place to make it happen. So ask yourself exactly 'how' that will come about.

Internet trading has already shown a wide range of success criteria, and some of the key criteria for success are described in the following section.

Seven Keys to Success in Internet Trading

It sometimes seems there are as many experts on internet trading as there are trading web sites. However, much of what they say overlaps and seems grounded in solid marketing theory plus a good helping of online experience.

Key 1 - Cost and Value

Cost is not just about minimising consumer prices. The internet trader must determine how price-sensitive a product or service really is. Some products are selected mainly on price (sensitive), while for others issues like customer support and perceived quality reduce price sensitivity.

It is necessary to obtain a clear impression of the true market situation. If a product is highly sensitive on price then a strategy of price reduction mass marketing may be the only approach (e.g. IT equipment), whereas other products may require careful planning to ensure appropriate sales criteria are in evidence (perceived exclusivity, 'lifestyle' branding, help-lines, service agreements, etc.).

Cost is not only about money, but value - what the customer gets out of a product/service.

Key 2 - Image and Branding

This success key is all about whether a brand image and product identity (or corporate identity) can be created (or already exists) or be promote as attractive and of high value. This relies on standard techniques that can be extended to on-line usage. The more people are aware of your company, your site, and the products and services offered there, then the more visits and the greater likelihood of sales. People go where the signposts point

Key 3 - Trading Site Content

All of the marketing pandits agree on one thing. Success in online selling is about three things 'content, content and content'. Good sites grab attention and are compelling. They provide plenty to look at and plenty to read, but is not just about loading the pages with words. Successful traders know that buyers want to browse, to compare products or services, and to give some time to choosing the 'best option'. For branded goods that are well known (e.g. a pair of Levi jeans) they may just want to know the price. For a whole range of goods and services they want details, images, reviews (to help with opinion formation), and as much as you can supply to support them as if they were in your shop or showroom. The biggest letdown of internet purchasing is not being able to turn to someone and ask that critical question, which will allow you to makeup your mind people need advice and information!

Key 4 - Trading Site Interactivity

Have spoken about cost and value, image and branding, and the necessity of supportive content. But even if you are seen as having good value, desirable goods, and lots of supportive information, you have to be sure people can make use of all that they buy online.

A recent study showed a huge proportion of retailers online failed to make sales simply because people could not work out how to complete the tasks of buying goods. Purchasing tasks are well known to all of us, yet system designers can make it very hard to spend. Buyers need to find target goods, they need to compare similar offerings, they need to check product features - and when they decide, they need to easily tell the system what they want. For most of us spending is not just a task, it is recreational. We should be having fun. Buyers want to enjoy spending!

Key 5 - Management of Internet Trading

The process of trading on-line can be quite different from the traditional business. There are new skills, new people and new processes to be integrated in the business. It is therefore critical to ensure that the new processes are defined as something SMEs can manage effectively and easily. Processes for fulfillment, customer support, catalogue management, etc. need to be carefully built into the overall business structure in an integrated way.

Internet trading allows companies to adapt and to automate business processes. Data captured at a web site (e.g. visitors, sales, and enquiries) can be handled by background software to automate processes such as targeted marketing, supply management, and customer support. The trader can also respond quickly and cost-effectively to new opportunities as they arise (knowledge in time).

The dynamic and linked nature of on-line systems means that business processes involving supply chain partners can be either automated or made more efficient. Creating links between information and communication systems allows trading partners to be part of a 'virtual' enterprise with a real level of integration and cooperation. Until recently only megastores like supermarkets could advise suppliers of replenishment levels in real time. Now, any web site with suitable background software can communicate selected information to any other SMEs via internet. Orders for fulfillment can be automatically sent to partner companies, and stock levels can be signaled for replenishment.

It requires commitment and plenty of energy to create a new on-line business while keeping the existing business running satisfactorily. But an internet trader can then be very flexible, due to the nature of the internet, and so can be efficient, responsive, and able to exploit well-integrated and automated business processes. The internet can be an extension of your business!

Key 6 - Relationship Building

Internet traders can exploit new ways of building relationships online.

Customer Relations can be improved by providing information as required, plus after sales support, all via Internet (e.g. e-mail). This will increase the level of customer loyalty.

Customer Communities can be facilitated by providing support for customer communication. For example, ebay links customers and encourages feedback to be shared, as does Amazon. SMEs can facilitate sharing of information and communication between other companies in the supply chain. These kinds of activities encourage people to feel part of a 'user community' (retail) or a 'business network' (SMEs chains).

Trading Partners can be involved in a more organised network of information and support, and can even help each other increase presence through large scale inter-working (e.g. Web Rings) or smaller scale support (e.g. web site links). Partnerships of this kind can even allow SMEs to extend business scope by providing fulfillment in areas where a specific business cannot or does not want to extend (e.g. holiday supplier and car rental company in partnership). The internet and web provide an infrastructure for communities of interest.

Key 7 - Lifestyle and Shared Vision

Following on from key 6, it is worth emphasising that communities of interest are a boost to trade and rely on shared information and resources. However, their identity as a community relies on more than just shared information. Groups rely on shared identity at some level, and that usually means shared vision, and an identified shared lifestyle at some level. Offline communities and on-line communities do not overlap greatly. A critical reason is that on-line nobody can see you, so the social and group bonds are derived from what we do, what we buy and what we enjoy. This means the process of group interaction on-line has a more dreamlike quality - it's almost a cross between catalogue shopping and watching TV. In the on-line world people will make choices they might not make when surrounded by other people (whose perceived opinions may 'ground' the prospective buyer). On-line, a person is more likely to go for personal fulfillment (I want what I want) - so understanding and appealing to lifestyle and group image is very important. A common feature of 'customer build up' is to recognise that those buying online at the moment are social innovators - they are leading edge people and recognise it. So many on-line vendors treat them that way. However, as internet trading matures more care will be needed in appealing to lifestyle and group identities. Buyers need to be recognised for who they are!

The 7 keys to success is simply to repeat the final statements under each:

- Cost is not only about money, but value. So it pays to know the customer's basis for judgment! Value is what the buyer gets out of the product or service,
- People go where the signposts point,
- People need advice and information when they arrive,
- Buyers want to enjoy spending,
- The internet can be an extension of your business,
- The internet and web provide an infrastructure for communities of interest, and
- Buyers need to be recognised for who they are.

Using the Guidelines for Business Benefit

This final section explores the guidelines for SMEs internet traders based around the seven keys to success identified earlier. Considerations are derived from a wide range of on-line and off-line sources including marketing texts, case studies, and research reviews. They are not exhaustive and are offered as a set for consideration in beginning or improving existing internet trading. The nature of electronic business is such that the range of available advice will grow steadily for years to come, so our best advice is to keep looking and listening to the developments in e-business - nobody knows exactly where it all may lead.

Cost and Value

Costs

For the new entrant, competing on price may seem an obvious strategy. However, the cost equation includes not just costs to the buyer, but also costs to the provider. The provider can reduce the costs of setting up an internet trading operation, but these will never be zero, and if expansion is contemplated, a sophisticated trading site can be a lot more expensive than a 'do it yourself', or simple off-the-shelf solution. Expansion is not all investment and is justified by a larger turnover, so economy of scale should be factored into your planning. The 'do it yourself' approach is one way of reducing startup costs. However, this can only be contemplated by traders with the necessary skills. Needless to say it is easier for technology companies to build their own trading sites since technology is their business. It means that for a large number of SMEs the path to cost reduction at installation is to find an affordable and suitable ready-made solution. Many new entrants ignore the fact that costs can be reduced in other areas to balance investment. Taking orders online will reduce the unit cost fraction for order taking, and automation of fulfillment can make substantial saving (see also partnerships).

Value

Perceived value is quite a complicated construct. Put simply, an expensive item may appear to be good value because there is substantial value added. For a simple example - paying 10 per cent more for an electrical appliance may be acceptable if there is a 5-year guarantee. In more complex scenarios we see people paying twice the price for a shirt that we feel must cost the same to manufacture, but its lifestyle value may owe as much to the logo on the breast pocket as it does to the material. In internet trading, added value can be a nebulous a concept. Certain sites have become the 'place to buy' and so can push margins further than less well-established entrants. However, its not all about lifestyle, and the majority of sites have to add 'real' value (perceived value based on actual additional services or features). This means a new trader may have to compete by adding real investment at the back end (good information, better support, etc.). Remember, value is not only what you put into a product or service, but what your customer gets out of it. This requires commitment (see also management) and dedication - something not usually lacking in small business.

Image and Branding

Brand and image promotion is especially difficult for small traders because of the resource requirements, yet the more successful ones seem to recognise its value and take pains to ensure their presence. Low cost methods of promotion are readily available.

Internet and SMEs should pay attention to on-line directories and search engines to make sure they can be found easily. Promotion of URL's on hard copy such as letterheads, advertising and product literature is a must!

- Apply standard marketing methods to on-line image creation.

- Create a meaningful identity for your company (name and logo), product brand (name and logo) and web site (name). The test of attractiveness - does the searcher click on that name when presented with the top ten finds for a specific search.

- Promote your own web site and keep abreast of current methods (e.g.www.webpromote.com).

- Place links in any relevant portal sites (portal sites are gateways for a particular market, market sector, user group, or geographical region. Offer the opportunity to allow other sites to easily put an attractive link from their site to yours.

- Get your web site mentioned in print as much as possible- place the URL in all printed materials, get the local paper to do a feature, place small ads which highlight the URL.

- Trade banners (adverts plus dynamic links) with trading partners.

- Join any relevant web rings. A web ring is a set of traders in a related field who link to each other - the rationale is that it is better to be one of a set of competitors people choose from than to be a singleton whose site is not found.

- Put your URL on your business cards and all promotional materials - you would be surprised how many people don't.

- Join your chamber of commerce and get your web site listed in their directory - you would be surprised how many enquiries chambers get from new companies looking for local suppliers. Even chambers are going online, so make your links available.

- Make sure you have an accurate entry in any available directories and be sure to include your e-mail address and web site URL.

Trading Site Content

The content of a site has to do a multitude of jobs. It must be attractive and encourage people to stay and browse (like a shop window). It must be accessible, people want to wander at will, look where they choose, and examine everything - just like in a real shop or showroom. The more mysteries there are the less they like it (so beware the trendy designer who wants to add tricky features loved by experts and hated by many buyers).

The worst offence to commit as an online trader is to forget that buyers want support 'when they want it', yet hate it to be offered it at the wrong time. The expert assistant seems to appear by magic at the right moment - so it should be easier on-line.

The information should be relevant to the kinds of buying decisions to be made at that time - if the potential buyer of a digital camera cannot work out whether it plugs into her/his type of VCR they cannot proceed. Try to predict what kind of assistance they need at any point and make it usable and friendly - and help them to spend!

- Make it immediately obvious what is on offer - some sites do not.

- Describe products and services briefly and accurately.

- Give space to featured items - the shop window display.

- Keep the site structure obvious - people get tired of hunting to find the 'hidden' links.

- Make the site as fast as possible. Designers love graphics, but buyers want them at the chosen moment. So provide thumbnails for fast loading, and let buyers decide what to inspect (so make it clear they can be enlarged).

- Let people 'click through' by making options visible quickly. They will take the door they want as soon as they see it, so don't force them to enjoy the full tour.

- Despite the above, ensure that your site 'looks the part'. If it looks like 'Joe's Discount Bazaar' you will not sell antiques! The reverse is also true, so aim for realism and remember to appeal to the likely 'lifestyle' and image values of the customer.

- Avoid plug-ins and non-standard features unless you really need them. Some traders put FLASH animation on the front page and do not realise there are buyers who only see a blank screen. Do not let designer enthusiasm get in the way of sales.

- Make sure you have good security.

- Update regularly but not for the sake of it. Search engines give ratings for recency, but do not irritate customers by drastically changing fundamental layout for no reason.

- Remember that spending should be fun. Do not rely on your own judgment. Get a sample of people to give you honest feedback

- Ensure your text is readable. Explorer uses one size larger text than Netscape for display, so avoid tiny text, but try not to get the Explorer 'big print edition' look either. Look at your site on different platforms and ensure it looks right everywhere.

4.5.4. Trading Site Interactivity

Interactivity is crucial for successful sites. The buying experience must be informative, under user control, and enjoyable. So there is some overlap between issues here and in content design. It has to be assumed that a potential buyer can use a computer and can click around a site and fill in forms. So long as they can do that they are looking for a good buying experience and that is what will bring them back. This is as true for retail as it is for business to business - whether we model a site on a trade show or a department store. There is one general rule - the experience of the site must fit with the expectations of your customer, and so must reflect their image of themselves (the right store for the right lifestyle) and their intended purchase (the right products and services for people like me). Examine the 'content' recommendations; a lot of those are about interactivity too. Make buying easy. Let people find what they want quickly, and let them pay with ease- but do not rush them through (see content - it should be user paced).

- Re-use data and do not ask people to retype things.

- Make the security obvious and reassure them that the site is completely safe.

- Offer alternative payment means if the customer is nervous print a form and fax it with credit card number inserted.

- Make the delivery arrangements clear and allow the customer to have a copy of the order forms and delivery details to print or save.

- If the product is downloaded (e.g. software, fonts, etc.) make sure you can ascertain that download is successful before processing final stage of payment (see OECD guidelines).

- If you use a 'shopping cart' metaphor, make sure the customer can look into and adjust their cart with a single click no matter where they are in the site.

- Arrange that clicking on cart items takes them back to the page where they 'selected' the item (they may want to change size, colour, quantity, etc)

- Read some stuff on good web site design - a pleasing layout is part of the interactive experience.

- Allow people to examine features of goods of interest. Remember, branded goods need less supporting information - novel items need more.

- Create regular customer identities so that routine data can be entered for them, but corrected if required.

Management of Internet Trading

Management of Internet trading is not unlike management of off-line business - it requires defined and workable procedures and processes which can be monitored, evaluated for performance, and adjusted to meet changing needs. For on-line trading these processes may look quite different, but most include familiar features (also see earlier section on management). The most novel feature is "automation" coupled with "integration" - either with upstream supply chain, or downstream (forward), or both. It also requires quite a high level of commitment in-house since new forms of trading have to be developed in parallel with maintenance of current business.

- Ensure site content is under complete control and can be adjusted at any time. Avoid hard coding data into HTML documents and use external databases to ensure flexible redefinition of product catalogue, pricing, special offers, delivery data, etc. If you are outsourcing site design, make sure the designer can explain in detail, how you control input data with ease (and with normal office skills). If you are buying an off the shelf package, make sure you can answer the same questions from the specification document, or ask the supplier why not - and think about continuity of software supply!

- Automate customer-ordering processes where possible. That means ensuring the on-line trading processes deliver data to back-office or fulfil applications and processes but retain transparency for quality assurance and monitoring. Integrate online systems with back office (and legacy) systems. Database connectivity is a key issue for integration of larger trading systems and cannot be ignored. Allowing automated systems to generate marketing information to customers and to process customer incoming data will greatly reduce costs and simplify process management. Reengineer legacy systems to allow internet processes seamless access.

- Develop flexible processes to ensure easy adaptation as future trading develops.

- If you have Quality processes in place, make sure the web trading operation conforms to a similar standard (e.g. ISO 9000).

- Quality assures the delivery chain - especially if fulfilment is outsourced.

- Make sure supply chain partners are using Internet trading methods as well - even if only e-mail. Try to move them towards a similar level of commitment so that you can achieve a similar level of technology usage (and integration).

- Track customers - who they are and where they come from. Traffic movement can be arranged to tell you what links are working (so long as the links declare their identities - a software design issue), and where business comes from. That allows better targeting in marketing.

Relationship Building

Internet traders must carefully consider the effect of on-line trading on the many relationships required for successful trading. These include relationships between supplier and end-customer, relationships between the trader and trading partners (including supply chain), and relationships between customers (the customer community).

The end-customer is probably the most important, since without the final sales the whole supply chain breaks down. Good customer relations always rely on customer contact and what happens there. So for the on-line trader that means interactivity (see 5.4) and how that is used to foster relationships which encourage loyalty and trust. Speed of response is one way to establish that you are 'really there', and that you treat your customer as important.

Soliciting their opinions, allowing them to make enquiries online and setting up mail lists to channel product information (e.g. newsletter) and 'offers' are some of the many ways to mimic the natural flow of interactions between supplier and customer on-line. Look at the example of the modern courier services that now let customers track deliveries worldwide. That not only tells the customers they are open, honest, and can be trusted, but it also removes a large part of the tracking cost - the enquiry agent!

The **supply chain** and trading partners are another source of important trading relationships. These range from intermediate customers (such as integrators, dealers and other downstream companies) to trading partners such as outsourced fulfillment companies, sub-system manufacturers, and marketing (e.g. web ring) associates. Given the complexity of the web, and the simplicity of its usage and development, it is possible to develop a wide range of partnerships for different business reasons.

Customer community building is an area that is made much easier by on-line methods. It is increasingly attractive as traders realise it encourages increased sales through relationship with a large community in which brand awareness and loyalty can be encouraged. Its main value, however, is in encouraging loyalty in customers who feel they belong to a group.

Guidelines for the SMEs in the Internet

End Customers

- Be consistent in customer care - trust builds up over time, and reliability is required.

- Be quick in responding to requests - not just sales, but requests for information, support, or whatever. Speed equals caring to most customers.

- If customer support is a big feature of your business, create an on-line help facility and make clear how it is used (including callback facilities if available).

- Make key contacts accessible via e-mail, and put their details on-line.

- Allow customers to join mail-groups for newsletters or product news / offers.
- Have your marketing people contact site users to find out what they feel, and what they would like changed / added.
- Always clearly state terms of sales, deliveries, and after sales care to ensure customers know there is nothing hidden.

Supply Chain / Partners

- Outsource fulfillment where possible to reduce costs, and exploit on-line processes for 'virtual enterprise' to increase effectiveness and reliability.
- Exploit opportunities to deliver on behalf of others, including promotion of their goods and services as part of a partnership deal. This increases the range of goods and services offered while only increasing costs for order taking. It also creates opportunity to develop new product and service lines in-house based on success of partnerships.
- For service companies, increased mass (size of contracts) and increased competence (range of services) can be achieved by virtual partnerships, which can be managed through on-line processes.
- Becoming part of trade associations, web rings, chamber listings, etc. can increase opportunities for business and increase physical contacts with likely trading partners.

Customer Community

- Group communication techniques such as forums are the most successful. Ones. Forums can be web-based, in which case customers must 'go' there, or can be mail-group based so that the discussion arrives 'at their door' (suitable so long as there is not too much volume). Some sites combine these (especially software user sites) to ensure a history of discussions is maintained (also benefits new users), and break down larger discussion areas into subjects (so users can select the ones of interest).

- Allow mail-groups to be self-moderating (either as a group or via an elected moderator). Some topics risk offensive comments / discussions more than others, so let the community decide. Group information can be easily maintained, such as links to related sites of interest that can be contributed by users. For example, if you trade dance wear then links to theatre listings, and museums of dance, might be valued. People will learn about these and come to your site for them - and may become customers.

- Make sure groups know who the 'in-house' expert is for their topic, and have that person monitor group discussions to keep pace with interests, concerns and needs.

Conclusion

Put simply, people identify with others on the basis of cues, and so on-line presentations should be sensitive to the existence of current trends, group behaviours, and tokens such as logos, emblems, buzzwords, etc. The person shown on your front page may be enough to encourage some people in, and others out, depending on the products and services offered. It may therefore be wise to appeal to the real target customer base for your product - if there is one. If there is not, then you should try to make it clear that the product or service is generic, or simply try to be free of lifestyle cues (i.e. neutral design).

- Decide if there is 'lifestyle' value in your product or service (i.e. trend or specific cultural group). If so, pay very careful attention to on-line image.

- Make it clear to your target customer from the presentation (style and content) that 'for specific reasons people like you rate products and services like these'.

- If your product or service is highly lifestyle or image sensitive, make the usual checks and tests with sample users before letting new material go public. A turn-off may be hard to turn on again, and the ease of web publishing can accelerate the time between ideas and public presentation (so reduce test time). Be consistent, and stay with the image focus you have established. If you are trading products and services that appeal to more then one specific group it can be quite easy to differentiate via separate trading sites (with different approaches) while managing fulfilment from an integrated back-end process.

References

Levy, M, Powell, P. and Galliers, R (1999), "Assessing Information Systems Strategy Development Frameworks in SMEs, "**Information and Management,** 36: 247-261.

Levy, M and Powell, P (2000)", IS Strategy in SMEs: An Organisational Perspective", **Journal of Strategic Information Systems.**

Levy M, Pwwell P and Yetton P (2001),"SEMs: Alignin IS and the Strategic Context" **Journal of Information Technology,** 16:133-144.

Levy, M, Powell, P and Yetton, P (2002)," SMEs: The Dynamics of IS Development", **Small Business Economics,** forthcoming.

Lunati, M (2000). **SMEs and Electronic Commerce,** OECD, DST/IND/PME, 11.

Costello, Tuche, J (1998), "A Comparative Study of Business to Consumer Electronic Commerce with in the Australian Insurance Sector", **Journal of Information Technology,** 13: 153-167.

Nath, R., Hjelm, K., Sakaguchi, T. and Schultz, M. (1998) "Electronic Commerce and the Internet: Issues, Problems and

Perspectives", **International Journal of Information Management,** 18(2): 91-101.

Poon, S and Swatman, P. (1999). "Exploratory Study of SME Internet Commerce", **Journal of Information and Management,** 35:9-18.

Poon, S and Swatman, P (2000), "Internet-based SME Communication", **Electronic Markets,** 7(2).

Schumpeter J., (1962), **Capitalism, Socialism and Democracy,** New York.

Venkatraman, N (1994), "IT-Induced Business Transformation: From Automation to Business Scope Redefinition", **Sloan Management Review,** winter: 73-87.

Willcocks, L, Sauer, C and Associates (2000),. **Moving to E-Business,** Random House Business.

14

E-Commerce and Small Enterprises

SoundaraPandian, M Renganayaki, R

Abstract

'Invent' and 'innovate' have become the key mantras of modern marketing. In this process, marketers have evolved newer modes of marketing one after another to meet the requirement of their customers. Electronic commerce, popularly known as 'E-Commerce', has emerged as the modern day avatar in marketing. It has become the buzzword of the day. It has been assuming acceptability and popularity by leaps and bounds in the present day business. Given such backdrop it seems pertinent to examine and explore the suitability of e-commerce for small enterprises in our country. This paper deals with the various aspects of e-commerce such as evolution and growth, benefits, suitability and challenges for small enterprises.

Introduction

'Invent' and 'innovate' have become the key mantras of modern marketing. In this process, marketers have evolved newer modes of marketing one after another to meet the requirement of their customers. Electronic commerce, popularly known as 'E-Commerce', has emerged as the modern day avatar in marketing. It has become the buzzword of the day. It has been assuming acceptability and popularity by leaps and bounds in the present day business. Given such backdrop, it seems pertinent to examine and explore the suitability of e-commerce for small enterprises in our country.

At the outset e-commerce is not about reinvesting business, it is about streamlining current business process to improve operating efficiencies which, in turn, will strengthen the value to provide to customers, which in turn will provide the competitive advantage over competitors. In simple words, electronic commerce is the process of doing business electronically or over internet.

According to the WTO says Production, distribution, marketing, sale or delivery of goods and services by electronic means. A commercial transaction can be divided into three main stages: advertising and searching stage; ordering and payment stage; and delivery stage. Any or all of these may be carried out electronically and may, therefore, be covered, by the concept of electronic commerce.

Evolution and growth

The evolution of e-commerce can be traced back to 1970's with the emergence of internet. E-commerce was developed for the business in the early 1970s to facilitate processing high volume and high value transactions electronically. Electronic Data Interchange (EDI) was the first business-to-business (B2B) application. Subsequently, internet added a prodigious new dimension to e-commerce. The power of the Internet, as a global access, was realized with the arrival of the World Wide Web (WWW) in 1994. Never in the history of mankind has a popular innovation spread as fast as internet. It has been considered the leader in the application of e-commerce. The quick spread of internet in US can be gauzed from the fact that it took 16 years for telephones to be used by a quarter of all US households and 133 years for the cell-phones to be so widely used, but internet has made similar penetration in less than five years. Further, e-commerce in US is taking place more in the service oriented activities than the product oriented ones. This is because of the fact that no two products are the same. But, services have a commonality that makes it a more general applicable whether it is hospitality or airlines, transport services, banking, reading of books and alike. After its fast debut in US, e-commerce is rapidly spreading beyond US boundaries and is growing speedly global. E-commerce success stories are aplenty in Europe.

The origin of e-commerce in India coincides with the introduction of Internet connectivity throughout the country in 1989. As such, e-commerce in India is in its infancy. Historically, Rediff-on-the-net, one of India's leading online services, set up India's first e-commerce on August 13, 1998. Then, India entered the age of e-commerce the day the government deregulated the Internet Service Provider (ISP) policy in November 1998. Since then, there is no looking back and the country is proliferating in Internet. The rate of growth of penetration of Internet has been spectacular. It took radio 50years to have 50 million owners, T.V. 16 years and personal computers 17 years. But it has taken Internet only 4 years to reach that figure after the invention of WWW and browsers.

Till now, Internet penetration in India is about 0.5 percent of the population against 50 percent in Singapore. Nevertheless, India is fast emerging as the largest country for registering domain names in the entire Asia-Pacific region. According to the latest dotcom index for the year upto February 2000, India occupies 11th place in it after US, UK, Korea, Canada, France, Germany, Japan, China, Spain and Italy. Presently India has nearly 35 ISPs in various stages of operations. Added to these are 187 more ISPs granted licenses. The popular ISPs already providing access to internet in the country are the Videsh Sanchar Nigam Limited (VSNL), Mahanagar Telephone Nigam Limited (MTNL), Satyam Online, and BT internet, Intel India, Max India, Quark, HCL Perot, Infosys, Future Devices and Dishnet. Satyam Online, India's largest ISP mega corporation has got over 1, 15,000 subscribers across the country. As of March 31, 2000, there were 7.5 lakh Internet connections in the country with 3.2 million Internet users. According to Forrester Research, over 27 million households in India will access the Internet by 2003.

NAASSCOM (National Association of Software and Service Companies), the apex body and Chamber of Commerce of India's software-driven IT industry, has recently released findings of its survey to evaluate the E-Commerce scenario in India. As per the findings of the survey, the total volumes of e-commerce transactions in India were about Rs. 131 crore in the year 1998-99. Out of this volume, about Rs.12 crore were contributed by retail internet or business-to-consumer transactions and about Rs.119 crore were contributed by business-to-business transactions. The figure for the year 1999-2000 was estimated to reach Rs. 4502 crore. Here, it is significant to note that India's experience in e-commerce transactions is compatible with that of US and other countries where percentage share of B2B remained much larger than that of B2C. This implies that businesses are more willing and able than individuals to use e-commerce technology.

This is attributed to the fact in B2B transactions, both buyers and sellers are known to each other and enjoy sufficient mutual trust. Added to it is that B2B transactions are relatively of higher value in nature and companies trading on Internet offer very high and attractive cost-saving options. But, such a situation is not obtainable in case of B2C transactions. Very possibly, the same explains why e-commerce in this area has still not taken off. That this trend is also expected to continue in future as indicated by a serious study forecasting B2B transactions' share of the order of 79 percent of the total e-commerce business in India by the year 2002.

Benefits

E-commerce is a win-win situation for the consumer and the product / service provider. The distinct advantages e-commerce can offer to the consumer are:

1. Consumers have a much wider choice available on the cyber market.

2. They can compare products, features, prices and even, look up reviews before they select what they want.

3. They also have the convenience of having their orders delivered right at the door-step.

4. Finally, consumers are driven to e-shopping in hordes as even branded goods cost less on the Net.

The Major Advantages

It minimises inventory cost: E-commerce venture need not maintain huge inventories or expensive retail showrooms. Their marketing and sales force is a fraction of that of traditional mortar-based businesses. E-commerce can minimize inventory costs by adopting just-in-time system enhancing the firm's ability to forecast demand more accurately.

It can improve customer services: It has been found that providing both customer and after-sale services account for upto 10 percent of the operating costs. By putting these services on-line under e-commerce, these costs get reduced, on one hand, and simultaneously the quality of services also get improved, on the other. High quality customer relationship called "customization" is crucial for retaining customers in the e-commerce environment. That is the reason why customer relationship management (CRM) has become the buzzword.

It helps business globalise: E-commerce by minimizing cost enables companies, especially small ones, to make information on its products and services available to all the potential customers spread over world wide.

It helps market products more quickly: By taking the entire product design process on line, drawing partners and customers into the process and removing the traditional communication barriers, companies can bring products and services to market far more quickly.

E-Commerce Suitability for Small Enterprises

Like elsewhere in the world, small enterprises play a vibrant and vital role in the Indian economy as well. They contribute significantly to the national production, employment, equity and export. With this strong realisation, small enterprises worldwide are turning to the use of modern technology to compete with their big brothers-medium and large size enterprises. According to a survey conducted by the Yankalovick Partners Inc., 90 per cent of the small enterprises in US are using wired technology in their operations. Numerous e-commerce success stories circulate galore in other countries as well.

The information revolution has opened up a great deal of potential for small enterprises in the marketing field. The excellent opportunities e-commerce offers to small enterprises are:

- Access new markets

- Improve customization
- Lower various kinds of costs
- Reduce the size of the enterprise
- Sell products / goods in global market

E-commerce has emerged as an opportunity for small enterprises. Not making use of it will turn into a threat to their very survival. The adoption of e-commerce in small enterprises has reached global presence and is offering stiff competition to their big brothers. It is noticed that web based big companies eventually have forced numerous small companies to go online for their business operations.

The scope for adoption of e-commerce is likely to be enlarged with cable, telephones and TVs making inroads in rural areas in the country. 'Sankhya Vahini' a massive project commissioned by the Government of India is likely to focus on activities such as tele-agriculture and tele-medicine in rural areas. Thus, there exists good scope for e-commerce to be adopted in small enterprises in the country.

Prospective Areas

E-Commerce is ideally found suitable for certain types of products and services amenable to online transactions. The products that are already being traded electronically mainly in small enterprises and are also expected to record high growth rate include computer products, books, music, gifts and flower, clothing and food items.

In India, small sector is an all embracing term. Small enterprises in India include agriculture and agro-based industries, handicrafts, readymade garments, footwear, professional services, electronic and engineering, chemicals, pharmaceuticals, gems and jewellery, cosmetics, furniture, poultry, bakery, retail trade, entertainment, health care, tourism, education, social service, and public utilities, Whatever e-commerce has so far taken place in India is concentrated in the metropolitan cities. Due to the dismal penetration of PCs and telephones into rural economy, the vast potential for e-commerce offered to rural areas so far remains untapped. There is no denying the fact that rural sector is the main stay of the Indian economy that supports nearly three-fourths of the country's population. Hence, there is a need for e-commerce to make inroads in rural areas of the country.

It is a happy augury that the government has also come forward to encourage e-commerce application in small enterprises. With this objective in view, the Ministry of Small Scale Industries has formulated a comprehensive plan to prepare small-scale industry (SSIs) for e-commerce with required infrastructure support in the country.

Challenges

(1) **Infrastructural Problems:** Internet is the backbone of e-commerce. Unfortunately, Internet penetration in India is so far dismally low at 0.5 per cent of the population against 50 per cent in Singapore. Similarly, penetration of personal computer (PC) in India is as low as 3.5 per thousand of population compared to 6 per thousand in China and 500 per thousand in US. Internet is still accessible through PCs with the help of telephone lines. Given the penetration of telephone only 2.1 per cent of population, e-commerce remains far away from the common man. It is difficult for e-commerce to reach to 1000 million population spread over 37 million households in 604374 odd villages and 5000 towns and cities. Besides, the cost of both PCs and internet access in India are quite high.

(2) **Absence of Cyber Laws:** Another big challenge associated with e-commerce market is the near absence of cyber laws to regulate transactions on the net. WTO is expected to enact cyber laws soon.

(3) **Privacy and Security Concern:** As of to-day, the vulnerable issues related to e-commerce are privacy and security. So far, there is no protection offered either by Website or outside watchdogs against hazards created through instruction of company's privacy.

(4) **Payment and Tax Related Issues:** Problems related to payment and tax are yet another problem continuously hunting e-traders. The electronic payment is made through credit card or plastic money which could, however, not become popular so far in India mainly due to two reasons. First, the penetration of credit card in India is very low (2 per cent of the population). Second, the Indian customers are quite skeptical of paying by credit card with the increasing threat of fraudulent hackers. Like elsewhere, credit card could not gain growth in India mainly because of authentication and recognition problems of electronic signatures.

(5) **Virus Problem:** That computer virus is also a formidable problem in the execution of e-transactions is confirmed by the recent computer virus originated in Manila. A computer virus logged 'I Love You' originated in Manila, Philippines on May 2000 ripping across the world, infected millions of computer files causing colossal loss of US $ 7 billion to the governments and the businesses. The offenders causing 'virus' must be awarded deterrent punishment, otherwise similar assaults in future can cause lasting blows to the quite young e-commerce in India as well.

(6) **English Specific:** The software so far in the country is English specific. But, in order to make e-commerce reach small enterprises, it needs to be available in the languages (regional) of the owners of the small enterprises to enable them to adapt e-commerce processes in their operations.

Sooner it is done the better will be it for small enterprises to adapt e-commerce.

Conclusion

Electronic commerce is doing business over internet. E-commerce originated way back during 1970s in US. In India its origin coincides with Internet connectivity in 1989. Since the introduction of www in 1984, expansion of e-commerce in the country is continuously spreading across country. At present there are 3.2 million internet users giving a total volume of Rs.131 crores e-business. The distinct advantages such as improvement in customer service reduction in inventory and distribution costs, speedy delivery of goods and services and globalisation of business, e-commerce provides make it suitable for small enterprises in the country. Certain types of products such as computer products, books, music, gifts and flowers, readymade garments and food items and certain types of services such as advertising, marketing, financial, insurance, tourism, entertainment and information services are amenable to online transactions. Lack of infrastructural facilities, absence of cyber laws, payment and tax related maters and virus problems are the major challenges before e-commerce in India,, that could be easily solved.

References

www.google.com

www.yahoo.com

Part – III
Strategies for SMEs Sustainability

15

Industrial Clusters for Encountering Challenges of Globlisation in Small Scale Sector

Srinivasan, R

Abstract

This paper traces the aspects of globalisation that have implications for the growth of small scale sector in India, the current status, possible strategies for its growth in the open economy with special emphasis on industrial clusters. The industrial cluster may facilitate free flow of capital, credit, skilled man power to Small Scale Industries (SSIs). It also protects the flexibility of SSI units and help to reap the benefits of economies of scale of operation.

Introduction

Independent India protected the domestic manufacturing sector from the rest of the world by erecting tariff and other restrictive barriers for imports of goods and services, restricting the inflow of foreign capital and technology and following fixed and information across countries without any hindrances such as tariffs, quantitative restrictions and licensing. This essentially requires a flexible exchange rate system as well. The integration of national economies makes the entire world a unified market for a manufacturer and the world a factory. The unrestricted flow of goods and services across the borders of the countries aided by the improvement in transport and communication systems has benefited the enterprises to visualise the entire world as the market for its commodity. The technological revolution has made it possible to segregate the production process into simple units and position the particular process in a country where it is cost advantageous to do that particular process. In other words, the production process is sliced into different stages and each stage is located in different geographical location to benefit from better access to inputs and markets. The production sharing requires efficient transportation system and sophisticated information and communication technology. The production sharing also increases foreign direct investment flow into a country and promotes industrialisation.

Given the aspects of globalisation described above the SSI sector faces both threats and opportunities. If the SSI produces final consumption goods then it is placed at a disadvantageous position to face the competition from large and medium industries, be they indigenous or foreign. If the SSI is a producer of an intermediate commodity, then it has the chance of participating in the globally spread production process of a multinational manufacturer. This chance is not restricted to producer of goods but modern technology helps even the provider of services to be at a distant land, like a Business Processing Outsourcing company in India providing consumer services to the customers of a bank in the USA.

The SSI sector faces many more challenges, which are not the immediate effects of globalisation, but can be definitely associated with the process of globalisation. The declining trend in lending to SSI sector by the banking sector, higher interest rate compared to the rest of the world, neglect of providing infrastructure facilities at affordable prices, lack of government intervention for providing capacity building with reference to WTO agreements and decisions are some of the problems that the SSI sector faces in India.

Status of SSI Sector in India

Let us take a snap shot of the status of SSI in the post-2000 era. The SSI sector is seemingly better today as revealed by the statistics in Table1. All the major indicators point out that the SSI sector has been growing over the last few years. But the ratios of the total production of the SSI sector to GDP as well as to the output of industrial sector show a moderate decline. In the period under consideration, the industrial sector has been one of the fastest growing sectors in India. If the SSI sector, which is a part of the industrial sector, has not been able to keep pace with the growth of the entire industrial sector then there is enough reason to get worried about the future of this sector. The data shown in Table 1 are based on the sample survey conducted every year by the State Directorates of Industries and District Industrial Centers. SSI units, which have a turn over of above Rs. 1 crore, are included in the sample survey. Besides the number of SSI units engaged in service delivery is on the rise and they are not included in this sample.

Let us move on to another set of data available, which is more reliable as it is a census survey of all the SSI units in organised and unorganised sectors and is engaged in the production of both goods and services. Data presented in Table 2 are with reference to organised sector of SSIs. Though the proportion of registered SSI units is only 13 per cent, they have 59 per cent of investment and contributed 59 per cent of total production as per the third SSIs census. The fixed investment per unit, and fixed investment per employee have shown exorbitant increase in 1988-2002 periods than in the period 1972-

Table 1: Status of Small Scale Industries in India

Years	*No. of Unit (lakh)*	*Total Fixed Investment (Rs.in lakh llalakh)*	*Total Production (Rs.in lakh)*	*Emplo-yment*	*Output per employer (Rs.in Lakh)*	*Output / GDP (in %)*	*Output / Industrial Production (in %)*
2000-01	101.10	146845	26128900	239	109325.94	6.86	39.91
2001-02	105.21	154349	28227000	249	113361.44	6.67	39.63
2002-03	109.49	162317	31199300	260	119997.30	6.82	39.48
2003-04	113.95	170219	35773300	271	132004.79	6.71	39.42
2004-05	118.59	178699	41826300	283	147796.11	-	-

Source: Annual Report 2005-06, Ministry of Small Scale Industries, Government of India.

Table 2: Results of the Three Small Scale Industries Censuses

Sl. No	*Particulars*	*1972-73*	*1987-88*	*% change*	*2001-02*	*% change*
1.	Fixed Investment per unit (Rs. in lakh)	0.76	1.60	110.53	6.68	317.50
2.	Investment in plant and Machinery per unit (Rs. in lakh)	0.38	0.95	150.00	2.21	132.63
3.	Employment per unit (in Number)	12.00	6.29	-47.58	4.48	-28.77
4.	Value of output per unit (Rs. In lakh)	1.86	7.38	296.77	14.78	100.27
5.	Fixed Investment per Employee (Rs.in 000)	6.38	25.36	297.49	149.25	488.53
6.	Value of output per Employee (Rs.000)	15.74	117.22	644.73	329.91	181.44
7.	Value of Output/investment in fixed assets	2.47	4.62	87.04	2.21	-52.16

Source: Economic Survey 1993-94, Report of SSI Census 2002, Government of India.

1988. The rates of increase in investment in plant and machinery per unit, value of output per unit, and value of output per employee have marginally declined. Whereas, there have been negative growth rates in the employment per unit and value of output per unit of fixed investment. These statistics show that the SSI sector is no more an employment generating industry and the capital intensity of production is on the rise. Moreover, the decline in output per unit of fixed investment is a pointer to the fact that the capital is also not very efficient in this sector. Nearly 34.45 per cent of the registered SSI units covered in the third Census are service and business enterprises. Though the output and investment figures are not strictly comparable as they are at current prices, they unequivocally point out that the SSI sector is in trouble now.

Let us take a look at the status of the unregistered SSI units as given in the Third SSI census. Compared to 22.6 lakh registered SSI units there are 91.46 lakh unregistered SSI units. Of the unregistered SSI units, 61.25 per cent are service and business enterprises. This is higher than the proportion of service and business enterprises in the organised SSIs sector. The employment per unit is 2.05, which is lower than corresponding figure for registered SSI units. But for every unit of investment, say rupees one lakh, and the unregistered units generate 3 units of employment where as registered units generate only 0.67 units of employment. Nearly 43.20 per cent of unregistered units are in urban areas compared to 58.18 per cent of urban registered units.

Between the second and third SSI census the proportion of working units in the SSI sector has declined. Though the number of sick SSI units is on the decline in recent years, the amount of outstanding loans from sick units is on the decline in recent years, the amount of outstanding loans from sick units is on the rise. As there is no estimation regarding the loss of output and employment opportunities due to the sickness prevailing in the SSI sector, we cannot calculate the economic loss arising out of industrial sickness in SSI sectors. But lack of demand and non-availability of working capital are the two most important reasons for the sickness in SSI sector. These two are quite interrelated. The fact that the demand for the goods and services produced by the SSIs sector is declining. This shows that globalisation has increased the number of choices made available in the market for the customers by the large business houses both in the domestic and foreign economies. Moreover, mass production by the large scale industries should have also substantially reduced the prices of commodities in the market. Similarly, the other fact is that SSI units are unable to compete with the large scale industries in the current dispensation, and their credit worthiness in the bank system has come down and hence the declining trend in bank lending to the SSI sectors. Though as per the existing banking regulations 10 per cent of the Net Bank Credit should be allocated for SSI sectors in 2005 the percentage of bank credit allocated to SSI sector was only 9.4 per cent. Even within this, a substantial amount of bank lending went towards subscribing the bonds of SIDBI.

On the whole, the registered SSI units though contribute substantially to the national income, their share in either the national income or industrial production is declining; they are neither labour intensive nor capital efficient. Comparatively the unregistered SSI units are more labour intensive and have larger rural bases. Larger proportions of both the registered and unregistered SSI units are engaged in service and business activities and therefore their engagement in manufacturing is correspondingly lower. The increasing number of non-working and sick SSI units and the increasing amounts of outstanding loans from such units are really a cause for concern. The flow of bank credit to SSI sector is also inadequate. The question that arises here is whether the SSI sector is sustainable in the era of globalisation and if so, what are the support systems needed from the government in this regard.

Strategies to Counter Challenges of Globalisation

There are different views on the strategies to counter challenges of globalisation in the SSI sectors. One, the free market advocates and also argues that only the survival of the fittest could continue in the face of globalisation; two, the welfare government supporters argue for a reasonable state intervention that is needed to help the SSIs to survive and develop in the global market; three, the anti-globalisation supporters argue that the government should provide all sorts of protection to the SSIs because the local industry should always be preferred to a foreign company and all aspects of globalisation should be countered.

The free market supporters advocate total *laissez faire* policy, which wants the government to provide only the minimum services to the citizens of a country like providing defense, public administration, public utilities and protecting private property. This is an extreme view, which treats local and foreign companies on the same footing and does not advocate even the reasonable support that could be provided to the SSIs like providing technical help and bank credit.

As per the on-going process of globalisation unfolding in the various international forums, like the WTO, and the World Bank, globalisation process offers both opportunities and threats to the SSI sector. To seize of the opportunities the SSI sectors should be empowered to counter the threats. This stand is different from protecting the SSI sector from threats like imposing huge tariffs on imports and reservation of items for SSI's production. This strategy is being followed in most of the countries now.

The third view can be called the localisation theory. As per the localisation theory all the activities in a locality should be within that region, that is, every region should be self-reliant in all aspects and should contact the external world only in an extreme situation where the region is totally unsuitable to produce certain essential commodities. Here the local region is specified; and the exposure to the rest of the world should be very much restricted. Thus, localisation opposes any liberalisation of trade and finance.

Given the two extreme position, the middle path seems to be a feasible one, because we have reached a reasonably advanced stage of globalisation today. The challenges that the SSI sector faces today are mainly the technological backwardness, non-availability of skilled manpower, lack of knowledge of market conditions and non-availability of cheap finance.

Industrial Clusters in India

Many of the challenges that the SSI sector faces can be solved through formation of Industrial Clusters. Industrial Clusters are geographical concentration of industries that have strong inter-industry linkages, both forward and backward. Clusters are attractive because they help to retain the flexibility of small scale industries as well as reap the benefits of economies of scale as a group of inter-related firms. The clusters have specific advantages like sharing the infrastructure cost, accessing foreign market and technology related information, inputs and marketing at low costs. These facilities should improve the credit worthiness of individual SSIs and ensure of adequate flow of credit to them.

Though the Government of India does not have special policies for the promotion of clusters, the government, through its financial institutions and with the aid of international agencies like UNIDO, has been promoting clusters in the country. Clusters are not something new to our country. Many of the clusters have been naturally formed like textile clusters in

Tirupur and leather clusters in Chennai and its neighborhood. There are many such naturally developed clusters all over the country.

The Third SSI census survey conducted in 2002 identified 1223 clusters in organised sector and 819 clusters in unorganised sector. The organised sector clusters contribute 17 per cent of total SSI output using 19 per cent of fixed investment and 28 per cent labour force in SSI sectors. The unorganised sector clusters contribute 21 per cent of unorganised sector output using 22 per cent of fixed investment and 35 per cent of labour force in unorganised sector. The difference between organised and unorganised sector in these indicators are in line with the general trend in these sectors.

The Government of India, with the support from the UNIDO, state governments and financial institutions has implemented Small Industry Cluster Development Programme for developing 25 sectoral clusters located in 60 centers in India. The main thrust of this programme is to upgrade the technologies in the SSIs situated in the recognised clusters through all possible means and also to improve their creditworthiness and ensure adequate flow of credit to them. Several studies, both by the official organisations and independent researchers have shown that the naturally formed clusters are more viable than artificially promoted ones. This does not mean that the government has to wait for the natural development of clusters. Rather the government should facilitates at affordable costs, technological upgradation of SSIs through fastening the tie-up between industry and research institutions, organising programmes for the flow of foreign technology to SSI sector and above all making a timely availability of credit at subsidised interest rate.

Conclusion

To recapitulate, the SSI sector in the country is passing through a face of transition. The process of globalisation has both threats and opportunities for the SSI sectors. The opportunities are the global market unfolding before them to access inputs as well as to market their products and they can participate in the production sharing process that has developed out of this globalisation and development in information and communication technology. SSIs are no longer labour intensive; moreover they should be made capital efficient. The flow of technology, credit and skilled manpower to the SSI sectors could be better achieved through the state facilitated formation of industrial clusters, as industrial clusters protect the flexibility of SSI units at the same time help to reap the benefits of economies in the scale of operation.

16

Managing Micro, Small and Medium Enterprises: Thanjavur Art Plate Cluster

Rathakrishnan, L Sriraman, V.P

Abstract

The role played by MSMEs in the world economy cannot be over ruled owing to the fact that more than 95 per cent of all enterprises in the world economy belongs to this group. This paper tries to bring together some of the interesting works in this area. It discusses the contributions made by this sector in various world economies and also the way in which MSMEs are defined in these economies. It then looks into the concept of globalisation and the importance of Governments in protecting /helping these MSMEs to stand against the formidable competition from global multinational corporations. It cites some of the recent fillips given by the Indian government to this important sector. Among the MSMEs the paper specifically looks

into the area of traditional industries as they herald the culture of Indian economy. As this area is vast, the present paper takes a specific case of Thanjavur Art Plate Industry that falls into the broad area of handicrafts. The present paper hence looks into the handicrafts sector and its performance over the years. It then presents the problems and challenges these units are facing, in particular about the marketing and finance aspects.

Introduction

Worldwide, Micro Small and Medium Enterprises (MSMEs) play a crucial role in sustaining and accelerating the competitiveness of an economy and in turn form an integral part of economic growth, providing significant contributions to every aspect of economic development namely, industrial prosperity, industrial output, exports, employment and social progress, reducing economic disparity between urban and rural areas, development of entrepreneurial class and the generation of innovations, there by contributing to the economy's productivity. In India, more than 90 per cent of Small and Medium Enterprises (SMEs) are in the hands of private sector. There are 12 million SMEs located in India, forming 91 per cent of total industrial units, nearly 40 per cent of total industrial production, producing over 6000 products, employing around 29 million people, and contributing to 34 per cent of national exports. In addition, the SMEs contribute about 7 per cent of India's Gross Domestic Product (GDP). The average growth of SMEs sector in the last years has been 8 per cent, whereas for the industrial sector, it has been only 5 per cent. According to UNIDO, the SME segment is estimated to comprise almost over 90 per cent of all enterprises in the world and account for 50-60 per cent of total employment.

The Bologna Ministerial Conference on "Enhancing the Competitiveness of SMEs in the Global Economy : Strategies & Policies" which was jointly conducted by Organisation for

Economic Co-operation and Development (OECD) and the Italian Ministry of Industry held at Bologna, Italy in June 2000 identified the following roles of SME's in an economy:

(a) SME's economic contribution is increasing;

(b) SMEs are active in the technology-intensive and business services sectors;

(c) SMEs are heavily involved in the innovation process; and

(d) SMEs are relatively local in their orientation but increasingly active internationally, generally through inter-firm linkages and clusters.

Contribution and Importance of MSMEs – Worldwide

The contribution of MSME's in the Asian and ASEAN countries is summerised in Table 1.

SMEs account for 99.7 per cent of business enterprises in **Japan**, with retail and manufacturing being the most popular industries (Organisation for Small and Medium Enterprises and Regional Innovation, Japan (SMRJ), 2004). This segment accounts for about 74 per cent of employment in the manufacturing sector, 85 per cent of total employment in the finance and insurance sectors and almost 96 per cent of employment in the real estate services sector. SMEs accounted for almost 50 per cent of the total manufacturing exports in Japan during the decade of the nineties.

In **Hong Kong** a total of almost 270,000 SMEs accounted for over 50 per cent of employment, providing job opportunities to almost 1.2 million people. The majority of enterprises were in the services sector, specifically import and export, and wholesale and retail trade.(Government of Hong Kong Trade and Industry Department, 2006).

In **Korea**, the SME segment represents 99.8 per cent of total business enterprises, accounting for 86.5 per cent of total

Table 1
Contribution of MSMEs

S. No	*Name of the Country*	*Popular Industries*	*% of MSMEs total industries*	*Employment (in %)*
1.	Japan	Manufacturing and service	99.7	74.00
2.	Hong Kong	service	56.00	50.00
3.	Korea	manufacturing	99.80	86.50
4.	Philippines	Agri.& Manufacturing	90.00	50.00
5.	Pakistan	Agri & Manufacturing	99.00	78.00
6.	Bangladesh	Agri & Manufacturing	80.00	80.00

employment. Whereas in the **Philippines**, SMEs are estimated to account for 90 per cent of registered business enterprises, contributing to about 25 per cent of GNP and accounting for almost 50 per cent of total employment.

In **Thailand**, commonly cited as a successful model in SME development in ASEAN, the SME contribution is at just below 40 per cent of Gross Domestic Product and total industrial export. The SME segment constitutes about 99 per cent of total business enterprises in **Pakistan**, accounting for about 78 per cent of industrial employment and contributing 35 per cent to total value addition. In **Bangladesh**, there are approximately 6 million micro, small, and medium enterprises with less than 100 workers, out of which around 27,000 are SMEs, The sector contributes 40 per cent of gross manufacturing output, 80 per cent of industrial employment and 25 per cent of the total labor force, micro, small, and medium enterprises provide more than 75 per cent of the income of the households in Bangladesh, SMEs contribute nearly 25 per cent of the GDP of the country.

As noted by Vattanapruttipaisan (2004), SME in ASEAN contribute a disproportionately limited share of 20 per cent - 30per cent to gross sales value or manufacturing value added and only between 10 - 20 per cent to export earnings. Comparatively in the developed nations, SMEs contribute about 50 per cent of total value added in EU, between 40 per cent - 50 per cent of manufacturing output in Japan, Republic of Korea and Taipei, China and the United States.

The following charts highlight the Importance of SME's to the Indian economy.

Defining MSMEs

World wide, there are varying definitions for MSMEs, some countries take the number of employees to define MSMEs,

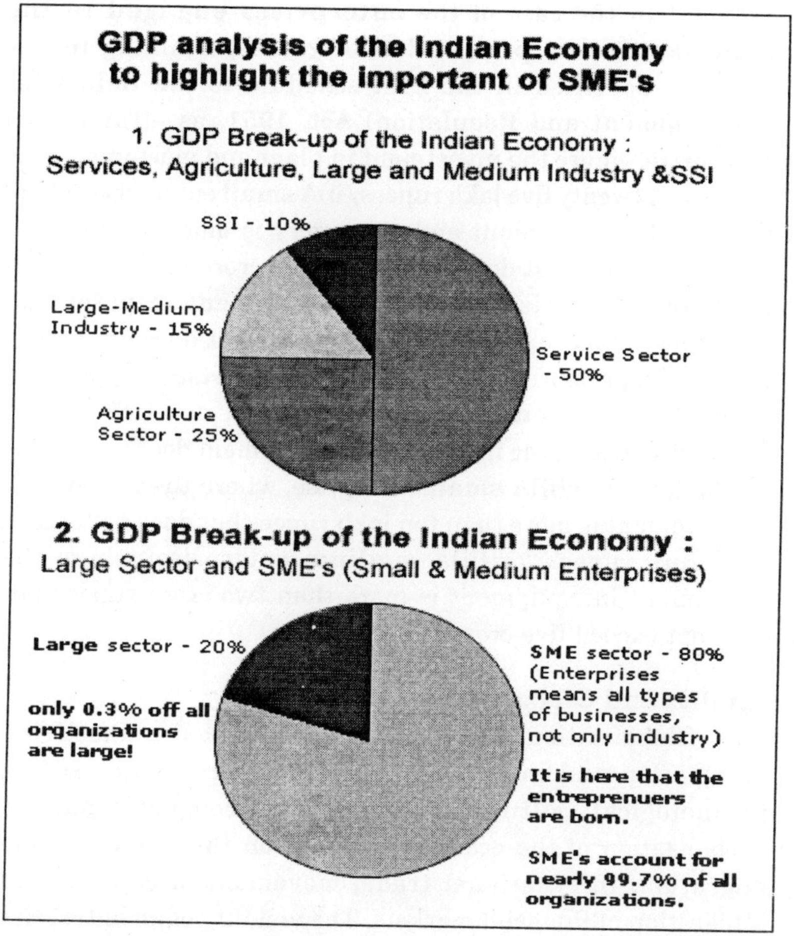

Source: www.wakeupcall.org

while others take the investment in plant and machinery, or paid-up capital, or turnover per year or a combination of these factors. In **India** the Micro, Small and Medium Enterprises are defined by the size of 'initial fixed assets investment', i.e., the 'plant and machinery (excluding land & building). Recently, with the enactment of "The Micro Small and Medium Enterprises Development Act 2006 (MSMED Act 2006), that came into effect from 2nd October 2006, MSMEs are defined as

(a) In the case of the **enterprises engaged in the manufacture or production** of goods pertaining to any industry specified in the first schedule to the Industries (Development and Regulation) Act, 1951, as –(i)A **micro** enterprise, where the investment in plant and machinery does not exceed twenty five lakh rupees;(ii)A **small** enterprise, where the investment in plant and machinery is more than twenty five lakh rupees but does not exceed five crore rupees; or(iii)A **medium** enterprise, where the investment in plant and machinery is more than five crore rupees but does not exceed ten crore rupees;(b) In the case of the **enterprises engaged in providing or rendering of services**, as –(i)A **micro** enterprise, where the investment in equipment does not exceed ten lakh rupees;(ii)A **small** enterprise, where the investment in equipment is more than ten lakh rupees but does not exceed two crore rupees; or(iii)A **medium** enterprise, where the investment in equipment is more than two crore rupees but does not exceed five crore rupees

MSMEs and Globalisation

Globalisation refers to increasing global connectivity, integration and interdependence in the economic, social, technological, cultural, political, and ecological spheres. Globalisation of the economy depends on the role of human migration, international trade, movement of capital, and integration of financial markets. The viability of an enterprise in such a dynamic environment necessitates the upgradation of technologies and more importantly the adoption of new technologies, building new capabilities, seamless integration of supply chums and value chains across the globe to reduce the cycle time and lead time, waste reduction and recycling, cost competitiveness and hence increasing the value for money. For this to happen, Indian MSMEs needs all support infrastructures to be in its place. By support infrastructure we mean all physical, legal, credit and other supporting stakeholders.

The formidable challenges created by the liberalisation of the Indian economy, as well as its closer integration within the global economy, have generated a great deal of interest within India on novel approaches to SMEs development. As a result, both private and public sector institutions at the Central as well as the State levels are increasingly undertaking cluster development initiatives to increase the competitiveness of this sector.

In the increasingly knowledge-driven economy, emerging trends are key consideration in day-to-day business decisions. New products, technologies and creative designs appear almost daily on the market and are the result of continuous human innovation and creativity. Small and medium-sized enterprises (SMEs) are often the driving force behind such innovations. Their innovative and creative capacity, however, is not always fully exploited as many SMEs are not aware of how these emerging trends can help and safeguard them. To help SMEs more fully utilise the emerging trends in their business activities, they need to know more about these trends.

Government has been focusing on the SMEs ever since the economic reforms taken place in the country and has formulated several policy reforms and initiatives. Some of the latest ones include the following.

- A single comprehensive legislation for the promotion, development and enhancement of the competitiveness of the MSME sector – Micro, Small and Medium Enterprises Development Act, 2006 came into effect from October 2006.

- Revised strategy of lending and introduction of newer measures, such as the scheme to establish Small Enterprises Financial Centers (SEFCs) for strategic alliance between branches of banks and SIDBI branches located in 388 clusters identified by the ministry of MSMEs.

- Production and financial support for credit-cum-performance rating in MSME sector in India to facilitate greater and easier flow of credit from banking sector to SMEs.

- National Manufacturing Competitiveness Council (NMCC) is set up to energise and sustain the growth in manufacturing sector.

- New promotional package for MSMEs and focus on accelerating development of clusters.

- Proposal for doubling the credit flow to MSMEs sector in another 5 years.

- Setting up of the National Commission for Enterprises in the Unorganised Sector (NCEUS) to bring about improvement in the productivity of these enterprises for the generation of large scale employment opportunities on a sustainable basis, particularly in rural areas.

- Facilitation of Technology Transfer through the Technology Bureau of Small Enterprises (TBSE)

- Scheme of Fund for Regeneration of Traditional Industries (SFURTI).

- Guarantee coverage under Credit Guarantee Fund for Small Enterprises expanded substantially.

- New legislation on Limited Liability Partnerships.

- Emphasis on bi-lateral / Multi-lateral partnerships at multiple levels

- A package for Promotion of Micro & Small Enterprises has been approved recently to address most of the concerns in the areas such as credit, cluster-based development, infrastructure, technology, and marketing. Capacity building of MSME Associations and support to women entrepreneurs are the other important features of this package.

- An empowered group of Ministers (EGoM) under the Chairmanship of the external Affairs Minister has been set up to lay down a comprehensive policy for cluster-development and oversee its implementation.

- Under the Credit Guarantee Scheme, life insurance cover for chief promoters of units providing guarantee cover by the Credit Guarantee Fund Trust for Small Industries (CGTSI) has been introduced. Further, the one-time guarantee fee under the scheme has been reduced from 2.5 per cent to 1.5 per cent with effect from April 1, 2006.

- After due consultation with the stakeholders, 180 items reserved for exclusive manufacture in micro & small enterprises have been de-reserved on May 16, 2006 and 87 such items have been dereserved on January 22, 2007.

Traditional Industries

Within the category of MSMEs, tradition industries assume importance. Tirthankar Roy, of IGIDR was discussed in his book 'Traditional Industry in the Economy of Colonial India' five important craft-based industries during the colonial period, namely Handloom Weaving, Gold Thread (Jari), Brassware, Leather and Carpets. Among these traditional industries, Indian handicrafts have withstood competition from machines over the years. The skills are passed on from one generation to the next. The handicraft and handloom sector is a major source of rural employment and earns substantial foreign exchange

Indian Handicraft Sector: An Analysis

The history of Indian crafts is indeed very old, going back to almost 5000 years.. The first examples of Indian crafts can be found from the Indus Valley Civilisation (3000 B.C – 1700 B.C). The craft tradition in India has revolved around religious beliefs, everyday needs of the common people, as well as the special needs of the patrons and royalty: There was the influence of foreign and domestic trade as well.

These craft traditions have withstood the ravages of time and numerous foreign invasions and continue to flourish till date, owing to the assimilative nature of Indian culture and willingness of the craftsmen to accept and use new ideas.

The craft or handicraft sector is the largest decentralised and unorganised sector of the Indian economy, and is among India's highest foreign exchange earners (Vijayagopalan, 1993). Craftspeople form the second largest employment sector in India, second only to agriculture. Handicrafts are rightly described as the craft of the people: There are twenty-three million craftspeople in India today (Jaitly, 2001). In India, craft is not merely an industry but the produce is viewed as a creation symbolising the inner desire and fulfilment of the community.

The handicraft sector occupies an important place in the country as it provides employment to 6.2 million persons (2004 estimates) and export earnings of Rs.14, 526.85 crores in 2005-06. It is expected to grow at 2.5 per cent to 3 per cent per annum. Looking at its importance, the Government of India set up All India Handicrafts board in 1952 under the Chairmanship of Ministry of Textiles with Development Commissioner (Handicraft) as Member Secretary. The trend in the export of Handicrafts is given in Table 1.

The major export items among the handicrafts include Art Metalware, Woodware, Handprinted Textiles & Scarves,

Table 2
Export of Handicrafts

(Rs. in Cr.)

Item	*1999-00*	*2000-01*	*2001-02*	*2002-03*	*2003-04*	*2004-05*	*2005-06*	*2005-06**	*2006-07**
1. Art Metal ware	1,497.18	1,778.10	1,758.90	2,165.21	2,642.42	3364.93	3662.98	2803.96	3178.49
2. Wood ware	394.95	434.44	431.88	511.35	609.07	721.18	853.06	478.58	651.94
3. H.P. Textiles & Scarves	1,158.05	1,276.75	1,221.59	1,466.52	1,611.43	1848.76	2053.70	1650.84	1947.86
4.Embroidered and Crochet goods	1,584.36	1,964.78	1,931.97	2,477.75	3,286.05	4199.86	4711.45	3024.47	3659.62
5. Shawls as Artwares	21.5	27.2	27.01	32.7	43.27	53.65	110.23	66.16	133.64
6. Zari and zari goods	83.52	142.32	134.04	159.47	210.54	252.28	347.05	196.08	222.18
7. Imitation jewellery	113.64	121.68	117.53	138.79	161.9	200.56	274.86	162.35	224.05
8. Misc Handicrafts	1,116.40	1,210.08	1,146.58	1,391.62	1,900.46	2391.48	2513.52	1696.58	1810.07
Total	**5,969.60**	**6,955.35**	**6,769.50**	**8,343.41**	**10,465.14**	**13032.70**	**14526.85**	**10079.02**	**11827.85**

Note: (* - April – December)

embroidered and crocheted goods, shawls as artwares, Zari & Zari goods, Imitation Jewellery & Miscellaneous handicrafts.

Table 2 shows that the exports of handicrafts have seen an increase of Rs. 14526.85 during 2005-06 from Rs.5969.60 during 1999-2000, an increase of 17.41 per cent in rupee terms over a period of 5 years. Also looking at the last two columns, which portray the export figures during April-December of 2005-06 and 2006-07, the exports increased by 17.35 per cent in rupee terms. During the period of April-December of 2005-06 and 2006-07, the increase in exports of all the main items showed an increasing trend as mentioned, namely Art Metalware (13.36%), Woodware (36.22%), Handprinted Textiles & Scarves (17.99%), embroidered and crocheted goods (21%), shawls as artwares (102%), Zari & Zari goods (13.31%), Imitation Jewellery (38%) & Miscellaneous handicrafts (6.69%). Looking at the trend between 1999-2000 and 2005-06, of the total export of handicrafts, embroidered and crocheted goods had increased from 27 per cent to 32 per cent, while hand printed Textiles & Scarves shows the downward trend from 19 per cent to 14 per cent. While others more or less remain same, Wood ware and miscellaneous handicrafts are showing slight down trend.

Handicrafts in Tamil Nadu

The origin of most of the arts and crafts tradition of the state of Tamil Nadu can be related to the influence of temple economy that prevailed for a long time in this part of the country. The rich temples of the region not only gave patronage to the craftsmen but constant construction work in these temples helped the craftsmen regularly upgrade their knowledge and experience. Today, the craft traditions of the state have developed into a full-fledged industry by itself.

The Handicrafts industry falls under the Tamil Nadu Handlooms, Handicrafts, Textiles and Khadi Department of the Tamilnadu Government. Under the initiative of the state

Government, the Tamilnadu Handicrafts Development Corporation Limited, popularly known as Poompuhar was established. The objective of Poompuhar is to improve, and promote the welfare of the artisans of Tamil Nadu. For over 25 years, Poompuhar has been involved in the promotion handicrafts such as stone sculptures, Bronze icons, Thanjavur Art plates, Brass lamps, Rosewood carving, Sandalwood carvings, Country wood carvings, and Thanjavur picture paintings.

Among the Handicrafts, the metal-crafts sector plays a vital role in providing employment to rural population. In India there are about three million handicraft artisans and most of them are working in metal ware sector. These metal ware artisans display inherent creativity and play a significant role in protecting the traditional art and culture of our nation.

Metalware in Tamil Nadu

The famous brass and copper metalware has a rich and ancient tradition in Tamil Nadu. These metal objects are used for both religious and secular purposes, though utility is a primary consideration. The deepam or lamp is regarded as a symbol of Agni, which is auspicious and is the best known of the State's metalware. There is a good variety of lamps that include standing lamps, aarathi (votive lamps), deepalakshmis, hand lamps and chain lamps. Patterned trays and shallow dishes in circular, hexagonal, octagonal and oval shapes are widely used in Tamil Nadu and are made out of bronze or sheet brass. The popular Thanjavur art plates feature designs of deities, birds, flowers, and geometric patterns beaten out from the back of copper and silver sheets and subsequently encrusted on a brass tray, kudam or panchpaathra. Metal toys include models of horses, cows or elephants made chiefly of brass. A whole range of attractively polished and finished utensils of utilitarian value are also made.

Thanjavur– The cultural citadel

Thanjavur has been a flourishing centre for cottage industries and handicrafts over centuries. Mat weaving is spread over a number of places and superior varieties of mats are made in Vilankudi, Chakkrappalli and Madukkur. This district is also famous for a wide range of utility and decorative articles like Thanjavur bell metal plates, bronze icons, inlay work, musical instruments and silver metallurgy. The handloom sector also occupies an important place in the economy of Thanjavur District. It provides employment to more than 60,000 people.

The Thanjavur art plate and Bronze (Panchaloha) icon making is one type of traditional handicrafts, which shows minute craftsmanship and exquisite beauty. The traditional art and the skill are taught and handed over from generation to generation, with major developments taking place over the last 300 years or so. This art is confined to certain number of goldsmith families of the viswakarma community over the ages and is more inherited than acquired. For the members of the community, this art is a way life. The Thanjavur art plate manufacturing is recognised as cottage industry, as the manufacturing takes place at the household level. Women are not given any role but boys are encouraged to learn the techniques. The production of Thanjavur art plate requires different types of skill and experience. The base plate, which is the first stage, is prepared only by a heavy metal worker. The preparation of the reliefs is done only by a jewel maker and the encrusting of the relief on the base plate is done by a diamond – setter. Thus, it is a co-operative work or team work done either among the artisans or artisan families. Thus, inter-firm linkages or cluster strategy is working well with the art plate industry.

The Thanjavur art plate has three components, namely the base plate, the primary relief and subsidiary reliefs. The main raw materials required for making the art plates are:

(a) Brass sheets, from which the base plate is made;

(b) Silver sheets are used for making reliefs;

(c) Lead in used for making moulds, used for depicting 3-D figures;

(d) Asphalt or wax is used for the base board.

The Thanjavur Art Plate is composed of units performing various specialised functions that form part of the production process. The main production processes are:

I. Preparation of the base plate;

II. Preparation of casting copper plate;

III. Preparation of casting moulds;

IV. Preparation of the reliefs using casting copper plate cast dyes ;

V. Encrusting the reliefs on the base plate and engraving the floral design round the reliefs; and

VI. Finishing touches to the art product

Problems and Challenges

Some of the problems / challenges that are faced by SMEs in general and by this cluster in particular are:

- Inability to capture market opportunities, which requires large production facilities; and thus could not achieve economies of scale, homogenous standards and regular supply;

- Small size hinders the internalisation of functions such as market research, market intelligence, supply chain, technology, innovation, training, and division of labour that impedes productivity;

- Absence of a wide range of financing and other services that are available to raise money and sustain the business;

- Absence of infrastructure, quality labour, business acumen and limited options /opportunities to widen the business; and

- Poor IT Knowledge and infrastructure.

Marketing

The art plates are manufactured both for domestic consumption as well as export purposes. However, depending on the geographic location and the marketing complexities, including logistics and procedural formalities involved, the products are sold directly by the artisans or through show rooms of handicraft organisations or through merchant exporters. The merchants will act as middlemen, and export the product to other states and foreign countries.

The domestic middlemen are jewellery shops gift shops, handicraft showrooms owned by state government and private parties and Khadi sales Bhavan. The Thanjavur art plates are also sold in special fairs/exhibitions abroad. The Victoria Technical Institute, Chennai, the Handicrafts and Handlooms Export Corporation of India, and Central Cottage Industries Corporation of India Limited, are the other agencies promoting marketing of finished goods. The handicraft and handlooms export Corporation undertakes and executes wholesale orders, conducts retail sales operations through retail outlets abroad and participates and sells in major exhibitions of the world.

The Cluster Development model can be usefully adopted not only to promote manufacturing but also to renew industrial towns and build new industrial townships. The model is now being implemented, in one form or other, in nine sectors falling under different Ministries. The sectors include Khadi and Village Industries, handlooms, handicrafts, textiles, agricultural products and medicinal plants.

Finance

Most of the artisans are weak in finance barring a few. Since the market is limited and shrinking and also new markets could not be tapped (like exporting) due to lack of knowledge and risk taking abilities and also due to high competition from within, this trade is in a bad shape today. Most of the artisans are not using the traditional bank channel itself for their financing needs. This is partly due to the bank's insistence on collateral and the general perception that bank would not give credit and even if it gives, considering the present conditions, the artisans worry whether they can repay . On the flip side, one good news is the emergence of self help groups. Many small artisans have become members of these SHGs for personal use. But again, the role that these SHGs play in the lives of these artisans is not well established as of now. The general view is that instead of going for informal sources of financing, they can use the credit provided by the SHGs for the present one. The view that the micro-credit will provide a way to encourage entrepreneurship is yet to be seen here.

Other Issues

There were more than 300 families making these art plates in Thanjavur. As the time pass by, due to various reasons like competition from within, inability to market the product, change in customer style, increased cost of basic metals, increased cost of labour, migration of next generation to other businesses etc, the number of craftsmen making this classic work has been shrinking and presently there are only about 20-25 families actively involved in the making of art plate. All other people who were the producers before have started to work for the bigger/ major ones. Currently, there are about 160 members in the society, most of whom are working for the major players. Recently Self Help Groups (SHGs) were formed and the activities of most of the SHGs are found to be satisfactory.

The issues at hand could be summarised as: a) to find out the exact reasons for the people to move out of this trade, b) possible ways of overcoming the problems of credit and marketing, c) identifying ways to enhance the domestic sales and exports, d) educating the people on the newer ways of finding the markets like e-commerce, and, e) motivating the worker class to become entrepreneurs etc.

Conclusion

Thanjavur art plate manufacturing units are concentrated in Thanjavur, which is known as "rice bowl" of Tamil Nadu. Thanjavur stands for agricultural production and again called as "granary" of South India. Nonetheless, the district is industrially backward. Small and medium industries located in the district are also being managed by particular caste group. Being traditional, the industries are managed in a poor manner. Many new management strategies need to be adopted, if the industry is to compete with global players.

References

Background paper on **'India Global Summit on MSMEs'** (2006), www.ciionline.org

Chidambaram P, **Indian Union Budget** 2006-07, www. indiabudget. nic.in/ub2006- 07/ubmain.htm

http://handlooms.nic.in/hl_sch_rebate.pdf

http://www.india-crafts.com/indian_states_crafts/tamilnadu.html

http://indiaheritage.org/creative/creative_metal_work.htm

http://www.indiasite.com/tamilnadu/arts.html

Jaitly, J (2001), **Visvakarma's Children:** Concept Publishing Company, New Delhi.

Lalitha, Sridhar (2007), **'Thanjavur: Summer of Discontent'**, India Together.

http://www.indiatogether.org/2004/apr/eco-thanjavur.htm

Sood, Anubha (2002), **Crafts as Sustainable Livelihood Option in Rural India'**,

London School of Economics and Political Science, University of London, http://www.livelihoods.org/lessons/lessons_ dissertations. html

Tiwari, Bhupesh (2002), **'Cluster Development Programme: India Diagnostic Study – Artisan**, The Bell Metal Cluster, Kondagaon (Chhattisgarh)

Vijayagopalan S (1993), **"Economic Status of Handicraft Artisans"**, National Council of Applied Economic Research, New Delhi.

www.epch.com

17

Cluster Approach in Small and Medium Enterprises in Tirupur, Tamil Nadu

Sumithra Devi, N

Abstract

As the countries integrate into a global village, the business enterprises, particularly, SMEs will have to respond accordingly and thus deserve special attention. Recently the debate and relevance of clustering as an alternative strategy for industrial development in developing countries is being dominating various discussions in economic literature. The constraints faced by SMEs in developing countries are not only accentuated with ineffective policy design, but also by market failures in the region. Experts in development economics and industrial organisations have therefore, shown some empirical evidences that small firms in developing countries can grow and be competitive as well, through cluster formations. This paper pursues the line of cluster approach in networking strategy of SMEs. This paper is divided into two parts. The first part deals with the concept and dimensions of cluster approach, factors behind the growth path of clusters, value chain and promotion of clusters in India, the ability of SMEs dynamics to penetrate into the large market and institutions strengthening the clusters. The second part of this paper discusses cluster development in Tirupur regarding Hosiery units clusters, historical background, characteristics of clusters, economy of clusters, entrepreneurial innovations in hosiery clusters, linkages with industry and employment creation by clusters in Tirupur. The paper concludes with suggestions for further development of clusters in Tirupur such as providing support through technical education and training, upgradation of clusters by implementing technical agreements, outsourcing, and purchase of needed equipment.

Introduction

The concept of industrial clusters is one of the most successful innovations. In industrial clusters, one can see that the town and its population whether young or old, rich or poor, are working like one big-networked company, as in a Honey Beehive. The cluster concept has proved helpful in building local capabilities, competence building, public private partnerships, skill upgradation, technological development and a host of other aspects necessary for the growth of SMEs. The clusters help small enterprises to overcome growth constraints and compete in international markets. In the context of emerging technologies, linking stakeholders in dynamic clusters is believed to enhance competition and regional innovation (OECD, 1999).

In an era of globalisation, dynamic clusters are becoming key factors in a country's capacity to attract international investment that generates new technological expertise, to interest investors in innovation (venture capital, etc.) and to benefit from the international mobility of skilled personnel. The forms of co-operation between agents within the cluster in terms of sharing of resources, information, technical expertise and knowledge help to reduce transaction costs. This in turn can strengthen the competitiveness as well as in facilitating learning and technical innovation. In recent times, the cluster has moved to high flexibly specialised form of production organisation with more emphasis on high quality standard. Apart from the above factors, clusters also play predominant role in creating employment opportunities for both rural and urban population of the country.

Meaning of Cluster

A simple definition of a cluster suggests that it is a network made for information and resource sharing between people. Clusters are formed based on the concept of two hands together is better than one. In economic literatures, it can be defined in various forms. Porter (1990) defined cluster as a group of firms engaged in similar or related activities within a national economy. Schmitz (1992) on the other hand defined cluster as a group of enterprises belonging to the same sector operating in close proximity to each other. Clusters mean geographical concentration of interconnected firms and institutions in a particular sector. The linkages existing between the firms are very important in strengthening competition.

The Cluster Concept

Sector-specific and geographically bounded clusters seem to be a common phenomenon for small-scale manufacturing in developing countries. Most of them have been very successful, primarily based on tacit and accumulated knowledge through learning by doing and learning by interaction. Thus, the cluster concept primarily requires knowledge sharing between elements of cluster. The clusters thus may be local, national or regional.

Local Cluster

Local cluster is developed easily in India as most of the times business is handled by a group of family members having different companies in the same industry (Desai 2000). For example, in Rajkot Diesel Engine Industry, most of the entrepreneurs involved in the business of manufacturing diesel engines are from the same caste and nearly same family background. There are certain characteristics of the local clusters, which as observed are as follows:

1. The creation of local cluster is due to the business being family business.
2. The state government support is higher.
3. Most entrepreneurs are from the same locality or of the same caste.
4. The business style or pattern followed is also very similar.
5. They all have similar competitive advantage.
6. Finance is generally generated within the family, that too from agricultural resources (e.g. Rajkot Diesel Engine Industry).
7. They possess high knowledge about each other but less about their competencies

National Clusters

Generally, resource rich countries like India have more than one cluster in the same industry. They are differentiated with their location. The national cluster is basically a group of local clusters spread geographically. For diesel engine industry, the national cluster consists of different local clusters based at Rajkot, Puna, Punjab, Coimbtore etc. National Clusters also have similar kind of advantages and characteristics like local clusters.

Some of the characteristics of national clusters are shown below:

1. The creation of national cluster is also due to the business being the family business.

2. The state government support is not as high as that given to local clusters.
3. They are treated as an industry by the central government.
4. Most entrepreneurs belong to the same caste or caste groups.
5. The business style or pattern followed is similar.
6. They all have similar competitive advantage.
7. Finance is generally generated within the family, and from other resources. But not from banks.
8. The entrepreneurs possess less knowledge about each other; as a result they are unable to identify competencies.

The major hurdle to national cluster concept is regionalisation prevailing in the country. Due to regionalisation, the state government's support to the cluster as a local cluster is there but when it comes to national cluster it is low. Even the central government treats it as an industry and all kinds of levies and taxes are imposed on the entrepreneurs, who in turn are small-scale manufacturers.

Natural Clusters

It has been noticed that clusters have normally emerged for such products produced in a traditional manner and which have no exposure to technology changes, design and manufacturing process. Gradually, similar types of industries grow in number utilising the existing pool of trained workers who shift from one unit and to another. Such clusters are classified as natural clusters. These clusters have grown spontaneously and are not consequent to a policy framework of the government.

Induced Clusters

On seeing the advantages of clusters, Government and other agencies have been promoting clusters through the creation of infrastructure, which is accompanied by a range of technical services (designed to cater to a group of units in the local area / industry). Such clusters are termed as induced clusters.

Need for Clusters

SMEs clustering are common in a wide range of countries and sectors. In India cluster approach enabled SMEs to reach high levels of growth and leadership in profitable niches of world markets (e.g. leather goods, textile, jewelry, ceramic tiles, and auto component). Similar accounts exist from other developed countries such as Germany, the USA, and Japan. Evidences on clusters are in Latin America, Asia, and to a lesser extent in Africa. The guiding principle of cluster approach towards SMEs is to facilitate small enterprises to play key role in triggering economic growth and equitable development in developing countries. Cluster development helps the firms in various ways, such as,

- Enables the SMEs to capture market opportunities with the help of large production quantities, homogenous standards, and regular supply.

- Helps them in achieving economies of scale in the purchase of inputs (such as equipment, raw materials, finance, consulting services, etc.)

- Assists SMEs in the process of upgradation of various internal functions such as training, market intelligence, logistics and technology innovation - all of which are at the very core of firm dynamism.

- Facilitates small scale units to achieve specialised and effective internal division of labour that fosters cumulative improvements in productive capabilities and innovation.

- Cluster approach provides assistance to small-scale entrepreneurs in developing countries to introduce innovative improvements to their products and processes and enables them to look beyond the boundaries of their firms to capture global market potentials.

- Cluster development helps the SMEs to access private equity and venture capital and have a vast access to secondary market instruments.
- Assists SMEs to have easy access to inter-state and international markets.

Cluster development also gives the residents of particular city an opportunity to undertake some activities directly or indirectly linked to the particular organisational framework apart from the web of SME. For example in Tirupur, most of the housewives and old people undertake hosiery related works like fixing buttons, embroidery works, sequins works, etc,.

Factors Behind the Growth Path of Clusters

1 Size of the Market and Nature of Products

The size of market is reflected in the number of participants and its geographical spread. Market size is an important factor for cluster development because the scale of product demand determines the growth rate of the producer. The quality of the products offered to final consumer also plays an important role to the growth of any SMEs cluster. The traditional quality standard of any product is measured by the value of the product characteristics. This implies that the durability, the reliability, and the conformity to specification and safety standards of the products are considered as important criteria.

2. Ability of the Firm to Enter into Large Markets

The ability to penetrate larger market is important in SMEs cluster dynamics. Reaching larger market will not only induce proportionate increase in productivity but also lead to increasing returns. Increasing returns are the result of economies of scale. Stock of economies of scale that induces increasing returns are measured by the following factors:

- ability of the firms to reach more markets
- ability to acquire more capital goods,
- Effective managerial skills
- Opportunity to enjoy division of labour in the production.

Tirupur hosiery units and engineering units in Coimbatore are found to be organised in production activities and they are able to invest more funds in capital goods. Whereas the lock making units in Dindigul show different picture, namely low investment on capital goods and lack of division of labour in production which make the enterprises remain weak

Economies of Scope

Economies of scope crop up due to the efficiency of the firm to engage in more than one activity successively. The major factors that influence the economies of scope are:

- ability of the enterprises to diversify their products with the least possible output costs (e.g. fabricating bakery ovens/palm kernel nut crackers).
- organisational ability of the enterprises to integrate factors of production in an effective production system.
- sharing of technical know-how and skilled workers by small firms.

Upgradation of Clusters

Upgrading of clusters enables the enterprises to meet the needs of markets quicker than the rivals. Upgrading is important for firms. The upgradation processes are systemic in nature and are achieved effectively when firms are linked together. It is important to understand the concept of value chain in order to get a true picture of upgrading. The relationship between value chain and upgrading are based on identifying not only the key problems in entire production organisation but also the methods through which upgrading can occur. Upgrading can occur at each stage of the chain as shown

Process of Value Chain

Value chain is the process which is required to bring a product or service from the consumption of raw material, through the intermediary phases of production, then delivery to the final consumers and finally disposed of after use (Kolinsky, 2000). Upgrading can be done in different chains:

- process upgrading,
- product upgrading,
- functional upgrading, and
- chain upgrading

Process upgrading: It occurs when SMEs can improve effectively by organising the internal working process of entire production system better than their local rivals.

Product upgrading: It entails ability to introduce new products or improve old products faster than the local rivals.

Functional upgrading: It takes place in firms where productivity is increased by improving the quality of the management skills and the organisation of labour factor.

Chain upgrading: It means moving to new value chains. An example is, moving from household products to industrial input products (Humphery and Schmitz 2000 and Kaplinsky and Read man 2001).

Clusters versus Networks Characteristics

It may be argued that clusters and networks are different yet interdependent, whereby small business network structures under pin the growth and sustainability of clustering. Clusters and networks should hence be seen as two separate constructs, each with its own distinctive characteristics.

Government Support for the Promotion of Cluster

In order to enable SMEs to mitigate their problems and enhance their access to new technologies for increasing their

Table 1

Clusters versus Networks Characteristics

Networks	*Clusters*
Networks allow firms access to specialised services at lower costs	Clusters attract needed specialised services to a region
Networks have restricted membership	Clusters have open membership
Networks are based on contractual agreement	Clusters are based on social values that foster trust and encourage reciprocity
Networks make it easier for firms to make complex products	Clusters generate demand for other firms with a variety of similar and related capacities
Networks are based on cooperation	Clusters take both cooperation and competition
Networks have common business goals	Clusters have collective visions

competitiveness in the international market, it is imperative to give them a friendly environment, which includes:

(a) formulation of appropriate national policies and programmes;

(b) building up technological capacity;

(c) knowledge flows and technology databases and

(d) R&D institutions and inter-firm linkages.

Formulation of Appropriate National Policies and Programmes

Conducive policy environment is a pre-requisite. The post-liberalisation era in the Indian economy has enhanced opportunities and challenges for small industries sector. The ultimate objective of promotional policies is to enhance SMEs capacity to grow so that they become viable units.

Building up Technological Capacity

In the present scenario of globalisation, knowledge of and access to latest advances hold the key to international competition. In this venture the industrial sectors which are able to identify their technology needs and adapt in time, will benefit the most. In India, the traditional sector which has shown this remarkable ability to adapt to technological change is leather. Central Leather Research Institute (CLRI), Chennai, India, has successfully introduced microprocessor control in tannery wet processing at industry level and promoted cleaner processing, quality consistency, and international equivalence. Anticipating the impact potential of computer-aided technique in footwear and garment design, CLRI alerted and prepared the industry so well that CAD is today widely employed by export manufacturers of footwear and garments.

Knowledge Flows and Technology Databases

Dynamism of SMEs is crucial for their long term competitiveness. For this they need to focus on systems of knowledge accumulation rather than just production system (Bell and Albu 1999). The SMEs should have capabilities for generating, accessing and diffusing knowledge and also have openness to external sources of knowledge including new technology data bases. In India, an important technology information data bank is the National Research and Development Corporation (NRDC), which serves as an important link between research and SMEs. NRDC acquires, evaluates, develops and transfers all worthwhile technologies generated at various national laboratories.

R & D Institutions and Inter Firm Linkage

At present, in India there are 2900 R&D institutions in total, of which 1350 are in the private sector. Out of these, over 1,250 are in-house R and D units, employing over 45,000 scientific and technical personnel and incurring an expenditure of the order of seven billion rupees per annum. However, the small scale sector is largely devoid of such facilities and is mainly supported by public R&D for acquisition of new technologies. As most SMEs lack financial resources, the best way is to enter into linkages and partnerships with other enterprises, academia and/or R&D institutions.

The Institutions Supporting the Cluster

It is now generally accepted in economic discussions that institutions are important not only in industrialisation process but also to development in general. Clustering can foster economic exchange quickly. Therefore, it is important that a third party is available in order to support the transactions. Furthermore, the quality of the service rendered by the institutions should be dynamic and in line with the growth-path of the cluster. In India the following institutions are established to promote SMEs.

Central Government

- Development Commissioner, (SSI), Ministry of Small Scale Industries
- Khadi and Village Industries Commission (KVIC), Ministry of Small Scale Industries
- Development Commissioner (Handicrafts), Ministry of Textiles
- Textiles Committee, Ministry of Textiles
- Department of Science and Technology, Ministry of Science and Technology

National Support Institutions

- State Bank of India (SBI) Uptech Programme
- Small Industries Development Bank of India (SIDBI)
- National Bank for Agriculture and Rural Development (NABARD)
- National Small Industries Corporation (NSIC)
- Entrepreneurship Development Institute of India (EDII)

- National Institute for Small Industry Extension Training (NISIET)

Collaborative Working in Cluster Development

Working in clusters is all about collaborative working in two ways: collaboration on backward and forward linkages.

Collaboration on backward linkages

- Common raw material procurement
- Common consultants
- Common testing facility centre

Collaboration on Forward Linkages

- Cross reference business
- Joint marketing executive
- One stop solution to customers for all their problems
- Consortia of smaller companies for subcontracting relationships with large companies
- Joint participation in exhibition/trade fairs
- Joint offices for service after sales, etc.
- Common world class marketing brochures
- Joint exploration of export markets - common dealers
- Common warehousing
- Common after sales setups
- Common advertisements

Indian Scenario

In India, at present, there are about 138 industrial clusters, which are engaged in specialised industries such as: locks at Aligarh and Dindigul, leather footwear at Agra and Kanpur; cotton hosiery at Calcutta and Delhi; blankets in Panipat; power looms at Bhiwadi; diesel engines in Rajkot, diamond polishing in Surat. Space bound "dense clusters" related to a specialised industry are even more pronounced in the State of Punjab with woollen garments, bicycle and bicycle parts, sewing machine parts and machine tools in Ludhiana; printing and printing goods, water pipes and bathroom fixtures in Jallandhar; foundries in Balata, etc. Of these, the one at Ludhiana is one of the very successful clusters, having a wide range of diverse products which include sewing machines parts, bicycle and bicycle parts, auto parts components and machine tools. Ludhiana is also better known as the Manchester of India, which alone contributes to the production of 95 per cent of the country's woolen knitware, 85 per cent of country's sewing machines and 60 per cent of the nation's bicycles and bicycle's parts. Agra cluster makes 0.15 million pairs of shoes per day with a production value of 1.3 m US$ and exporting shoes worth US $ 57.14 million per year (Juneja, 1998). Knitwear cluster in Tiruppur, Tamil Nadu is responsible for 85 per cent of Indian market and its export earnings have expanded from US$ 25 million in 1986 to US$ 636 million in 1997. What is interesting about Tiruppur cluster is that it is organised in a web of small work places through which the entire town works like a living industrial organisation (Chari 2000).

The Indian experience shows that the local and national clusters sharing are mostly informal. Information regarding the latest development and competency understanding is much less. Even though the product and technology used by the entrepreneurs are similar; the tendency to share is less among the cluster participants. And as most clusters are made for production related issues such as procurement of raw material, maintenance and corrective actions. the marketing related issues are never dealt with. The marketing related issues are the real differentiators between a multinational company and the SMEs entrepreneurs. With the creation of local and national clusters the SMEs entrepreneurs can compete with the multinational company on the issues of quality and other production aspects. But when it comes to market, the multinational companies (MNCs) are much ahead of the small-scale entrepreneurs. With the marketing muscle the multinational companies take away the market share from the small-scale entrepreneurs.

Further, local and national clusters are mostly formed for production purposes, i.e. for the issues related to production, like procurement, assembling, and maintenance. The clusters are not formed for marketing the products. As such, in local and national clusters, the entrepreneurs are less aware or even unaware of the competitors' strengths and weaknesses. Thus, the local and national clusters do not really serve the purpose of clusters for which they are created. The local and national clusters nearly miss the vital factor of knowledge sharing between elements of cluster and united marketing to face the competition from the MNCs. On the other hand, it is very well noticed in Italy. The creation and use of specific data basis from production to marketing (as in Italy and UK) is wanting.

The Road Ahead

In this era of globalisation, mergers and acquisition, collaboration at local and national level is not sufficient. We have seen the pros and of cons of local and national clusters. A very important point that local and national clusters both miss is the competitiveness at the international level. A global cluster will change the threat of WTO for SMEs to their advantage. It is basically a cluster that is created between local clusters in different countries of the world. Applications of information technologies have facilitated this process to a great extent. A global cluster nearly overcomes the hurdles, which are faced by the local and national clusters.

As global cluster is an international phenomenon, entrepreneurs are very keen about what is happening. As the entrepreneurs are more interested in the information about what is happening between the clusters all over the world, information sharing is much higher than normal. Due to more information sharing the local clusters' entrepreneurs understand other entrepreneurs' competencies in a better way which in turn leads them to work sharing between them. With a global clusters, the SMEs can compete with MNCs in a better way with the work sharing and joint efforts coming into existence. As the world has become one marketplace, any entrepreneur who has an added advantage over others can sell easily anywhere in the world. The Asian countries have an easy and cheap labour advantage over the others. They can use this advantage to reduce the prices and sell more products and generate more profits.

Cluster Development in Tirupur

> "Tirupur has not only evolved as the most noteworthy
> Apparel cluster in the country but it has also served as
> A pathfinder to the rest of the clusters in the country"
>
> \- Dr. A.P.J. Abdul Kalam.

Tirupur is one of the crown jewels in the small and medium scale enterprises. It is a textile town where commerce precedes everything. Tirupur is a textile District of Tamil Nadu and is popularly known as Banian City / Knit City. Tirupur is situated at 50 Kms. east of Coimbatore and the town is spread over 27.20 Sq.Kms. with a population of around 7.00 lakhs. The rich availability of raw materials, being in close proximity to

Table: 2
Highlights of Hosiery Cluster in Tirupur

- It contributes to more than 56% of India's total Knitware Exports
- It has earned the name **"Town of Export Excellency"** under Exim Policy of 2002-2007.
- Annual Growth Rate is 12%.
- Can deliver customised samples in less than12 hours;
- Half a million pieces can be produced in a matter of days.
- Buyers from 35 countries frequently visit Tirupur regularly
- Earning Rs. 5000 crore in terms of foreign exchange

Coimbatore which is a major centre of cotton spinning industry in the country makes Tirupur one of the Jumbo foreign exchange earner of the nation, earning Rs.5000 crores through 7000 units provides ample employment opportunity to around 6 lakh people. Due to its national and international importance, Tirupur is now separated from Coimbatore and declared as a separate district in 2009.

Historical Background

Today Tirupur is probably the best-known garment town in India, and one of the largest garment manufacturing and exporting clusters in South Asia. It has boomed almost without interruption since the early 1970s when the first garment manufacturers began to experiment with export orders. Starting from modest beginnings as a place known for its ginning and textile mills in 1930s and 1940s, the town transformed itself first into a leading centre of underwear garment manufacturing for the domestic market in the 1950s and 1960s, and since the late 1970s into a major export town of knitwear garments for the world market.

The first hosiery factory with hand-operated machines was set up in 1935 and for more than 30 years they were producing mainly grey and bleached banian. It is in the late 60s that the Industry slowly diversified towards manufacturing other inner garments. The strength of Hosiery Industry in Tirupur in 1961 was 200 units.

During 1970's this town was mainly producing under garments namely banian and underwear consumed largely by the domestic market. Fortune took dramatic turn in the early 1980's when Tirupur suddenly woke up to launch its entry into export arena. Early in the 80s, export of knitwear, mainly basic T-Shirts were made in small quantities. Export of other items of knitwear gained momentum from 1985 onwards.

With a beginning of Rs.19 Crores in the year 1985, exports of knitwear from Tirupur rose to Rs.3937 crores during the year 2003. In the late 80s, knitwear industry diversified very quickly and took up manufacture and export of other outer garments, namely cardigans, jersey, pullovers, ladies blouses, dresses and skirts, trousers, nightwear, sportswear and even industrial wear.

With the commendable interest shown by the entrepreneurs, cluster development and the support from the Government in the form of higher investment limit allowed for ancillary industrial undertakings including Hosiery Industry to avail facilities of SSI Units. With this impressive growth over a period of about two decades, Tirupur has emerged as the country's highest knitwear export centre. In terms of quantity also there has been a parallel growth pattern. Having exported 172 lakh pieces in the year 1985 the number of pieces exported during the year 2003 stands out at a gigantic figure of 3704 lakhs pieces.

Table 3
Number of Units at Tirupur

Knitting and / or stitching units	2500
Dyeing and / or bleaching units	750
Printing Units	300
Embroidery units	100
Other (compacting, raising, calendering)	200

Reasons Behind the Success Story of Hosiery Cluster in Tirupur

The main reason for the successful/phenomenal growth rate in exports of knitwear items from Tirupur over a period of about two decades, ultimately goes to its export culture, which is not found anywhere else and also due to the following:-

- Cluster approach in production of Readymade Garments
- Easy availability of Hosiery yarn
- Availability of cheap/rural labour
- Flexible attitude of entrepreneurs in meeting the demands of the buyers
- The strong entrepreneurial plan and personalised management
- Direct control of operations causing cost effective competitiveness of the Industry;
- Quick delivery and quality products add dimension to Tirupur's prowess as a centre to outsource excellent products.
- Disbanding of their garment manufacturing due to pollution and high cost of labour, of most western countries.
- Movement of the Asian Tigers Japan, Hong Kong, Taiwan and South Korea to hi-tech areas thus enabling Tirupur to capitalise the opportunity of penetrating into the European Market.

Infrastructure Facilities in Tirupur

In ord:er to augment the export of knitted garment an Inland Container Depot was opened in Tirupur.

- A Knitwear Fashion Institute in collaboration with National Institute of Fashion Technology (NIFT) and TEA-NIFT has been set up to conduct diploma courses and certificate courses with a duration of 3 years and one year respectively. 300 students are admitted each year in the institute.

- In its endeavor to produce excellent work, AEPC has set up an AEPC-SITRA Knitwear Service Centre, which has been functioning in Tirupur. It offers services such as testing of samples of various quality entrepreneur development programmes, imparting training in various disciplines of garment manufacturing, etc.

- New Tirupur Area Development Agency, a joint venture company with equity participation from the State Govt., Central Government, Industrial Leading and Financial Services (IL &FS) and Tirupur Exporters Association came into being for the purpose of promoting infrastructure facilities in Tirupur.

- It is a matter of deep satisfaction that the knitted sector of the garment industry, which traditionally was a laggard, has become aware of the changes taking place in the domestic and international arena and has already, geared itself to seize the opportunities that present themselves to this sector. This is evident from the growth of this sector during the decade as compared to the overall growth of the garment industry.

Present Scenario

Knitting industry in Tirupur has emerged as a premier supplier of value added items earning high foreign exchange.

Table 4

Export Performance of Tirupur Kint Wear Industry

Details	*Year*	*Qty.in lakh pices*	*Value In Lakh US $*	*Value in Crore Indian Rs.*
Tirupur	1996	2,574 (47.87%)	5,443 (38.29%)	1,892 (38.16%)
Knitwear	1997	2,943 (46.54%)	6,042 (37.77%)	2,214 (37.81%)
Exports as A	1998	3,385 (49.63%)	6,168 (37.91%)	2,540 (37.79%)
% to all India	1999	3,680 (48.52%)	6,897 (36.58%)	2,968 (36.55%)
Knitwear	2000	4,104 (49.58%)	7,616 (37.28%)	3,423 (37.29%)
Exports	2001	3,724 (51.87%)	7,186 (40.30%)	3,389 (40.30%)
		3,448 (52.83%)	6,667 (41.78%)	3,239 (41.78%)
		3,704 (54.57%)	7,935 (43.62%)	3,700 (43.61%)
Jan-Mar	2002	1,187 (55.26%)	2,327 (43.05%)	1,112 (43.08%)
Jan-Mar	2003	1,243 (56.17%)	2,826 (47.20%)	1,279 (47.25%)

Source: Tirupur Export Association, Tirupur.

For the past 6 years, there was a phenomenal change in technology and large number of sophisticated computerised knitting and embroidery machines, full fledged processing units, individual machines, compacting machines and other machinery required in knitwear manufacturing have been imported. Moreover exporters have started concentrating on value added products and high unit value realisation.

Suggestions For Further Growth Of Tirupur Clusters

- The labour standards adopted in the Tirupur knitwear industry have come under critical scrutiny of European garment sourcing multinationals. Customers in Europe/ US insist on the concept of "Green Cloth" that is, the products sold to them are produced under good/fair conditions without any kind of exploitation of workers, especisilly child labour. Therefore, efforts should be taken to improve the working conditions of labour and national laws to be followed in respect of minimum salary, overtime compensation etc

- Measures should be taken to evolve a collective brand for garments originating from Tirupur. Brand promotion is a long term exercise and the benefits accruing from this will also be for a long time.

- Hosiery units here are said to have been affected by the "unhealthy competition" in the last two years. Those producing large quantities were offering prize and gift schemes for the wholesale dealers. Further, the price quoted by them was lower than the "normal" price. Others, especially the smaller units, were hit hard by this as they were unable to offer the products at such low prices. In order to overcome this problem "Code of Conduct" should be insisted on the enterprises either by the government or Knitwear associations.

- Knitwear exporters from Tirupur are concerned over volatile fluctuation in rupee-dollar exchange rates seen in recent times and its adverse impact on their exports. Therefore, the finance ministry has to work out some mechanism to impart exchange rate protection so that currency fluctuations do not affect the export prices

Conclusion

The export committee on Small Enterprises (Abid Hussain Committee) observed that "the center- piece of the new approach is an increasing public private partnership in setting up support systems for small scale enterprises". such public private partnership would thrive particularly in clusters of small scale enterprises. As a matter of fact, spontaneous growth of over 300 clusters has already taken place in the country mostly unaided by the state. This growth has been fuelled by access to domestic and international markets and cheap labour. However, further progress in clusters is restrained by

- Lack of knowledge sharing between the entrepreneurs
- United marketing to face the competitions from minds
- Improve infrastructure
- Technological obsolescence.

World wide experience confirms that growth in clusters can be improved by institutional development, aided by abundant provision of services, and infrastructure development. The thrust of the future policy for SSIs should be to boost the growth of existing clusters by:

- Redirecting the current investment in backward areas
- Common information system (located within the clusters) that provide software databases on the status of units.
- Provision for procuring and storing inputs in bulk for each group of units.

- Liaison department to interact with traders, exporters and government agencies.

- Aiming for organizing trade fairs, exhibitions, group advertisements and the common branding of cluster products.

Abdul Kalam, the former President of India has emphasised the need for productive work rather than productive employment as means to our vision 2020. Cluster development is one of the most successful approaches to escalate the productive work.

> "The vision must be followed by the venture. It is not enough to stare up the steps we must step up the stairs."

References

http://www.smallindustryindia.com/
http://www.kvic.org.in/
http://texmin.nic.in/
http://textilescommittee.nic.in/
http://www.statebankofindia.com
http://www.sidbi.com

18

Lock and Iron Safety Box Manufacturing Units in Dindigul District, Tamil Nadu: An Appraisal of the Cluster

L. Rathakrishnan

Abstract

The lock industry is a traditional cottage industry in India. Aligarh and Dindigul are famous for lock industry hub in India. Lock and safety box making is a promising industry in Dindigul. This chapter traces the growth and decay of lock industry and its future. Modernisation, mechanisation, financial accessibility and innovation are the pre-requisite for the survival of lock and safe industry in the 21st century.

Introduction

The Small Scale Industries play an important role in the economic development of the country. The definition for small scale industry is changing from time to time. In the earlier days the small scale industries was classified into two categories, namely using power and no power. According to the definition, using power with less than 50 employees or using no power but the strength of employees is more then 50 but less than 100 were called small scale industries. In recent times, the SSIs are also called as micro, small and medium enterprises (MSMEs). As such, the small enterprise is the one where the investment in plant and machinery is more then Rs.25 lakh but does not exceed five crore rupees. The medium enterprise is the one where the investment in plant and machinery is more then five crore rupees but does not exceed Rs.10 crore. A micro enterprise is the one where the investment in plant and machinery does not exceed Rs.25 lakh.

The SSIs account for more than 95 per cent of firms and provide employment to 60 per cent to 70 per cent employees. The SMEs are active in the technology intensive and business services sectors. SMEs are heavily involved in the innovation process. Although, they spend less on research and development than larger firms, they innovate in other ways, either by treating or re-engineering products or services or by inventing new organisational approaches. The SMEs are relatively local in their orientation but interestingly active internationally, generally through inter-firm linkages and clusters. Networking allows SMEs to project their advantages of smaller science and greater flexibility with economies of scale and scope.

There are 12 million SSI units functioning in India in various sectors. Their contribution in the total industrial production is approximately 40 per cent. The growth rate of SSIs was 9.96 per cent in 2004 – 05 and the growth rate of SSIs to overall industry sector was 8.4 per cent. These industries contribute about 6-7 per cent to gross domestic product (GDP).

Lock Making in Earlier Days

Although locks of some sort had been used throughout history, lock making as a profession went back to1485. Lock making became a promising enterprise in European countries due to changing social conditions and aspirations, increasing wealth and capital accumulation,. Lock making at the initial stage was started as a local trade, but market demand forced lock makers into being professional one. The British rule in the country was instrumental for India to enter into lock making. Eventhough lock making as a profession went back to the period of 1485, it was popularised in India only in 1870. Johnson & Co. initiated manual production of locks on a small scale by cutting the metal and manufacturing it with the process of moulding.

Skills were passed on from parent to child and from master to apprentice. In the earliest lock making times the makers would have been one family outfits. In course of time, as market expanded, firms could grow larger and eventually become very large and independent. By the end of the 17th century, lock making was well established and certainly it became more than a total trade. The industry made from the ordinary gate lock and padlock to the secret bag lock and motor vehicle lock. More then 24 different types of locks are manufactured now. Several patents were taken out by local men even before large manufactures moved in.

Now, lock is manufactured almost in all countries. There is foreign competition, mainly from United Kingdom, America, France, Italy, Germany and China. But the strength and practical use–wise Indian locks are better than any other lock. In general, the locks were made by small master men in tiny places at the rear of their own homes. No machinery was used until 1856. Even large manufacturers such as Messrs. Chubb of Wolver Hampton (UK) made their locks entirely by hand.

Use of machinery was popularised only in the first half of the 20th century. In the meantime cooperative society had also joined in lock making. But they were not successful, except when they sold their production to cooperative retailers. Among the few surviving cooperative lock makers, the Dindigul Lock

Workers Industrial Cooperative Society is the one doing its business successfully.

The handicraft lock industry in India became sick due to lack of demand and higher finished goods inventory caused its demise. In addition, price of iron also went up very steep. The invasion of machinery, competition from larger firms, emergence of registered limited liability company with access to the necessary capital, liberalisation of the economy consequently allowing cheap lock manufactured in China to Indian market, issues related to child labour in lock industry resulted in the closure of many lock units in India.

At some point the lock making industry added safe making. The lock making industry diversified its role into other security devices as well. It started to concentrate on strong rooms and linings, safe deposit systems, burglar and fire-resisting safes, steel grilles and gates, safe deposits, certified safe cabinets, safe files, ledger containers, wall safes, cash and deed boxes, and all types of locks.

The twentieth century witnessed the disappearance of many back-yard lock makers due to competition from larger firms and poor capital investment. This century also experienced closures, take over and amalgamations. Small numbers of traditional lock makers are in the trade, hence, this study was undertaken.

Surendra Kumar (1950), an advocate by profession and son of a barrister was recorded as the man behind the manufacturing of modern locks in India. By 1957 Aligarh and Dindigul emerged as the hub of large number of lock manufacturing units. As far as India is concerned and particularly Aligargh and Dindigul, many muslim industrialists made significant contribution in the manufacturing of locks from sheet metals with the help of machines. Prominent among these were

Jemco and Rose lock brands, which were very popular in 1970. During the same period the lock makers also stepped into the field of manufacturer of locks for scooters and motors.

Lock Industry in Aligarh: Case Analysis

Aligarh is famous for its locks. Over 6000 manufacturing units of locks are found here. More than 25,000 employees are working in these units. About 30 per cent of total products are exported to foreign countries. The annual turnover of the lock industry in the Aligarh is Rs.200 crore. Even after the entry of Chinese locks into Indian market, locks made in India are still demanded in the market. Working hours have been 6 a.m to 7 p.m in winter and from 7 a.m to 8 p.m in summer. But in many instances these hours go beyond. Only 10 per cent of the work force is women. Boys are widely employed. Sunday and Monday are treated as week end break. 70 per cent of the artisans are members of friendly societies. 50 per cent can read and write. 15 per cent are members of a mechanics institute. 10 per cent have accounts with the post office savings bank and five per cent are the owners of the freehold cottages in which they reside. The locksmiths are assisted by their wives and members of their families, together with one or two apprentices. Children are treated as cheap labour. The children are exploited heavily. They are forced to work long hours; and the poor food has wrought havoc with their frail bodies and the death rate amongst them is high.

Recommendations of the Earlier Studies

Studies conducted earlier suggested the following recommendations for survival of lock industry.

(i) Government should import advanced lock manufacturing machine to suit the Indian conditions, which should be made available at reasonable rates to the manufacturers.

(ii) Supply of electricity should be given at low rates;

(iii) Loan should be provided at cost effective/reasonable rates;

(iv) A considerable family contribution comes through child labourers including girls, whose involvement should be avoided or banned

(v) Lack of new technology and training, non-availability of facilities, poor salary, lack of diets and environment faced by the labourer must be removed;

(vi) Cooperation and encouragement on the part of the government will provide the necessary fillip to the business; and

(vii) Prosperity of industry depends upon unified approach of government and industry on issues related to establishing training centers, supply of raw materials at low rates, amendment of labour laws and ban on the contract system.

Government Initiative

In order to promote lock industry, the government of India has set up national programme. The key players are small scale industry (SSI), UNIDO, SIDBI, NSIC, All India Lock Manufacturers Associations (Aligarh), and Dindigul Lock Workers Industrial Cooperative Society (Dindigul). The objectives of the programme was to upgrade technology of Indian lock industry, creation of common facility centre for the lock artisans at Dindigul, Tamil Nadu, establishing market network, and sourcing of lock components by leading lock manufacturers (e.g. Godrej)

Locks and Safety Box Industry in Dindigul

Materials and Methods

A study on lock and iron safety box manufacturing industry in Dindigul district, Tamil Nadu, was Conducted in 2009 to trace the development of lock and iron safety box manufacturing industry in Dindigul district, to find the economies of operation, and to identify the problems faced by the industry.

Both primary and secondary data were collected for the study. Interview schedule was used to collect the primary data from the lock and iron safety box manufacturers. The secondary data was collected from the records maintained by the various lock and iron safety box manufacturers in the selected district. Census method was followed for selecting the respondents. Thus, 25 lock and safe box industry owners were interviewed. The primary data was collected in January 2009. Simple statistical tools were used in the study.

Results and Discussion

Three types of lock and safety box industry were found in the selected district, namely private lock unit owners, Dindigul Lock Workers Industrial Cooperative Society, and safety box manufacturers.

The lock industry in Dindigul is a traditional industry, surviving for quite a long period. The Dindigul Lock Workers Industrial Cooperative society has been functioning since 24 November 1957. The major objective of the lock industry is to provide continuous employment, produce quality locks and market it at reasonable price. The lock unit in the district manufactures various types of locks, namely, pad locks, almirah locks, door locks and drawer locks.

14 private lock units, one cooperative society lock making unit and 10 safety box manufacturers were interviewed and data was collected from the field. Thus, the total sample comes to 25. The private lock manufacturers and safety box manufacturers were working as sole proprietorship pattern but the Dindigul Lock Workers Industrial Cooperative society was functioning on cooperative pattern.

Geographical Location of the Lock Units

The lock manufacturing units have been distributed in different places in the district. They are located in Dindigul,

Paraipatti, Mettupatti, and Nallampatti, out of which 56 per cent of the units are located in Dindigul itself. The remaining units are distributed in other places in the same district (Table 1).

Table 1
Geographical Location of the Units

S.No.	*Name of the Place*	*No of units*			*Total*	*%*
		Lock	*Safety Box*	*Cooperative Society*		
1.	Dindigul	4	9	1	14	56
2.	Paraipatti	2	1	-	3	12
3.	Mettupatti	3	-	-	3	12
4.	Nallampatti	5	-	-	5	20
	Total	14	10	1	25	100

Source: Computed from primary data

The year of establishment of the lock units is explained in Table 2. The lock units have been functioning since 1950. The table highlights that 68 per cent of the lock units were established before 1990. Only 32 per cent came to the market after 1991. Interestingly the private lock industries (85%)

Table 2
Year of Establishment of the Units

S.No.	*Year of Establishment*	*No of Units*			*Total*
		Lock	*Safety Box*	*Cooperative Society*	
1.	1950 – 1970	3 (21)	1 (10)	1 (100)	5 (20)
2.	1971 – 1990	9 (64)	3 (30)	-	12 (48)
3.	1991 – 2000	2 (15)	3 (32)	-	5 (20)

S.No.	Year of Establishment	No of Units Lock	Safety Box	Cooperative Society	Total
	After 2001	-	3 (30)	-	3 (12)
	Total	14 (100)	10 (100)	1 (100)	25 (100)

Source: Computed from primary data.
Note: Figures in parentheses indicate per cent to total

established their unit before 1990. The Dindigul lock workers Industrial Cooperative Society has been functioning since 1957.

Investment

Investment pattern of the lock and safety box industry is shown in Table 3. The owners of the lock manufacturers have invested money from Rs. 27, 000 to Rs.14 lakhs. 60 per cent of the respondents have invested up to a maximum of Rs. one lakh. Another 20 per cent had invested to the tune of up to Rs. three lakhs. Since the Dindigul Lock Workers Industrial Cooperative Society falls under the category of cooperative society, the average investment was found higher (Rs.14, 36,500). The least amount was invested by the private lock units (average investment was Rs.1, 58,071). The safety box unit holders have invested on an average of Rs.2, 03,000.

Sources of Finance

The financial accessibility is a great burden to the small scale industries. As government financial institutions are reluctant to issue loan to the lock manufacturers majority of the owners (88%) have invested money on their own. The owners had contributed 66 per cent of the total financial requirement of lock industry. Only one safety box owner has received rupees five lakh from South Indian Bank.

Table 3

Investment on the Unit

S.No	Capital Investments	No of Units				
		Lock	Safety Box	Cooperative Society	Total	%
1.	Less than 50,000	9 (2,34,000)	-	-	9 (2,34,000)	36
2.	50,001 – 1,00,000	1 (64,000)	5 (5,65,000)	-	6 (6,29,000)	24
3.	1,00,001 – 3,00,000	2 (2,65,000)	3 (7,65,000)	-	5 (10,39,000)	20
4.	3,00,001 – 5,00,000	-	2 (7,00,000)	-	2 (7,00,000)	8
5.	More than 5,00,000	2 (16,50,000)	-	1 (14,36,500)	3 (30,86,500)	12
	Total	14 (22,13,000)	10 (20,30,000)	1 (14,36,500)	25 (56,79,500)	100
	Average	1,58,071	2,03,000	14,36,500	2,27,180	

Source: Computed from primary data.

Note: Figures in parentheses indicate actual investment by the respective category.

Table 4
Sources of Finance

S.No	Types of the Industry	Sources of finance: Own	Members Government of Tamil Nadu Share Capital	Bank	Cooperative Bank	Total
1.	Lock	14 (22,13,000)	-	-	-	14 (22,13,000)
2.	Safety Box	9 (15,30,000)	-	1 (5,00,000)	-	10 (20,30,000)
3.	Cooperative Society	-	- (11,36,500)	-	1 (3,00,000)	1 (14,36,500)
	Total	23 (37,43,000)	(11,36,500)	1 (5,00,000)	1 (3,00,000)	25 (56,79,500)
	Average	1,62,739	11,36,500	5,00,000	3,00,000	2,27,180

Source: Computed from primary data.
Note: Figures in parentheses indicate actual amount.

The Dindigul lock workers industrial cooperative society has received three lakh rupees from the cooperative bank as loan. The Tamil Nadu government and members of the Co-operative Society contributed Rs.11, 36,500 as share capital. Thus, the investment made by the society was found higher. Nonetheless, the bank contribution to the lock and safety box manufacturers was found less (9%). Table 4 explains financial source details of lock and safety box manufacturers in Dindigul district.

Sources of Raw Material

The lock and safety box units received raw material such as iron, brass, lever, steel, key, paint, and brush and iron plate from two sources. They receive raw material from government as well as private agencies. They do receive raw material within the district as well as beyond the district boundary. 88 per cent of the respondents received their raw materials within the district only. Iron and steel are the principal raw materials for this industry.

Cost of Production

The cost of production of lock and safety boxes is shown in Table 5. The cost of production varies from one industry to another industry depending upon the unit size and number of lock and safety box produced. The production cost ranges between 1,65,000 to 16,00,000. The highest number of respondents (80%) have spent between Rs.2,00,000 to Rs.10,00,000 on production.

Finished Products

88 per cent of the units produced up to the maximum of 5,000 units of locks and safety boxes. It was found from the study that the cooperative society has produced up to 14,400 pieces of locks in 2008 - 09. On an average the safety box units produced 80 boxes per year. The private lock owners produced on an average 2425 pieces during the year 2008 – 2009 (Table 6).

Table 5
Cost of Production

S.No	Cost of Production (in Rs.)	No of Units Lock	Safety Box	Cooperative Society	Total	%
1.	Upto 2,00,000	2 (3,29,520)	-	-	2 (3,29,520)	8
2.	2,00,001 – 5,00,000	9 (31,30,320)	1 (4,19,280)	-	10 (35,49,200)	40
3.	5,00,001 – 10,00,000	2 (12,33,240)	8 (53,72,044)	-	10	40
4.	10,00,001 – 16,00,000	1 (11,75,400	1 (11,29,800)	1 (16,72,300)	3 (66,05,284)	12
	Total	14 (28,68,480)	10 (69,21,124)	1 (16,72,300)	25 (1,14,61,904)	100
	Average	2,04,891	6,92,112	16,72,300	4,58,476	-

Source: Computed from primary data.
Note: Figures in parentheses indicate actual cost.

Table 6
No. of Finished Products Produced During 2008 - 2009

S.No	Particulars	No of Units				
		Lock	Safety Box	Cooperative Society	Total	%
1.	Less than 1,000	1 (720)	10 (804)	-	11 (1524)	44
2.	1001 – 5000	11 (22,440)	-	-	11 (22,440)	44
3.	More than 5001	2 (10,800)	-	1 (14,400)	3 (25,200)	12
	Total	14 (33,960)	10 (804)	1 (14,400)	25 (49,164)	100
	Average	2425	80	14,400	1966	-

Source: Computed from primary data.
Note: Figures in parentheses indicate actual number of finished products.

Sale of the Finished Products

The sale particulars of lock and safety box are furnished in Table 7. Normally, the finished lock and safety boxes are sold in the production spot itself. They also undertake production on the basis of previous orders. They receive orders from regular lock shop owners. As the demand for lock is higher, whatever produced was sold immediately. Where as the sale of safety boxes was slow. 80 per cent of the products were sold for cash and 20 per cent was sold for credit. Thus, the lock and safety boxes have high demand in the market. The finished products are also being sent to other states through parcel service.

Table 7
Sales of the Finished Products during the Year 2008 - 2009

S.No	Sales of the Products	No of Units				
		Lock	Safety Box	Cooperative Society	Total	%
1.	Less than 500	-	10 (648)	-	10 (648)	40
2.	501 – 1000	3 (2520)	-	-	3 (2520)	12
3.	1001 – 5000	10 (21,120)	-	-	10 (21,120)	40
4.	More than 5000	1 (7200)	-	1 (9600)	2 (16,800)	8
	Total	14 (30,840)	10 (648)	1 (9600)	25 (41,008)	100
	Average	2202	64	9600	1643	-

Source: Computed from primary data.
Note: Figures in parentheses indicate actual sale of finished goods.

Earnings

The sales return particular for the year 2008 – 09 is given in Table 8. Although, the lock and safety box manufacturers fall

Table 8

Sales Return for the Year 2008 - 09

S.No	*Sales of the Products (in Rs.)*	*No of units*				%
		Lock	*Safety Box*	*Cooperative Society*	*Total*	
1.	Less than 3,00,000	3 (7,06,720)	-	-	3 (7,06,720)	12
2.	3,00,000 – 5,00,000	4 (13,70,940)			4 (13,70,940)	16
3.	5,00,000 – 8,00,000	5 (27,26,900)	6 (40,70,000)	-	11 (67,96,900)	44
4.	8,00,000 – 10,00,000	1 (8,40,840)	2 (16,20,000)	-	3 (24,60,840)	12
5.	More than 10,00,000	1 (13,65,300)	2 (24,40,500)	1 (21,30,000)	4 (59,35,800)	16
	Total	14 (70,10,700)	10 (81,30,500)	1 (21,30,000)	25 (1,72,71,200)	100
	Average	5,00,764	8,13,050	21,30,000	6,90,848	-

Source: Computed from primary data.
Note: Figures in parentheses indicate actual sales amount.

under the category of micro enterprises (based on investment made on fixed capital), the demand for the product was found high. 72 per cent of the respondents had sold goods worth Rs.3,00,000 to Rs.10,00,000 during the year 2008 – 2009. On an average the cooperative society sold lock to the tune of Rs.21,30,000, but it was only Rs.5,00,764 by the private lock owners. Since cooperative society had larger network, they are able to sell large quantity of locks.

Inventory Management

Table 9 explains the inventory management practices of micro enterprises. It is clear from the table that the lock and safety box manufacturers maintain low inventory (16%). Interestingly, the private lock owners have a stock of only nine per cent at the year end. Whereas it is 33 per cent in the case of the cooperative society and 19 per cent in the case of safety box manufacturers. Thus, the private lock owners maintain good inventory management Practices.

Table 9
Inventory Management

S.No	*Types of Units*	*Production*	*Sales*	*Stock Inventory (balance)*	*%*
1.	Lock	33,960	30,840	3,120	9
2.	Safety Box	804	648	156	19
3.	Cooperative Society	14,400	9600	4,800	33
	Total	49,164	41,088	8,076	16

Source: Computed from primary data.

Net – Profit Earned

The net profit earned by the selected enterprise is shown in Table 10. It was found from the study that almost all enterprise earned profit. The profit ranges from Rs.12, 000 to

Table 10
Net Profit Earned

S.No	Net Profit (in Rs.)	No of units Lock	Safety Box	Cooperative Society	Total	%
1.	Less than 15,000	6 (72,600)	-	-	6 (72,600)	24
2.	15,001 – 25,000	1 (16,000)	5 (1,19,000)	-	6 (25,400)	24
3.	25,001 – 35000	3 (94,000)	3 (86,000)	-	6 (1,80,000)	24
4.	35,001 – 50,000	2 (48,000)	1 (98,000)	-	3 (1,46,000)	12
5.	More than 50,000	2 (1,42,050)	1 (60,000)	1 (2,86,050)	4 (4,88,050)	16
	Total	14 (3,72,600)	10 (3,63,000)	1 (2,86,050)	25 (10,21,650)	100
	Average	28,661	33,000	2,86,050	40,866	-

Source: Computed from primary data.
Note: Figures in parentheses indicate actual profit.

Rs. 2, 86,000 per year. 72 per cent of the respondents earned a profit of less than Rs. 35,000. The cooperative society earned highest profit (Rs. 2,86,050). On an average the safety box manufacturers earned a profit of Rs. 33,000 followed by the lock industry (average of Rs. 28,661). As the cooperative lock makers had produced higher number of lock besides market network, they earn high profit.

Employment

The number of person employed is shown in Table 11. On an average the industry provides employment to 6 people. These findings coincide with the case analysis of Aligarh lock industry, where, the lock industry gives employment to six workers in Aligarh lock cluster. Nonetheless, the Dindigul Lock Workers Industrial Cooperative Society provides employment to the tune of 19 people per year.

Table 11
Number of Persons Employed

S.No	Number of Persons Employed	No of units			
		Lock	Safety Box	Cooperative Society	Total
1.	Less than 5 person	9 (25)	4 (17)	-	13 (42)
2.	6 – 9	3 (18)	4 (24)	-	7 (42)
3.	More than 10 person	2 (30)	2 (25)	1 (19)	5 (74)
	Total	14 (73)	10 (65)	1 (19)	25 (158)
	Average	5	6	19	6

Source: Computed from primary data.
Note: Figures in parentheses indicate actual number of people employed in select industry.

Types of employment is shown in Table 12. It is found from the table that 77 per cent of the workers are skilled, 13 per cent of the workers are classified as managerial staff and 10

Table 12
Types of Employment

S.No	*Types of Labour*	*No of units*				*%*
		Lock	*Safety Box*	*Cooperative Society*	*Total*	
1.	Skilled	55	50	16	121	77
2.	Unskilled	10	8	-	18	11
3.	Managerial Staff	8	8	3	19	12
	Total	13	66	19	158	100

Source: Computed from primary data.

per cent of the workers are classified into unskilled workers. Hence, the industry needs skilled workers than unskilled workers.

Salary and wages

Salary and wage structure of the worker is shown in Table 13. The workers are paid in terms of wages as well as salary. 98 per cent of the workers have been classified in the category of wage receivers. They receive upto Rs.5, 000 per month. Only three managerial (2%) staff earn more than Rs.5, 000 as salary per month. They are working in the cooperative society.

The mode of wage/ salary payment ranges from daily wage to monthly salary. About 76 per cent of the respondents receive their salary either daily or weekly. 20 per cent of the respondents receive their wages on contract basis. This can be seen table 14. Only one manager in the cooperative society receives salary on monthly basis.

Problems of the Industry

Although the lock and safety box manufacturers fall under micro enterprise category and have a good demand for their products, they also face a number of problems, namely, capital, labour and marketing. 80 per cent of the respondents viewed

Table 13
Salary and Wage Payment

S.No	Salary / Wage	No of units Lock	Safety Box	Cooperative Society	Total	%
1.	Less than 3000	8 (17,900)	4 (8,800)	4 (8,400)	16 (35,100)	10
2.	3001 – 5000	64 (2,03,000)	61 (2,00,800)	14 (42,000)	139 (4,45,800)	88
3.	5001 – 7000	1 (6,000)	1 (6,500)	1 (6,200)	3 (18,700	2
	Total	**73 (2,26,900)**	**66 (2,16,100)**	**19 (56,600)**	**158 (4,99,600)**	**100**
	Average	**3108**	**3274**	**2978**	**3162**	-

Source: Computed from primary data.
Note: Figures in parentheses indicate actual salary / wage to the respective category.

Table 14
Problems of the Industry

S.No	*Problems*	*No of units*			*Total*	*%*
		Lock	*Safety Box*	*Cooperative Society*		
1.	Capital	9	8	-	17	68
2.	Labour	3	-	-	3	12
3.	Marketing	-	-	1	1	4
4.	No problem	2	2	-	4	16
	Total	14	10	1	25	100

Source: Computed from primary data.

that the capital and labour are the most important problems. The cooperative society has perceived that marketing is the only problem for them. Table 14 further explains that 16 per cent of the enterprise does not have any problem at all.

Conclusion

The lock and safety box manufacturers in Dindigul fall under the category of micro enterprises, which is also the traditional industry in Tamil Nadu. These industries were started in 1950 and leave now they have not adopted modern technology. Hence, many industries of this kind have become sick. Thus, large number of industries has been closed and only 25 lock and safety box making units are surviving including one lock workers industrial cooperative society. Hence, the industry has to adopt modern technology to increase the volume of production and economies scale of operation. Standardisation and quality maintenance are another important criteria to be adopted by the industry. Periodical meetings among the lock and safety box manufacturers must be conducted to find out the solution for the problems faced by them. Short term training programme can also be arranged to import knowledge on latest technology among lock manufacturers and also to encourage the would be entrepreneurs (who may likely to enter the lock and safety box manufacturing). Above all, financial support is very much the need of the hour for survival and growth of the lock and safety box manufacturing industry.

References

Batra G.G and A.C. Dangwal (2003), **Entrepreneurship and Small Scale Industries**, Deep & Deep Publications, New Delhi: 204.

Chandrasekhar N, Dhanalakshmi M, Dhanalakshmi N, and Ilamvazhuthi A, (2009), **A Study on Lock and Iron Safety Box Manufacturing Industry in Dindigul District, Tamil Nadu (Unpublished U.G. Dissertation),** Gandhigram Rural University, Gandhigram: 42.

Jim Evans (1998), **100 years Key Making: The History of Arthur Hough & Sons Ltd.,** Arthur Hough & Sons Ltd.

Joseph E, Sjepanek (1962), **Management of Small Industry,** ASIA Publishing House, Chennai: 256.

Nisar Ahmad (1987), **Problems and Management of Small Scale and Cottage Industries,** Deep and Deep publications, New Delhi: 272.

19

Strategies to Enhance Competitiveness of SMEs

Raja Alias Pranmalai K,
Thirumal Azhagan C, Varadaraj A,

Abstract

This paper discuses different strategies to be adopted by SMEs in the context by globalisation. Although they form the backbone of industries development they suffer from the problem of sub-optimal scales of operation and technological obsolescence. The paper suggests an effective technological capacity-building exercise to enhance the competitiveness of SMEs. Some of the issues discussed in this paper are knowledge acquisition and dissemination, new technology demonstration, technology net working, and financial support systems.

Introduction

The role of the SMEs in nation building is well recognised across the globe. The industrial engines of Japan, Germany and Taiwan are driven by the SMEs sector. Even in the United States, the home of many transnational corporations, SMEs enjoy an important place and are actively supported by the Small Business Administration through a number of policies and programmes. A small enterprise is generally born as an idea. It is only later that such ideas grow, find their place on the world stage and then become mega corporations. Small and Medium Enterprises (SMEs) have a very important place in the Indian economy. Their contribution in terms of production, exports, employment generation and all round growth of the country is well known. Spread across the country, the SMEs also help in the equitable distribution of wealth through entrepreneurs who set up SMEs in India. The SMEs form the backbone of industrial development. But these industries suffer from problems of sub-optimal scales of operations and technological obsolescence. This chapter addresses the issues and strategies to enhance the effectiveness of SMEs.

Need for Access to New Technology

Small enterprises in India, with their dynamism, flexibility and innovative drive are increasingly focusing on improved production methods, penetrative marketing strategies and modern scientific management capabilities to sustain and strengthen their operations. They are poised for global partnership and have the potential to absorb latest diverse technologies in industrial fields. Small scale industries in India is more than beautiful- it is efficient, adaptable and adds value in economic and social spheres. As the country integrates into the global village, the small and medium sectors will have to respond accordingly. They deserve special attention as they play a pivotal role in country's socio-economic development. The problems faced by the SMEs, particularly in accessing technology and maintaining competitiveness have been formidable. The reasons for the inability of SMEs to identify their technology needs are:

- **Poor financial situations and low levels of R&D;**
- **Poor adaptability to changing trade trends;**
- **Desire to avoid risk;**
- **Non-availability of technically trained human resources;**
- **Emphasis on production and not on production costs;**
- **Lack of management skills;**
- **Lack of access to technological information and consultancy services;**
- **Isolation from technology hubs.**

To enable SMEs to mitigate the above problems and enhance their access to new technologies for increasing their competitiveness in the international market, it is imperative to give them a conducive environment, which includes

(i) Formulation of appropriate national policies and programmes;
(ii) Building up technological capacity;
(iii) Knowledge flows and technology database and
(iv) R&D and inter firm linkages.

1. Formulation of Policies and Programmes

Conducive policy environment is a pre-requisite for technological development. Major policy reforms aimed at substantially deregulating industrial sector and liberalising foreign investment as well as technology imports, have been the most significant development since 1991. The post liberalisation era in the Indian economy has enhanced opportunities and challenges for the small industries sector. The ultimate objective of promotional policies is to enhance SMEs capacity to grow so that they become viable units.

2. Built up Technological Capacity

Access to advanced technologies and assistance in its adoption is crucial to built up Indigenous Technological Capacity (ITC) to face international competition. In the present scenario of globalisation, knowledge of access to latest advances holds the key to international competition. In this venture the industrial sectors, which are able to identify their technology needs and adopt in time, will benefit the most.

In India, the traditional sector which has shown this remarkable ability to adapt to technological change is leather. Central Leather Research Institute (CLRI), Chennai, has successfully introduced Microprocessor control in tannery wet processing at industry level and promoted cleaner processing, quality consistency and international equivalence. Anticipating the impact potential of computer-aided techniques in foot-wear and leather garment designs, CLRI alerted the leather industry to adopt CAD in their industries so as to export the finished leather garments to foreign countries. In another example, under NISTADS Bandura Project, a software package called 'MADHU' (Modernisation of Artistic Design for Handloom Unit) was developed in collaboration with Indian Institute of Technology, Kharagpur. National Institute of Science Technology and Development Studies (NISTADS) has set up a S&T field station at Bankura, India to upgrade the technologies for artisans and craftsmen through blending the traditional technologies with new technologies and promoting commercialisation. This CAD software package facilitates computerised digitisation of the picture/design produced by the artist/designer. This package has been successfully demonstrated to designers and weavers of Bankura. As a result, a large number of craftsmen have adopted blending of this new technology to increase efficiency, quality, flexibility and cost effectiveness. The above factors show that information technology can be of immense use to upgrade and modernise the small-scale sector.

3. Knowledge Flows and Technology Database

Dynamism of SEMs is crucial for their long-term competitiveness. For this they need to focus on systems of knowledge accumulation rather than just production system. The SMEs should have capabilities for generating, accessing and diffusing knowledge and also have openness to external sources of knowledge, including new technology databases. To do so the SSLs need efficient national information services and networks. In developing countries, most of the SMEs do not have access to well-researched technology databases that provide information pro-actively on a regular basis. The information usually remains in the banks untapped, while the purveyors of the information wait for the targeted beneficiaries to request it.

In India, an important technology information data bank is the National Research and Development Corporation (NRDC), which serves as an important link between research and SMEs. NRDC acquires, evaluates, develops and transfers all worthwhile technologies generated at the various national laboratories. The technologies available with NRDC for commercial exploitation cover a wide range of products, namely drugs and pharmaceuticals, pesticides and herbicides, plasticizers, resins, electro-chemical products, metals, paints and varnishes, leather chemicals and auxiliaries, electrical and electronic goods, building materials, etc. It provides a comprehensive international patent search and also has few renowned international databases online for carrying out the search. Through the Ministry of Science and Technology, the Government of India has also established information centers in specific areas for assisting academic institutions and industry under the scheme called National Information System for Science and Technology (NISSAT). There are information banks on food, leather, drugs and pharmaceutical, machine tools and aeronautics. SMEs can approach them for assistance, especially with regard to the latest developments in the field of technology.

4. R&D and Inter-firm Linkages

At present, there are 2900 R&D institutions functioning in India, of which 1350 are in the private sector. Out of these, over 1250 are in-house R&D units, employing over 45,000 Scientific and technical personnel and incurring an expenditure of seven billion per annum. However, the small-scale sector is largely devoid of such facilities and is mainly supported by public R&D for acquisition of new technologies. In general, SMEs are encouraged to invest in localised technological development. As most SMEs lack financial resources, the best way is to enter into linkages and partnerships with other enterprises, academia and/or R&D institutions. Over the past decade, emphasis in the concept of technology transfer has gradually shifted towards a new set of strategies, which can be described as 'creative partnerships' or 'strategic alliances' to form learning organisations the underlines the idea that technological cooperation is no longer 'one-way', but involves a longer-term mutual benefit beyond short-term financial success.

Role of Financial Institutions

The availability of financial resources on affordable terms and in a non-bureaucratic manner is yet another problem the SMEs confront, hindering access to new technologies. It is imperative, there for, to influence existing financial networks and, if need be, to set-up a separate mechanism for funding smaller enterprises, especially those categorised as micro-enterprises. One of the important ways to promote access to new technologies among SMEs in developing countries is to provide venture capital, which in a way helps in indigenous development of technologies. Financial institutions such as Industrial Development Bank of India (IDBI), Industrial credit and Investment Corporation of India (ICICI), and Industrial Finance Corporation of India (IFCI), are providing assistance for commercialisation of indigenously developed technologies and adoption of imported technologies for wider domestic applications through venture capital companies. SRISTI Venture Capital Fund is also supporting a large number of small innovations. One of the main factors of the success of knitwear cluster at Tripper is the state intervention in the supply of short-term credit to facilitate networked production. In order to create a business environment, with adoption and assimilation of new technologies that are resource-efficient and have little waste output, the supportive infrastructure also needs to be strengthened in many developing countries. There is a need for such institutions to deal exclusively with the myriad problems that SMEs face in their day-to-day work.

In India the Department of Scientific and Industrial Research (DSIR) is one such institution. It is engaged in technology promotion, development, utilisation of locally available R&D options through its major schemes, namely Programme Aimed at Technological Self-Reliance (PATSER), Scheme to Enhance the Efficacy of Transfer of Technology (SEETOT), Technology Bureau for Small Enterprises. The result of collaboration between APCTT and Small Industries Development Bank of India (SIDBI), represents under one roof, synergy of technology and finance which facilitates capability building and identifying market channels.

Employment Initiatives by SMEs

The small scale industrial sector is an important and vibrant constituent of the economic structure of the economy. Our country has about 35.31 lakh SSI units providing employment to more than 199.65 lakh persons. 40 per cent of the industrial production and 35 per cent of the National exports are contributed by the SSI sectors. As on 31st March 2004, there are 4.75 lakh registered SSI functioning units in Tamil Nadu having an investment of Rs.13, 292 corers, providing employment to 34.65 lakh persons.

To generate more employment in the agro-and-rural industries sector, the government has fixed a target of creating 25 lakh additional SSLs in rural area during the 10th plan period, which world be implemented through Rural Employment Generation Programme (REGp) under the organ of Khadi and Village Industries Commissions (KVIC). In the first two years of 10th plan 8.32 lakh job opportunities have already been created under the REGP 16.5 lakh employments have been fixed under the Pradhan Mantri Rojgar Yojana (PMRY) for the 10th Plan Period.

Employment generation has been encouraging not only in this sector but also in other sectors across the country. A study commissioned by the Ministry of SSLs reveals the export generated on the incremental direct employment of 10 lakh jobs in the year 2004-05 over the previous year. The total employment generated during the year corresponding to export activity valued at 78 billon was corer jobs of the direct employment in the logistics, transport and related sectors.

The SMEs now-a-days are gradually turning acillaries, which are keen to capitalise on the availability of abundant trained and dedicated man power", The report says further that an enterprise must bring together at each productive point the people with the right technological knowledge, equipment with the right technological capabilities, and materials suitable for the purposes and the moment it must also sustained. Thus, the people, and the enterprise can have a flexibility to select wisely among alternative technologies for each step in the process.

Conclusion

In conclusion, any effective technological capacity-building exercise to enhance competitiveness of SMEs will have to address issues that can be broadly classified under the generic heads of a conductive policy frame-work, knowledge acquisition and dissemination, new technology demonstration and networking, and financing and institutional support systems. In each of the above categories, the barriers must be clearly identified and enabling strategies developed so that the technological capacity-building process in SMEs becomes meaningful, in terms not only of international trade and business or of the environment, but also making it responsive to the needs of the people. Constant learning by doing adds interaction to the activities for innovation with tacit knowledge playing a crucial role, as exemplified by Indian SMEs and clusters. Here, human centered systems play a crucial role for flexible manufacturing and customer orientation. There have been many successful examples of industrial clusters in India, China, South Korea, Japan and European countries. The study of these innovation models can be highly useful for greater cross-culture exchange of experiences between different countries.

20

Value Added Services in Health Care Industry: A Tool to Overcome Competition

Nisha, J Sarata, A.V

Abstract

An often – heard quote about Service Organizations goes like this: In a Service Organisation, if you're not serving the customer, you'd be serving someone who is People – front – line employees and those supporting them from behind the scenes are critical to the success of any service organisation. Value added Services and Services marketing is about promises – promises made and promises kept to customers. Today we talk of emotional labor particularly in the Health Care Industry that goes beyond the physical or mental skills needed to deliver quality service. Friendliness, courtesy, empathy and responsiveness directed towards customers, all require huge amounts of emotional labour which is a critical factor, key to the success of any organization in today's competitive business world. This research paper focuses in particular the revolutionary changes taking place in the Health Care Industry in providing Value Added Services to customers, in order to stay competitive. A critical analysis is done to study the impact of Value Added Services, its implications on success, and suggestions are offered for future growth.

Introduction

India's health care sector has made impressive strides in the recent years. It has transformed to a Rs. 1000 billion industry today and is surging ahead with an annual growth rate of 17 per cent per annum. This industry is expected to grow to Rs. 1862 billion by the financial year 2005-06.

Reasons for the Revolution

Since healthcare is dependent on the people served, India's huge population of a billion people represents a big opportunity. At the same time, India has a very low density of doctors. The country has only 34 doctors for every 10,000 people. Compared to this, the US has 2340 doctors per 10,000. There is a huge shortage of hospital beds. According to a World Health Organization (WHO) report, India needs to add 80,000 hospital beds each year for the next five years to meet the demands of its population. Statistics also indicate that infant mortality is amongst the highest in India. Given these constraints, the demand - supply gap is widening each year with hospitals in India running at 80-90 per cent occupancy. However, serving India has its own challenges owing to the great urban – rural divide.

The Rural Health Care Domain

Data in the public domain reveal that there are severs disparities in distribution of health care resources as well as health outcomes across rural and urban areas. The situation in urban India is closer to developed country averages, whereas the rural scenario in India is one of the worst in the world. The disparity in infrastructure too is obvious with the difference in availability of hospital beds being as much as 15 times less in rural areas and public expenditures 7 times less. In case of health outcomes, the urban areas do nearly twice better than the rural areas.

The critical factor here is the investment of resources in rural and urban areas. The urban areas have received relatively adequate resources over the years and hence the infrastructure and facilities here are reasonable both in numbers and qualitative terms.

Growth in the Urban Healthcare Services Market

People are spending more on healthcare today in urban India. Today, a middle – level manager with a family of four, spends between Rs. 8,000 and Rs.12, 000 a year on healthcare, compared to just Rs. 2000 in the late 1980's. Moreover, most of them are paying from their own pocket and prefer private services to government ones.

The rise in literacy rate, the higher levels of income, and an increased awareness through the deep penetration of media, have contributed to greater attention being paid to health. The middle income group in this vast base constitutes a large 250 million. The proportion of households in the low income group has declined from 58.8 per cent in 1990, to 39 per cent in 2005-06.

Entry of Organised Private Health Care Service Providers

There are various gaps in the Indian healthcare market, which, apart from the population advantage, also present a vast opportunity. There is a major dearth in the provision of quality health care services and it is this gap that the corporates are looking to leap in. Major corporations like the Tatas, Apollo Group, Fortis, Max, Wockhardt, Piramal, Duncan, and Ispat have made significant investments in setting up state- of – the –art private hospitals in cities like Mumbai, New Delhi, Chennai and Hyderabad.

Using the latest technical equipment and the services of highly skilled medical personnel, these hospitals are in a position to provide a variety of general as well as specialist services. These services are available at extremely competitive prices, encouraging patients not only from developing countries, but even from a number of developed ones to come to India for specialised treatment.

Organised Healthcare Services Framework

Most of the corporate hospital chains have started taking efforts to adopt the best practices in hospital management in an attempt to differentiate their services in the healthcare industry. The management of these institutions has ensured that the services framework adopted could address areas such as Customer Relationship Management, Use of Information Technology etc.

Customer Relationship Management (CRM)

Relationship marketing concerns developing, and retaining customer relationship. Its central tenet is the creation of true customers – customers who are glad they selected a firm, who perceive that they are receiving value and feel valued, who are likely to buy additional services from the firm, and who are unlikely to defect to a competitor.

A good relationship between the buyer and a seller is one in which both parties could receive value in doing business with each other over an extended period of time. For customers, the value of the stream of benefits from an extended series of transactions must exceed the cost (money, time, and effort) involved. For the suppliers who are in business to make profit, the revenue from the stream of sales to a customer must exceed the financial cost of attracting the customer, establishing the relationship, and executing each transaction (variable cost of labor, materials, utilities plus a contribution to overheads).

Concept of CRM

- Relationships rather than transactions
- Assessment of a customer's value and value to a customer
- Technology enablers

Role of CRM

CRM can be a customer retention strategy in tough times, for many service sector companies. Better services, more customised services, and closer relationships can help retain customers in times of hyper competition. This may have to be combined with loyalty programmes that offer value, highest levels of service quality and an attitude that rewards customers continuously for choosing your brand.

Case Study

Dr. A. Govindarajan Eye Hospitals

History

Forty years of dedicated service in Eye Care, the hospital was founded by late Dr. A. Govindarajan as a six bedded hospital. Today the second generation of doctors are taken it ahead as a 100 bedded hospital. Equipped with the latest know how in the field of Ophthalmology, the hospital is fully furnished with State – of – the – art facilities.

The hospital offers quality service at affordable price covering districts in and around Tiruchirappalli namely Pudukottai, Thanjavur, Perambalur, Ariyalur, Karur, and Thuraiyur etc.

Free Eye Screening camps are conducted regularly as part of its outreach programmes making medical services accessible even to the poorest of the poor in remote villages.

Measuring Service Quality

A SERVQUAL scale was used to measure service quality offered by the hospital. A seven point Likert scale was used for measurement. The five broad parameters under which service quality is measured and the questions used to probe these areas are listed below.

Tangibles

- State of art medical facilities
- Cleanliness
- Facilities provided like pharmacy, lab and canteen
- Functional rooms
- Specialties offered
- Professionalism of staff
- Approachability and ambience of the Hospital

Reliability

- Professional acumen
- Service quality
- Timely attention

Responsiveness

- Commitment of staff
- Promptness in responding to calls
- Patient updates

Assurance

- Hospital reputation
- Doctors expertise and skill
- Reassuring behavior
- Patient satisfaction

Empathy

- Patient's waiting time
- Charges and timings
- Personalized and individual care

Findings

The results obtained on each parameter was tabulated and the combined score was reduced to a scale of 0 – 10 to present the final results.

The general findings from the study could be summarized as follows:

1. Dr. A. Govindarajan Eye Hospitals and Institute of Ophthalmic Research and Training scores substantially high in terms of tangibles. This is due to the extremely modern services provided and the relatively new infrastructure. The hospital keeps upgrading itself with the latest technology to remain competitive and offers quality service at affordable price.

2. The hospital receives a high score on empathy which may be in line with its mission "I care in Eye care"

3. The results also rate the hospital high on the responsiveness parameter. The patients report a homely atmosphere where every staff, including doctors, is equally approachable and accessible.

4. The reliability and assurance gets equal score, since the hospital has a long standing of 40 years with second generation doctors in the line. It is a family run concern offering personalized touch thus enhancing value added service.

Conclusion

From the study it is understood that in spite of the heavy competition in Tiruchirappalli town in the field of ophthalmology Dr. A. Govindarajan Eye Hospitals is rated high for its service quality and stands far ahead of its competitors due to its vision focused towards value added services. It has moved from service centric to patient centric strategies. The strength of the hospital is its relationship with patients. However, it was suggested that the staff should be put on a regular training programme to keep them abreast of the latest in technology and patient care by exploiting the aspect of emotional labor in service.

Bibliography

Alfred de Souza (1998), **THE INDIAN CITY (Poverty, Economy and Urban Development)**, Manohar Publications, New Delhi: 17.

Amal Mandal (2005), "Swarna Jayanti Gram Swarozgar Yojana and Self Help Group: An Assessment", **Kurukshetra**, 53 (3): 4-9.

Anschuliz, Eric.E. (1996)," **TQM in America,** Synergy Books International, Malaysia.

Anand, J.C. and Mani, S.B (1997), "Utilisation of Fruits and Vegetables Wastes"**, Indian Food Packer,** 51 (2): 45-63.

Anon (1998), **Emerging Micro-finance Innovations,** NABARD, Mumbai.

Andrea Frazeur, AG (1998), "Quality and Safety Conditions for Customer Satisfaction inthe Whole Meat Chain", **Innovation News**, Cacilin Hernandix, UrsulaRickert, Grehard Schiefer, University of Bon, 7 (2).

Anon (1998), "Byproducts from Food Processing Waste", **Yojana,** 39: 75.

Anon (1999), "Strategic Business Plan", **Center for Quality Management Journal, 8 (3),** http://cqmextra.cqm.org/cqmjournal.nsf/reprints/rp10700.

Anon (1999), **"Dairies Adopt TQM to Improve Milk Quality, Food Safety: News and Information Outreach",**

University of California, Agriculture and Natural Resources, California.

Anon (1999), **World Development Report 1999-2000: Entering the 21st Century: The Changing Development Landscape'**, Oxford University Press, New York.

Anon (2005), **Handbook of SGSY**, Dept of Rural Development, Government of India, New Delhi.

Anon (2006), **TQM Guidelines for Food Processing Industries**, Ministry of Food Processing Industry, New Delhi. www. mofpi.nic.in.

Anon (2007), "Total Quality Management: Lisa Lop", article id 552, issue id 44. www.Qualityassurance.com.

Appa Rao P.B (1998), **Personnel Management in Small Scale Industries**, Deep and Deep Publications, New Delhi.

Asokan R (2005), Micro-Enterprises, An Alternative Strategy for Poverty Alleviation", **Kissan World**, 32 (3): 49-50.

Ashok Kumar Mohanty and Durg Madhab Mahapatra (2007), **Financing of Small and Medium Enterprises in India**, Serials Publications, New Delhi.

Avvai Kothai, T.K. (2005), "The World Trade Organisation and SSIs in India", **Kisan World**, 32 (7): 25-26.

Batra G.G and A.C. Dangwal (2003), **Entrepreneurship and Small Scale Industries**, Deep & Deep Publications, New Delhi: 204.

Beck, T.H.L., Levine, R and Loayza, N (2000), "Finance and the Sources of Growth." **Journal of Financial Economics**, 58 (1-2): 261-300

Beck, Thoresten, Demirguc-kunt, Asil and Maksimovic, Vojislav (2002), "Financing Patterns Around the World: The Role of Institutions", **Policy Research Working Paper 2905**, The World Bank, Wasington D.C.

Beck, T.H.L and Torre, A.de la (2007), "The Basic Analytics of Access to Financial Service", **Financial Markets, Institutions and Instruments**, 16 (2): 79-117.

Behr, Patrick and Guttler, Andre (2007), "Credit Risk Assessment and Relationship Lending: An Empirical Analysis of German SMEs", **Journal of Small Business Management,** 45 (2): 194-213.

Beck, H.T.L., Demirguc-Kun, A., Laeven, L and Levine, R (2008), "Finance, Firm Size, and Growth", **Journal of Money, Credit and Banking,** 40 (7): 1379-1405.

Beck, Thorsten, Demirguc-kunt, Asli and Hanohan (2009), "Access to Financial Services: Measurement, Impact and Policies", **The World Bank Research Observer,** 24 (1): 119

Bhatia, B.S. and Batra, G.S. (2003), **Entrepreneurship and Small Business Management,** Deep and Deep Publications Pvt. Ltd., New Delhi.

Bharti D.K, L.S. Gangwar and Sendeep Kumar (2004), "Food Processing Industry in India: An Economic Analysis", **Agricultural Economics Research Review,** 17 (2): 191-192.

Binodhini Sethi and Atibudhi H, N (2001), "Microfiance: An Innovative Tool for Bank with Un-banable – A study in Kalahandi District", **Indian Journal of Agricultural Economics,** 56 (3): 478.

BIS. (2005), **The Role of Ratings in Structured Finance: Issues and Implications,** Committee on the Global Financial System, Publication Number 23.

Chadha, M. (1993), **Nutritional Evaluation and Utilisation of Guava,** Unpublished M.Sc. Thesis, CCS HAU, Hisar.

Chadha G.K and P.P. Sahu (2003), "Small Scale Agro- Industry in India: Low Productive is its Achilles Heel", **Indian Journal of Agricultural Economics,** 58 (3): 522-526.

Chinnaiyan.P and Krishnamurthi P. (2002), "A Study of Community Banking in Tamil Nadu," **Indian Economic Panorama,** 11 (2): 10.

Costello, Tuche, J (1998), "A Comparative Study of Business to Consumer Electronic Commerce with in the Australian Insurance Sector", **Journal of Information Technology,** 13: 153-167.

Dayanandan. R (2000), **Sustainable Development: Opportunities and Challenges**, Serials Publications, New Delhi.

Dasgupta, Rajaram (2005), "Microfinance in India: Empirical Evidence, Alternative Models and Policy Imperatives", **Economic and Political Weekly**: 1229-1237.

Dela Torre, Augusto, Gozzi, Juan Carlos and Schmukler, Sergio L (2007), **Innovative Experiences in Access to Finance: Market Friendly Roles for the Visible Hand?**, Policy Research Working Paper 4326, The World Bank, Washington D.C

Deepa Sharma (2004), "Family Quality Circles", **Indian Journal of Trading and Development,** XXX1V (2).

Dhawan (2001), "Potential of byproducts Recovery From Fruit Waste: A Review", **Beverage and Food World,** 28 (5): 5

Dickson D (1974), **Alternative Technology and the Politics of Technical Change**, Fontana/Collins, Glasgow.

Durairaj N and Soundara Nageswaran. M (1998), **Entrepreneurship in Small-Scale Industries in India**, Doss Printers, Tirunelveli,

European Commission. (2003), **Microcredit for Small Businesses and Business Creation: Bridging a Market Gap**, Enterprise Publications Report.

Goading, A and D.Gallear (1996), "Total Quality Management in SMEs Omega", **The International Journal of Management Science**, 24 (1): 83 -106.

Gordon Wilson and Richard Heeks (2000), "'Technology, Poverty and Development' in **Poverty and Development in 21st Century**, Tim Allen and Alan Thomas (Eds), Oxford University Press, Oxford.

Gopalakrishnan V (2004), "Financial and Social Constraints of Rural Women Entrepreneurs" **Rural Women Entrepreneurship,** Maria John.S, Discovery Publishing House, New Delhi.

Govindarajan, Vijay, and Chris Trimble (2005), **Ten Rules for Strategic Innovators: From Idea to Execution**, Harvard Business School Press, Hardward.

Gupta, S.R (1994), **Quality Circles Progress Through Participation,** Tata McGraw-Hill Book Company, New Delhi: 195-198.

Gupta N.S (1977), **Financing of Small Scale Industry**, S. Chand & Company Ltd, New Delhi.

Gunther, J., Hawkins, F. (1999), **Making TQM Work: Quality Tools for Human Service Organisations,** Springer Publishing Company, New York.

Hamilton, J.A., Coulson A.B., and Worthely S (2002), **Business Finance and Security Over Moveable Property**, Scottish Executive Central Research Unit. Edinburgh.

Heeks R (1998), **Management Information and Management Information Systems,** School of Oriental and African Studies, University of London, London.

Hermes, Niels and Lenssink, Robert (2007), "Impact of Microfinance: A Critical Survey', **Economic and Political Weekly**: 462 – 465

Hina Sidhu (1998), **Structural Changes and Productivity in Small Scale Industries,** Mittal Publications, New Delhi

Holder, Shabthana. R (2003), "Poverty Outreach and BRAC's Microfinance Interventions: Program Impact and Sustainability", **IDS Bulletin** 34 (4): 49

Honohan, Partrick. (2004), **Financial Sector Policy and the Poor: Selected Findings and Issues, Working Paper 43**, The World Bank, Washington, D.C.

Hrishikes Bhattacharyya (1984), **Entrepreneurs, Banker and Small Scale Industry**, Deep and Deep Publications, New Delhi.

Indira Misra (2004), **Micro Credit for Macro Impact on Poverty**, National Publishing House, New Delhi.

Jaya Prakash Reddy (1991), **Problems and Development of Small Scale Industries in India**, Ashis Publishing House, New Delhi.

Jaitly, J (2001), **Visvakarma's Children,** Concept Publishing Company, New Delhi.

Joseph E, Sjepanek (1962), **Management of Small Industry,** ASIA Publishing House, Chennai: 256.

Joseph, G. and Mahadeviah M (1988), "Utilisation of Waste from Pine Apple Processing Industry", **Indian Food Packer,** 42 (1): 46-58.

Joanna Chataway and Tim Allen (2000), "Industrialisation and Development: Prospects and Dilemmas" in **Poverty and Development in 21st Century,** Alan Thomas (Edi), Oxford University Press, Oxford.

Joel E.Ross (2000), **TQM - Text Cases and Readings,** Deep & Deep Publication, New Delhi.

Karlan, D., and Zinman, J. (2005), **Elasticities of Demand for Consumer Credit Working Paper 926**, Economic Growth Center, Yale University.

Khurana, I.R. (1988): 'Strategy for Rural Development", **Khadi Gram Udyog,** 34 (8), : 335-344.

Khanka S.S (2002), **"Entrepreneurial Development"**, S. Chand & Company Ltd., New Delhi.

Kharbande V.P (2006), "Facilitating Indian Small and Medium Enterprises", **Current Science,** 80 (3): 365.

Kiely R (1998), **"Industrialisation and Development: A Comparative Analysis"**, UCL Press, London.

Kumar, Anjali (2005) **Access to Financial Services in Brazil: A Study**, The World Bank, Washington D.C.

Kundu, Amitabh, Niranjan Sarangi and Bal Paritosh Das (2005), 'Economic Growth, Poverty and Non-farm Employment: An analysis of Rural-urban Inter-linkages' in **Rural Transformation in India**, Rohini Nayyar and Alakh N. Sharma (eds.), Institute of Human Development, New Delhi.

Lalitha, Sridhar (2007), **Thanjavur: Summer of Discontent**: **India Together,**http://www.indiatogether.org/2004/apr/eco-thanjavur.htm

Levy, M Powell P. and Galliers R (1999), "Assessing Information Systems Strategy Development Frameworks in SMEs", **Information and Management,** 36: 247-261.

Levy, M and Powell P (2000), "Is Strategy in SMEs: An Organisational Perspective", **Journal of Strategic Information Systems,** 56 (15): 227-230.

Levy M, Powell P and Yetton P (2001), "SEMs: Aligning IS and the Strategic Context", **Journal of Information Technology,** 16:133-144.

Levine, Ross (2005), **Finance and Growth: Theory and Evidence, Handbook of Economic Growth,** Elsevier Publications: 865-934.

Love, Inessa (2003), "Financial Development and Financing Constraints: International Evidence from the Structural Investment Model", **Review of Financial Studies,** 16 (3): 765-91.

Lunati, M (2000), **SMEs and Electronic Commerce,** OECD, DST/IND/PME, 11.

Lynn Mytelka and Rulvia Farinell (2000)," **Local Clusters, Innovation Systems and Sustained Competitiveness",** United Nations University, Institute for New Technologies, Maastricht: 37.

Martin, I., Hulme, David and Rutherford, Sturt (1999), **Financial Services for the Poor and Poorest: Deepening Understanding to Improve Provision,** Finance and Development Working Paper 9, Institute for Development Policy and Management, University of Manchester, England.

Malhotra, Mohini. (2004), **Microfinance Regulation, Framework and Guiding Principles,** Washington, DC: World Bank Institute.

Mahalingam N (2005), "Innovations in Science and Technology", **Kisan World,** 31(7): 3-4.

Mainuddin Afza (2005), "Superior Subordinates Relationship and Satisfaction in India", **Small Business Enterprises,** 30 (3).

Mathias Fink and Sascha Kraus (2009), **The Management of Small and Medium Enterprises**, Routledge Publications, New York.

Mohanty (2005), "Mega Socio-Economic Transformation Through Microfinance: The NABARD Experience", **Focus**: 9-22.

Mytelka (1999), "Competition, Innovation and Competitive Framework for Analysis" in **Innovation and Competitions in Developing Countries,** Pairs, OECD: 15-27.

Naik. Chitra (1996), "Social Welfare and Poverty Alleviation: Some Reflections", **Yojana,** 40 (1): 6.

Nath, R., Hjelm, K., Sakaguchi, T. and Schultz, M. (1998), "Electronic Commerce and the Internet: Issues, Problems and Perspectives", **International Journal of Information Management**, 18 (2): 91-101.

Nair, Tara S (2005), "The Transforming World of Indian Microfinance", **Economic and Political Weekly:** 1695-1704.

Nagarajan R.S. and A.A. Arivalagan (2005), **Total Quality Management,** New Age and International Publications, New Delhi.

Nelson, R.E (1985), **Entrepreneurship and Self Employment Training**, Asian Development Bank, Manila.

Neela Mukherjee (2000), **WTO and Indias Trade Policy in Services**, Vikas Publishing House, New Delhi.

Nisar Ahmad (1987), **Problems and Management of Small Scale and Cottage Industries,** Deep and Deep Publications, New Delhi: 272.

Platt L.J. & Wilson G.A (1999), "Technology Development and the Poor Marginalised: Context, Intervention and Participation", **Technovation,** 19 (6/7):139—40.

Poon, S and Swatman P (1999) "Exploratory Study of SMEs Internet `Commerce", **Journal of Information and Management:** 35: 9-18.

Poon, S and Swatman, P (2000), "Internet-based SMEs Communication", **Electronic Markets,** 7 (2).

Pugazhendhi, V (1995), **Transaction Costs of Lending to the Rural Poor: NGOs and SHGs of the Poor as Intermediaries for Banks in India,** FDC, Bangladesh: 70.

Rao, S.K. (1976) Entrepreneur Development in India- Is Achievement Training the Answer, **Laghu Udyog,** 4: 9-12.

Rao RV (1978), **Small Industries and the Developing Economy in India,** Concept Publishing Company, New Delhi.

Ramalingam. (1987), **Studies of SHGs of the Rural Poor,** NABARD, Bombay: 50.

Ramana, A. (2001), "Indias Policy on IPR's and Agriculture", **Economic and Political Weekly,** 26 (51): 1576.

Racal Schumann, Downa Prestwood, Alwin Tong John Vansto, (2005), **Innovation,** McgrawHill Inc., New Delhi.

ReVelle, J. (2003), **"TQM Tools Kit.",** http://www. qualit yam erica.com/knowledgecente/articles/revelle tqmtools. html.

Sart, Daniel (2001) "The Rise and Fall of the Rural Non-farm Economy: Poverty Impacts and Policy Options", **Development Policy Review:** 215-220.

Samuel Kho (2002), **TQM and Integrated Approach,** Crest Publishing House, New Delhi.

Sanchez, Susana M., Clarke, Georhe, Robert Cull, Maria and Soledad Martinez Peria. (2002), "Bank Lending to Small Businesses in Latin America: Does Bank Origin Matter?" **Journal of Money, Credit, and Banking,** 37 (1): 83-119.

Sayanthi kar a syravel Tyev (2009), "Bharat Rescues India", **Indian Management,** 48 (4): 12-22.

Schumpeter J., (1962), **Capitalism, Socialism and Democracy,** New York.

Schumacher E.F (1973), **Small is Beautiful: A Study of Economics as if People Mattered,** Blond and Briggs, London.

Shapiro, Stephen M (2001), **"24/7 Innovation: A Blueprint for Surviving and Thriving in an Age of Change",** McGraw-Hill, New Delhi.

Sharma, D.D (2003), **TQM Principles, Practice and Cases,** Sultan Chand and Sons, New Delhi.

Siwar, Chamhuri and Talib, Abd. Basri. (2001), "Micro Finance Capacity Assessment for Poverty Alleviation: Outreach, Viability and Sustainability", **Humanomics,** 17(1): 116-133.

Sinha, Sanjay and Patole, Meenal (2002), **Microfinance and the Poverty of Financial Services: How the Poor in India Could be Better Served,** Working paper 56, IDPM, University of Manchester, England.

Sinha, Frances (2005), "Access, Use and Contribution of Microfinance in India:Findings from a National Study." **Economic and Political Weekly**: 1714-1719.

Sood, Anubha (2002), **Crafts as Sustainable Livelihood Option in Rural India',** London School of Economics and Political Science, London.

Sridhara Bhat, K (2004), **"Total Quality Management",** Himalaya Publishing House, New Delhi: 328-330.

Sundara Raju, S.M (1995), **"Total Quality Management",** Tata McGraw-Hill, New Delhi: 16-18.

Syed Vazith Hussain (2003), **Small Scale Industries in the New Millennium,** Sarup & Sons, New Delhi.

Tiwari, Bhupesh (2002), **'Cluster Development Programme: India Diagnostic Study –Artisan,** The Bell Metal Cluster, Kondagaon (Chhttisgarh).

Trindade S., A.S. Bhalla A.S (1991), **Small and Medium Enterprises: Technology Policies and Options,** Intermediate Technology Publications, London.

Willem Hulsink, Tom Elfring and Louter Stam (2008), **"The Locus of Innovation in Small and Medium Sized Firms: The Importance of Social Capital and Networking in Innovative Entrepreneurship"**, Erasmusresear Institute of Management (ERIM), The Netherlands: 47.

Wurgler, Jeffrey. (2000), "Financial Markets and the Allocation of Capital." **Journal of Financial Economics,** 58 (1-2): 187-214.

Vasant Desai (1983), **Problems and Prospects of Small Scale Industries in India,** Himalaya Publishing House, Bombay

Varshney A.C (1987), **Rural Industrial Waste Management,** Associated Publishing Company, New Delhi: 205.

Venkatraman, N (1994), "IT-Induced Business Transformation: From Automation to Business Scope Redefinition", **Sloan Management Review,** Winter: 73-87.

Vijayagopalan S (1993), **Economic Status of Handicraft Artisans,** National Council of Applied Economic Research, New Delhi.

Vibha Mathur, (2000), **"Indian Economy and WTO Challenges and Strategies"**, New Century Publications, New Delhi.

Zoller C (2001), "Using TQM to Organise Labour and Work", **Buckeye Dairy News,** 4(1): 147.

Zoller C (2006), "Micro Finance Development Review: The Dynamics of Micro and Small Enterprises": **The Case of Mekelle, Ethiopia,** 5 (1): 181.

Index

D

E

N

U